经典回声 | Echoes from the Classics

彷徨 Wandering

鲁迅 著
杨宪益 戴乃迭 译
裘沙 王伟君 插图

外文出版社
FOREIGN LANGUAGES PRESS

目　　录
Contents

"一个人死了之后，究竟有没有魂灵的?"

"Do dead people turn into ghosts or not?"

福

祝福

The New-Year Sacrifice

祝福

4

旧历的年底毕竟最像年底，村镇上不必说，就在天空中也显出将到新年的气象来。灰白色的沉重的晚云中间时时发出闪光，接着一声钝响，是送灶的爆竹；近处燃放的可就更强烈了，震耳的大音还没有息，空气里已经散满了幽微的火药香。我是正在这一夜回到我的故乡鲁镇的。虽说故乡，然而已没有家，所以只得暂寓在鲁四老爷的宅子里。他是我的本家，比我长一辈，应该称之曰“四叔”，是一个讲理学的老监生。他比先前并没有什么大改变，单是老了些，但也还未留胡子，一见面是寒暄，寒暄之后说我“胖了”，说我“胖了”之后即大骂其新党。但我知道，这并非借题在骂我：因为他所骂的还是康有为。但是，谈话是总不投机的了，于是不多久，我便一个人剩在书房里。

第二天我起得很迟，午饭之后，出去看了几个本家和朋友；第三天也照样。他们也都没有什么大改变，单是老了些；家中却一律忙，都在准备着“祝福”。这是鲁镇年终的大典，致敬尽礼，迎接福神，拜求来年一年中的好运气的。杀鸡，宰鹅，买猪肉，用心细细的洗，女人的臂膊都在水里浸得通红，有的还带着绞丝银镯子。煮熟之后，横七竖八的插些筷子在这类东西上，可就称为“福礼”了，五更天陈列起来，并且点上香烛，恭请福神们来享用；拜的却只限于男人，拜完自然仍然是放爆竹。年年如此，家家如此，——只要买得起福礼和爆竹之类的，——今年自然也如此。天色愈阴暗了，下午竟下起雪来，雪花大的有梅花那么大，满天飞舞，夹着烟霭和忙碌的气色，将鲁镇乱成一团糟。我回到四叔的书房里时，瓦楞上已经雪白，房里也映得较光明，极分明的显出壁上挂着的朱拓的大“壽”字，陈抟老祖写的；一边的对联已经脱落，松松的卷了放在长桌上，一边的还在，道是“事理通达心气和平”。我又无聊赖的到窗下的案头去一翻，只见一堆似乎未必完全的《康熙字典》，一部《近思录集注》和一部《四书衬》。无

1. On the twenty-third of the twelfth lunar month the Hearth God was supposed to go up to make a report.

2. The Confucian school in the Song Dynasty (960-1279) which claimed that all things in the universe and the feudal order were ordained by “Reason” and could never change.

3. Referring to Kang Youwei, Liang Qichao and others who in 1898, supported by Emperor Guang Xu, started a bourgeois reform movement. After this was crushed by the die-hards, Kang Youwei and others fled abroad and organized a royalist group advocating constitutional monarchy, becoming a reactionary political clique.

4. A tenth-century hermit.

The end of the year by the old calendar does really seem a more natural end to the year for, to say nothing of the villages and towns, the very sky seems to proclaim the New Year's approach. Intermittent flashes from pallid, lowering evening clouds are followed by the rumble of crackers bidding farewell to the Hearth God[1] and, before the deafening reports of the bigger bangs close at hand have died away, the air is filled with faint whiffs of gunpowder. On one such night I returned to Luzhen, my home town. I call it my home town, but as I had not made my home there for some time I put up at the house of a certain Fourth Mr. Lu, whom I am obliged to address as Fourth Uncle since he belongs to the generation before mine in our clan. A former Imperial Academy licentiate who believes in Neo-Confucianism,[2] he seemed very little changed, just slightly older, but without any beard as yet. Having exchanged some polite remarks upon meeting he observed that I was fatter, and having observed that I was fatter launched into a violent attack on the reformists.[3] I did not take this personally, however, as the object of his attack was Kang Youwei. Still, conversation proved so difficult that I shortly found myself alone in the study.

I rose late the next day and went out after lunch to see relatives and friends, spending the following day in the same way. They were all very little changed, just slightly older; but every family was busy preparing for the New-Year sacrifice. This is the great end-of-year ceremony in Luzhen, during which a reverent and splendid welcome is given to the God of Fortune so that he will send good luck for the coming year. Chickens and geese are killed, pork is bought, and everything is scrubbed and scoured until all the women's arms — some still in twisted silver bracelets — turn red in the water. After the meat is cooked chopsticks are thrust into it at random, and when this "offering" is set out at dawn, incense and candles are lit and the God of Fortune is respectfully invited to come and partake of it. The worshippers are confined to men and, of course, after worshipping they go on letting off firecrackers as before. This is done every year, in every household — so long as it can afford the offering and crackers — and naturally this year was no exception.

The sky became overcast and in the afternoon it was filled with a flurry of snowflakes, some as large as plum-blossom petals, which merged with the smoke and the bustling atmosphere to make the small town a welter of confusion. By the time I had returned to my uncle's study, the roof of the house was already white with snow which made the room brighter than usual, highlighting the red stone rubbing that hung on the wall of the big character "Longevity" as written by the Taoist saint Chen Tuan.[4] One of the pair of scrolls flanking it had fallen down and was lying loosely rolled up on the long table. The other, still in its place, bore the inscription "Understanding of principles brings peace of mind." Idly, I strolled over to the desk beneath the window to turn over the pile of books on it, but only

论如何，我明天决计要走了。

况且，一想到昨天遇见祥林嫂的事，也就使我不能安住。那是下午，我到镇的东头访过一个朋友，走出来，就在河边遇见她；而且见她瞪着的眼睛的视线，就知道明明是向我走来的。我这回在鲁镇所见的人们中，改变之大，可以说无过于她的了：五年前的花白的头发，即今已经全白，全不像四十上下的人；脸上瘦削不堪，黄中带黑，而且消尽了先前悲哀的神色，仿佛是木刻似的；只有那眼珠间或一轮，还可以表示她是一个活物。她一手提着竹篮，内中一个破碗，空的；一手拄着一支比她更长的竹竿，下端开了裂：她分明已经纯乎是一个乞丐了。

我就站住，豫备她来讨钱。

"你回来了？"她先这样问。

"是的。"

"这正好。你是识字的，又是出门人，见识得多。我正要问你一件事——"她那没有精采的眼睛忽然发光了。

我万料不到她却说出这样的话来，诧异的站着。

"就是——"她走近两步，放低了声音，极秘密似的切切的说，"一个人死了之后，究竟有没有魂灵的？"

我很悚然，一见她的眼钉着我的，背上也就遭了芒刺一般，比在学校里遇到不及豫防的临时考，教师又偏是站在身旁的时候，惶急得多了。对于魂灵的有无，我自己是向来毫不介意的；但在此刻，怎样回答她好呢？我在极短期的踌躇中，想，这里的人照例相信鬼，然而她，却疑惑了，——或者不如说希望：希望其有，又希望其无……。人何必增添末路的人的苦恼，为她起见，不如说有罢。

"也许有罢，——我想。"我于是吞吞吐吐的说。

"那么，也就有地狱了？"

"阿！地狱？"我很吃惊，只得支梧着，"地狱？——论理，就该也有。——然而也未必，……谁来管这等事……。"

"那么，死掉的一家的人，都能见面的？"

5. Compiled by Luo Pei in the Qing Dynasty for use in the imperial examinations.

found an apparently incomplete set of *The Kang Xi Dictionary*, the *Selected Writings of Neo-Confucian Philosophers*, and *Commentaries on the Four Books*.[5] At all events I must leave the next day, I decided.

Besides, the thought of my meeting with Xianglin's Wife the previous day was preying on my mind. It had happened in the afternoon. On my way back from calling on a friend in the eastern part of the town, I had met her by the river and knew from the fixed look in her eyes that she was going to accost me. Of all the people I had seen during this visit to Luzhen, none had changed so much as she had. Her hair, streaked with grey five years before, was now completely white, making her appear much older than one around forty. Her sallow, dark-tinged face that looked as if it had been carved out of wood was fearfully wasted and had lost the grief-stricken expression it had borne before. The only sign of life about her was the occasional flicker of her eyes. In one hand she had a bamboo basket containing a chipped, empty bowl; in the other, a bamboo pole, taller than herself, that was split at the bottom. She had clearly become a beggar pure and simple.

I stopped, waiting for her to come and ask for money.

"So you're back?" were her first words.

"Yes."

"That's good. You are a scholar who's travelled and seen the world. There's something I want to ask you." A sudden gleam lit up her lacklustre eyes.

This was so unexpected that surprise rooted me to the spot.

"It's this." She drew two paces nearer and lowered her voice, as if letting me into a secret. "Do dead people turn into ghosts or not?"

My flesh crept. The way she had fixed me with her eyes made a shiver run down my spine, and I felt far more nervous than when a surprise test is sprung on you at school and the teacher insists on standing over you. Personally, I had never bothered myself in the least about whether spirits existed or not; but what was the best answer to give her now? I hesitated for a moment, reflecting that the people here still believed in spirits, but she seemed to have her doubts, or rather hopes she hoped for life after death and dreaded it at the same time. Why increase the sufferings of someone with a wretched life? For her sake, I thought, I'd better say there was.

"Quite possibly, I'd say," I told her falteringly.

"That means there must be a hell too?"

"What, hell?" I faltered, very taken aback. "Hell? Logically speaking, there should be too — but not necessarily. Who cares anyway?"

"Then will all the members of a family meet again after death?"

"唉唉，见面不见面呢？……"这时我已知道自己也还是完全一个愚人，什么踌躕，什么计画，都挡不住三句问。我即刻胆怯起来了，便想全翻过先前的话来，"那是，……实在，我说不清……。其实，究竟有没有魂灵，我也说不清。"

我乘她不再紧接的问，迈开步便走，匆匆的逃回四叔的家中，心里很觉得不安逸。自己想，我这答话怕于她有些危险。她大约因为在别人的祝福时候，感到自身的寂寞了，然而会不会含有别的什么意思的呢？——或者是有了什么豫感了？倘有别的意思，又因此发生别的事，则我的答话委实该负若干的责任……。但随后也就自笑，觉得偶尔的事，本没有什么深意义，而我偏要细细推敲，正无怪教育家要说是生着神经病；而况明明说过"说不清"，已经推翻了答话的全局，即使发生什么事，于我也毫无关系了。

"说不清"是一句极有用的话。不更事的勇敢的少年，往往敢于给人解决疑问，选定医生，万一结果不佳，大抵反成了怨府，然而一用这说不清来作结束，便事事逍遥自在了。我在这时，更感到这一句话的必要，即使和讨饭的女人说话，也是万不可省的。

但是我总觉得不安，过了一夜，也仍然时时记忆起来，仿佛怀着什么不祥的豫感；在阴沉的雪天里，在无聊的书房里，这不安愈加强烈了。不如走罢，明天进城去。福兴楼的清炖鱼翅，一元一大盘，价廉物美，现在不知增价了否？往日同游的朋友，虽然已经云散，然而鱼翅是不可不吃的，即使只有我一个……。无论如何，我明天决计要走了。

我因为常见些但愿不如所料，以为未必竟如所料的事，却每每恰如所料的起来，所以很恐怕这事也一律。果然，特别的情形开始了。傍晚，我竟听到有些人聚在内室里谈话，仿佛议论什么事似的；但不一会，说话声也就止了，只有四叔且走而且高声的说：

"不早不迟，偏偏要在这时候，——这就可见是一个谬种！"

"Well, as to whether they'll meet again or not..." I realized now what an utter fool I was. All my hesitation and manoeuvring had been no match for her three questions. Promptly taking fright, I decided to recant. "In that case...actually, I'm not sure.... In fact, I'm not sure whether there are ghosts or not either."

To avoid being pressed by any further questions I walked off, then beat a hasty retreat to my uncle's house, feeling thoroughly disconcerted. I may have given her a dangerous answer, I was thinking. Of course, she may just be feeling lonely because everybody else is celebrating now, but could she have had something else in mind? Some premonition? If she had had some other idea, and something happens as a result. Then my answer should indeed be partly responsible....Then I laughed at myself for brooding so much over a chance meeting when it could have no serious significance. No wonder certain educationists called me neurotic. Besides, I had distinctly declared, "I'm not sure," contradicting the whole of my answer. This meant that even if something did happen, it would have nothing at all to do with me.

"I'm not sure" is a most useful phrase.

Bold inexperienced youngsters often take it upon themselves to solve problems or choose doctors for other people, and if by any chance things turn out badly they may well be held to blame; but by concluding their advice with this evasive expression they achieve blissful immunity from reproach. The necessity for such a phrase was brought home to me still more forcibly now, since it was indispensable even in speaking with a beggar woman.

However, I remained uneasy, and even after a night's rest my mind dwelt on it with a certain sense of foreboding. The oppressive snowy weather and the gloomy study increased my uneasiness. I had better leave the next day and go back to the city. A large dish of plain shark's fin stew at the Fu Xing Restaurant used to cost only a dollar. I wondered if this cheap delicacy had risen in price or not. Though my good companions of the old days had scattered, that shark's fin must still be sampled even if I were on my own. Whatever happened I would leave the next day, I decided.

Since, in my experience, things I hoped would not happen and felt should not happen invariably did occur all the same, I was much afraid this would prove another such case. And, sure enough, the situation soon took a strange turn, Towards evening I heard what sounded like a discussion in the inner room, but the conversation ended before long and my uncle walked away observing loudly, "What a moment to choose! Now of all times! Isn't that proof enough she was a bad lot?"

我先是诧异，接着是很不安，似乎这话于我有关系。试望门外，谁也没有。好容易待到晚饭前他们的短工来冲茶，我才得了打听消息的机会。

“刚才，四老爷和谁生气呢？”我问。

“还不是和祥林嫂？”那短工简捷的说。

“祥林嫂？怎么了？”我又赶紧的问。

“老了。”

“死了？”我的心突然紧缩，几乎跳起来，脸上大约也变了色。但他始终没有抬头，所以全不觉。我也就镇定了自己，接着问：

“什么时候死的？”

“什么时候？——昨天夜里，或者就是今天罢。——我说不清。”

“怎么死的？”

“怎么死的？——还不是穷死的？”他淡然的回答，仍然没有抬头向我看，出去了。

然而我的惊惶却不过暂时的事，随着就觉得要来的事，已经过去，并不必仰仗我自己的“说不清”和他之所谓“穷死的”的宽慰，心地已经渐渐轻松；不过偶然之间，还似乎有些负疚。晚饭摆出来了，四叔俨然的陪着。我也还想打听些关于祥林嫂的消息，但知道他虽然读过“鬼神者二气之良能也”，而忌讳仍然极多，当临近祝福时候，是万不可提起死亡疾病之类的话的；倘不得已，就该用一种替代的隐语，可惜我又不知道，因此屡次想问，而终于中止了。我从他俨然的脸色上，又忽而疑他正以为我不早不迟，偏要在这时候来打搅他，也是一个谬种，便立刻告诉他明天要离开鲁镇，进城去，趁早放宽了他的心。他也不很留。这样闷闷的吃完了一餐饭。

冬季日短，又是雪天，夜色早已笼罩了全市镇。人们都在灯下匆忙，但窗外很寂静。雪花落在积得厚厚的雪褥上面，听去似乎瑟瑟有声，使人更加感得沉寂。我独坐在发出黄光的菜油灯下，想，这百无聊赖的祥林嫂，被人们

6. This was said by the Song Dynasty Neo-Confucian Zhang Zai.

My initial astonishment gave way to a deep uneasiness; I felt that this had something to do with me. I looked out of the door, but no one was there. I waited impatiently till their servant came in before dinner to brew tea. Then at last I had a chance to make some inquiries.

"Who was Mr. Lu so angry with just now?" I asked.

"Why, Xianglin's Wife, of course," was the curt reply.

"She's gone."

"Dead?" My heart missed a beat. I started and must have changed colour. But since the servant kept his head lowered, all this escaped him. I pulled myself together enough to ask.

"When did she die?"

"When? Last night or today — I'm not sure."

"How did she die?"

"How? Of poverty of course." After this stolid answer he withdrew, still without having raised his head to look at me.

My agitation was only short-lived, however. For now that my premonition had come to pass, I no longer had to seek comfort in my own "I'm not sure," or his "dying of poverty," and my heart was growing lighter. Only from time to time did I still feel a little guilty. Dinner was served, and my uncle impressively kept me company. Tempted as I was to ask about Xianglin's Wife, I knew that, although he had read that "ghosts and spirits are manifestations of the dual forces of Nature,[6]" he was still so superstitious that on the eve of the New-Year sacrifice it would be unthinkable to mention anything like death or illness. In case of necessity one should use veiled allusions. But since this was unfortunately beyond me I had to bite back the questions which kept rising to the tip of my tongue. And my uncle's solemn expression suddenly made me suspect that he looked on me too as a bad lot who had chosen this moment, now of all times, to come and trouble him. To set his mind at rest as quickly as I could, I told him at once of my plan to leave Luzhen the next day and go back to thc city. Hc did not prcss mc to stay, and at last the uncomfortably quiet meal came to an end.

Winter days are short, and because it was snowing darkness had already enveloped the whole town. All was stir and commotion in the lighted houses, but outside was remarkably quiet. And the snowflakes hissing down on the thick snowdrifts intensified one's sense of loneliness. Seated alone in the amber light of the vegetable-oil lamp I reflected that this wretched and forlorn woman, abandoned in the dust like a worn-out toy of which its owners have tired, had once left her own imprint in the dust, and those

弃在尘芥堆中的，看得厌倦了的陈旧的玩物，先前还将形骸露在尘芥里，从活得有趣的人们看来，恐怕要怪讶她何以还要存在，现在总算被无常打扫得干干净净了。魂灵的有无，我不知道；然而在现世，则无聊生者不生，即使厌见者不见：为人为己，也还都不错。我静听着窗外似乎瑟瑟作响的雪花声，一面想，反而渐渐的舒畅起来。

然而先前所见所闻的她的半生事迹的断片，至此也联成一片了。

她不是鲁镇人。有一年的冬初，四叔家里要换女工，做中人的卫老婆子带她进来了，头上扎着白头绳，乌裙，蓝夹袄，月白背心，年纪大约二十六七，脸色青黄，但两颊却还是红的。卫老婆子叫她祥林嫂，说是自己母家的邻舍，死了当家人，所以出来做工了。四叔皱了皱眉，四婶已经知道了他的意思，是在讨厌她是一个寡妇。但看她模样还周正，手脚都壮大，又只是顺着眼，不开一句口，很像一个安分耐劳的人，便不管四叔的皱眉，将她留下了。试工期内，她整天的做，似乎闲着就无聊，又有力，简直抵得过一个男子，所以第三天就定局，每月工钱五百文。

大家都叫她祥林嫂；没问她姓什么，但中人是卫家山人，既说是邻居，那大概也就姓卫了。她不很爱说话，别人问了才回答，答的也不多。直到十几天之后，这才陆续的知道她家里还有严厉的婆婆；一个小叔子，十多岁，能打柴了；她是春天没了丈夫的；他本来也打柴为生，比她小十岁：大家所知道的就只是这一点。

日子很快的过去了，她的做工却毫没有懈，食物不论，力气是不惜的。人们都说鲁四老爷家里雇着了女工，实在比勤快的男人还勤快。到年底，扫尘，洗地，杀鸡，宰鹅，彻夜的煮福礼，全是一人担当，竟没有添短工。然而她反满足，口角边渐渐的有了笑影，脸上也白胖了。

新年才过，她从河边淘米回来时，忽而失了色，说

who enjoyed life must have wondered at her for wishing to live on; but now at last she had been swept away by death. Whether spirits existed or not I did not know; but in this world of ours the end of a futile existence, the removal of someone whom others are tired of seeing, was just as well both for them and for the individual concerned. Occupied with these reflections, I listened quietly to the hissing of the snow outside, until little by little I felt more relaxed.

But the fragments of her life that I had seen or heard about before combined now to form a whole.

She was not from Luzhen. Early one winter, when my uncle's family wanted a new maid, Old Mrs. Wei the go-between brought her along. She had a white mourning band round her hair and was wearing a black skirt, blue jacket, and pale green bodice. Her age was about twenty-six, and though her face was sallow her cheeks were red. Old Mrs. Wei introduced her as Xianglin's Wife, a neighbour of her mother's family, who wanted to go out to work now that her husband had died. My uncle frowned at this, and my aunt knew that he disapproved of taking on a widow. She looked just the person for them, though, with her big strong hands and feet; and, judging by her downcast eyes and silence, she was a good worker who would know her place. So my aunt ignored my uncle's frown and kept her. During her trial period she worked from morning till night as if she found resting irksome, and proved strong enough to do the work of a man; so on the third day she was taken on for five hundred cash a month.

Everybody called her Xianglin's Wife and no one asked her own name, but since she had been introduced by someone from Wei Village as a neighbour, her surname was presumably also Wei. She said little, only answering briefly when asked a question. Thus it took them a dozen days or so to find out bit by bit that she had a strict mother-in-law at home and a brother-in-law of ten or so, old enough to cut wood, Her husband, who had died that spring, had been a woodcutter too, and had been ten years younger than she was. This little was all they could learn.

Time passed quickly. She went on working as hard as ever, not caring what she ate, never sparing herself. It was generally agreed that the Lu family's maid actually got through more work than a hard-working man. At the end of the year, she swept and mopped the floors, killed the chickens and geese, and sat up to boil the sacrificial meat, all single-handed, so that they did not need to hire extra help. And she for her part was quite contented. Little by little the trace of a smile appeared at the corners of her mouth, while her face became whiter and plumper.

Just after the New Year she came back from washing rice by the river most upset

刚才远远地看见一个男人在对岸徘徊，很像夫家的堂伯，恐怕是正为寻她而来的。四婶很惊疑，打听底细，她又不说。四叔一知道，就皱一皱眉，道：

“这不好。恐怕她是逃出来的。”

她诚然是逃出来的，不多久，这推想就证实了。

此后大约十几天，大家正已渐渐忘却了先前的事，卫老婆子忽而带了一个三十多岁的女人进来了，说那是祥林嫂的婆婆。那女人虽是山里人模样，然而应酬很从容，说话也能干，寒暄之后，就赔罪，说她特来叫她的儿媳回家去，因为开春事务忙，而家中只有老的和小的，人手不够了。

“既是她的婆婆要她回去，那有什么话可说呢。”四叔说。

于是算清了工钱，一共一千七百五十文，她全存在主人家，一文也还没有用，便都交给她的婆婆。那女人又取了衣服，道过谢，出去了。其时已经是正午。

“阿呀，米呢？祥林嫂不是去淘米的么？……”好一会，四婶这才惊叫起来。她大约有些饿，记得午饭了。

于是大家分头寻淘箩。她先到厨下，次到堂前，后到卧房，全不见淘箩的影子。四叔踱出门外，也不见，直到河边，才见平平正正的放在岸上，旁边还有一株菜。

看见的人报告说，河里面上午就泊了一只白篷船，篷是全盖起来的，不知道什么人在里面，但事前也没有人去理会他。待到祥林嫂出来淘米，刚刚要跪下去，那船里便突然跳出两个男人来，像是山里人，一个抱住她，一个帮着，拖进船去了。祥林嫂还哭喊了几声，此后便再没有什么声息，大约给用什么堵住了罢。接着就走上两个女人来，一个不认识，一个就是卫婆子。窥探舱里，不很分明，她像是捆了躺在船板上。

“可恶！然而……。”四叔说。

这一天是四婶自己煮午饭；他们的儿子阿牛烧火。

午饭之后，卫老婆子又来了。

“可恶！”四叔说。

because in the distance she had seen a man, pacing up and down on the opposite bank, who looked like her husband's elder cousin — very likely he had come in search of her. When my aunt in alarm pressed her for more information, she said nothing. As soon as my uncle knew of this he frowned.

"That bad," he observed. "She must have run away."

Before very long this inference was confirmed.

About a fortnight later, just as this incident was beginning to be forgotten, Old Mrs. Wei suddenly brought along a woman in her thirties whom she introduced as Xianglin's mother. Although this woman looked like the hill-dweller she was, she behaved with great self-possession and has a ready tongue in her head. After the usual civilities she apologized for coming to take her daughter-in-law back, explaining that early spring was a busy time and they were short-handed at home with only old people and children around.

"If her mother-in-law wants her back, there's nothing more to be said," was my uncle's comment.

Thereupon her wages were reckoned up. They came to 1,750 cash, all of which she had left in the keeping of her mistress without spending any of it. My aunt gave the entire sum to Xianglin's mother, who took her daughter-in-law's clothes as well, expressed her thanks, and left. By this time it was noon.

"Oh, the rice! Didn't Xianglin's Wife go to wash the rice?" exclaimed my aunt some time later. It was probably hunger that reminded her of lunch.

A general search started then for the rice-washing basket. My aunt searched the kitchen, then the hall, then the bedroom; but not a sign of the basket was to be seen. My uncle could not find it outside either, until he went right down to the riverside. Then he saw it set down fair and square on the bank, some vegetables beside it.

Some people on the bank told him that a boat with a white awning had moored there that morning but, since the awning covered the boat completely, they had no idea who was inside and had paid no special attention to begin with. But when Xianglin's Wife had arrived and was kneeling down to wash rice, two men who looked as if they came from the hills had jumped off the boat and seized her. Between them they dragged her on board. She wept and shouted at first but soon fell silent, probably because she was gagged. Then along came two women, a stranger and Old Mrs. Wei. It was difficult to see clearly into the boat, but the victim seemed to be lying, tied up, on the planking.

"Disgraceful! Still..." said my uncle.

That day my aunt cooked the midday meal herself, and their son Aniu lit the fire.

After lunch Old Mrs. Wei came back.

"Disgraceful!" said my uncle.

“你是什么意思？亏你还会再来见我们。”四婶洗着碗，一见面就愤愤的说，“你自己荐她来，又合伙劫她去，闹得沸反盈天的，大家看了成个什么样子？你拿我们家里开玩笑么？”

“阿呀阿呀，我真上当。我这回，就是为此特地来说说清楚的。她来求我荐地方，我那里料得到是瞒着她的婆婆的呢。对不起，四老爷，四太太。总是我老发昏不小心，对不起主顾。幸而府上是向来宽洪大量，不肯和小人计较的。这回我一定荐一个好的来折罪……。”

“然而……。”四叔说。

于是祥林嫂事件便告终结，不久也就忘却了。

只有四婶，因为后来雇用的女工，大抵非懒即馋，或者馋而且懒，左右不如意，所以也还提起祥林嫂。每当这些时候，她往往自言自语的说，“她现在不知道怎么样了？”意思是希望她再来。但到第二年的新正，她也就绝了望。

新正将尽，卫老婆子来拜年了，已经喝得醉醺醺的，自说因为回了一趟卫家山的娘家，住下几天，所以来得迟了。她们问答之间，自然就谈到祥林嫂。

“她么？”卫老婆子高兴的说，“现在是交了好运了。她婆婆来抓她回去的时候，是早已许给了贺家墺的贺老六的，所以回家之后不几天，也就装在花轿里抬去了。”

“阿呀，这样的婆婆！……”四婶惊奇的说。

“阿呀，我的太太！你真是大户人家的太太的话。我们山里人，小户人家，这算得什么？她有小叔子，也得娶老婆。不嫁了她，那有这一注钱来做聘礼？她的婆婆倒是精明强干的女人呵，很有打算，所以就将她嫁到里山去。倘许给本村人，财礼就不多；惟独肯嫁进深山野墺里去的女人少，所以她就到手了八十千。现在第二个儿子的媳妇也娶进了，财礼只花了五十，除去办喜事的费用，还剩十多千。吓，你看，这多么好打算？……”

“祥林嫂竟肯依？……”

"What's the meaning of this ? How dare you show your face here again?" My aunt, who was washing up, started fuming as soon as she saw her. "First you recommended her, then help them carry her off, causing such a shocking commotion. What will people think? Are you trying to make fools of our family ?"

"*Aiya*, I was completely taken in! I've come specially to clear this up. How was I to know she'd left home without permission from her mother-in-law when she asked me to find her work? I'm sorry, Mr. Lu. I'm sorry, Mrs. Lu. I'm growing so stupid and careless in my old age, I've let my patrons down. It's lucky for me you're such kind, generous people, never hard on those below you. I promise to make it up to you by finding someone good this time."

"Still..." said my uncle.

That concluded the affair of Xianglin's Wife, and before long it was forgotten.

My aunt was the only one who still spoke of Xianglin's Wife. This was because most of the maids taken on afterwards turned out to be lazy or greedy, or both, none of them giving satisfaction. At such times she would invariably say to herself, "I wonder what's become of her now?" — implying that she would like to have her back. But by the next New Year she too had given up hope.

The first month was nearing its end when Old Mrs.Wei called on my aunt to wish her a happy New Year. Already tipsy, she explained that the reason for her coming so late was that she had been visiting her family in Wei Village in the hills for a few days. The conversation, naturally, soon touched on Xianglin's Wife.

"Xianglin's Wife?" cried Old Mrs. Wei cheerfully. "She's in luck now. When her motherinlaw dragged her home, she'd promised her to the sixth son of the He family in He Glen. So a few days after her return they put her in the bridal chair and sent her off."

"Gracious ! What a mother-in-law!" exclaimed my aunt.

"Ah, madam, you really talk like a great lady! This is nothing to poor folk like us who live up in the hills. That young brother-in-law of hers still had no wife. If they didn't marry her off, where would the money have come from to get him one? Her mother-in-law is a clever, capable woman, a fine manager; so she married her off into the mountains. If she'd betrothed her to a family in the same village, she wouldn't have made so much; but as very few girls are willing to take a husband deep in the mountains at the back of beyond, she got eighty thousand cash. Now the second son has a wife, who cost only fifty thousand; and after paying the wedding expenses she's still over ten thousand in hand. Wouldn't you call her a fine manager?"

"But was Xianglin's Wife willing?"

“这有什么依不依。——闹是谁也总要闹一闹的；只要用绳子一捆，塞在花轿里，抬到男家，捺上花冠，拜堂，关上房门，就完事了。可是祥林嫂真出格，听说那时实在闹得利害，大家还都说大约因为在念书人家做过事，所以与众不同呢。太太，我们见得多了：回头人出嫁，哭喊的也有，说要寻死觅活的也有，抬到男家闹得拜不成天地的也有，连花烛都砸了的也有。祥林嫂可是异乎寻常，他们说她一路只是嚎，骂，抬到贺家墺，喉咙已经全哑了。拉出轿来，两个男人和她的小叔子使劲的擒住她也还拜不成天地。他们一不小心，一松手，阿呀，阿弥陀佛，她就一头撞在香案角上，头上碰了一个大窟窿，鲜血直流，用了两把香灰，包上两块红布还止不住血呢。直到七手八脚的将她和男人反关在新房里，还是骂，阿呀呀，这真是……。”她摇一摇头，顺下眼睛，不说了。

“后来怎么样呢？”四婶还问。

“听说第二天也没有起来。“她抬起眼来说。

“后来呢？”

“后来？——起来了。她到年底就生了一个孩子，男的，新年就两岁了。我在娘家这几天，就有人到贺家墺去，回来说看见他们娘儿俩，母亲也胖，儿子也胖；上头又没有婆婆；男人所有的是力气，会做活；房子是自家的。——唉唉，她真是交了好运了。”

从此之后，四婶也就不再提起祥林嫂。

但有一年的秋季，大约是得到祥林嫂好运的消息之后的又过了两个新年，她竟又站在四叔家的堂前了。桌上放着一个荸荠式的圆篮，檐下一个小铺盖。她仍然头上扎着白头绳，乌裙；蓝夹袄，月白背心，脸色青黄，只是两颊上已经消失了血色，顺着眼，眼角上带些泪痕，眼光也没有先前那样精神了。而且仍然是卫老婆子领着，显出慈悲模样，絮絮的对四婶说：

“……这实在是叫作‘天有不测风云’，她的男人

It wasn't a question of willing or not. Of course any woman would make a row about it. All they had to do was tie her up, shove her into the chair, carry her to the man's house, force on her the two of them into their room — and that was that. But Xianglin's Wife is quite a character. I heard that she made a terrible scene. It was working for a scholar's family, everyone said, that made her different from other people. We go-betweens see life, madam. Some widows sob and shout when they remarry; some threaten to kill themselves; some refuse to go through the cermony of bowing to heaven and earth after they've been carried to man's house; some even smash the wedding candlesticks. But Xianglin's Wife was really extraordinary. They said she screamed and cursed all the way to He Glen, so that she was completely hoarse by the time they got there. When they dragged her out the chair, no matter how the two chair-bearers and her brother-in-law held her, they couldn't make her go through the ceremony. The moment they were off guard and had loosened their grip — gracious Buddha! — she bashed her head on a corner of the altar, gashing it so badly that blood spurted out. Even though they smeared on two handfuls of incense ashes and tied it up with two pieces of red cloth, they couldn't stop the bleeding. It took quite a few of them to shut her up finally with the man in the bridal chamber, but even then she went on cursing. Oh, it was really...." Shaking her head, she lowered her eyes and fell silent.

"And what then?" asked my aunt.

"They said that the next day she didn't get up." Old Mrs. Wei raised her eyes.

"And after?"

"After? She got up. At the end of the year she had a baby, a boy, who was reckoned as two this New Year. These few days when I was at home, some people back from a visit to He Glen said they'd seen her and her son, and both mother and child are plump. There's no mother-in-law over her, her man is a strong fellow who can earn a living, and the house belongs to them. Oh, yes she's in luck all right."

After this event my aunt gave up talking of Xianglin's Wife.

But one autumn, after two New Years had passed since this good news of Xianglin's Wife, she once more crossed the threshold of my uncle's house, placing her round bulb-shaped basket on the table and her small bedding-roll under the eaves. As before, she had a white mourning band round her hair and was wearing a black skirt, blue jacket, and pale green bodice. Her face was sallow, her cheeks no longer red; and her downcast eyes, stained with tears, had lost their brightness. Just as before, it was Old Mrs. Wei who brought her to my aunt.

"It was really a bolt from the blue," she explained compassionately. Her husband

是坚实人，谁知道年纪青青，就会断送在伤寒上？本来已经好了的，吃了一碗冷饭，复发了。幸亏有儿子；她又能做，打柴摘茶养蚕都来得，本来还可以守着，谁知道那孩子又会给狼衔去的呢？春天快完了，村上倒反来了狼，谁料到？现在她只剩了一个光身了。大伯来收屋，又赶她。她真是走投无路了，只好来求老主人。好在她现在已经再没有什么牵挂，太太家里又凑巧要换人，所以我就领她来。——我想，熟门熟路，比生手实在好得多。……”

“我真傻，真的，”祥林嫂抬起她没有神采的眼睛来，接着说。“我单知道下雪的时候野兽在山墺里没有食吃，会到村里来；我不知道春天也会有。我一清早起来就开了门。拿小篮盛了一篮豆，叫我们的阿毛坐在门槛上剥豆去。他是很听话的，我的话句句听；他出去了。我就在屋后劈柴，淘米，米下了锅，要蒸豆。我叫阿毛，没有应，出去一看；只见豆撒得一地，没有我们的阿毛了。他是不到别家去玩的；各处去一问，果然没有。我急了，央人出去寻。直到下半天，寻来寻去寻到山墺里，看见刺柴上挂着一只他的小鞋。大家都说，糟了，怕是遭了狼了。再进去；他果然躺在草窠里，肚里的五脏已经都给吃空了，手上还紧紧的捏着那只小篮呢。……”她接着但是呜咽，说不出成句的话来。

四婶起初还踌躕，待到听完她自己的话，眼圈就有些红了。她想了一想，便教拿圆篮和铺盖到下房去。卫老婆子仿佛卸了一肩重担似的嘘一口气；祥林嫂比初来时候神气舒畅些，不待指引，自己驯熟的安放了铺盖。她从此又在鲁镇做女工了。

大家仍然叫她祥林嫂。

然而这一回，她的境遇却改变得非常大。上工之后的两三天，主人们就觉得她手脚已没有先前一样灵活，记性也坏得多，死尸似的脸上又整日没有笑影，四婶的口气上，已颇有些不满了。当她初到的时候，四叔虽然照例皱过眉，但鉴于向来雇用女工之难，也就并不大反

was a strong young fellow; who'd have thought that typhoid fever would carry him off? He'd taken a turn for the better, but then he ate some cold rice and got worse again. Luckily she had the boy and she can work — she's able to gather firewood, pick tea, or raise silkworms — so she could have managed on her own. But who'd have thought that the child, too, would be carried off by a wolf? It was nearly the end of spring, yet a wolf came to the glen — who could have guessed that? Now she's all on her own. Her husband's elder brother has taken over the house and turned her out. So she's no way to turn for help except to her former mistress. Luckily this time there's nobody to stop her and you happen to be needing someone, madam. That's why I've brought her here. I think someone used to your ways is much better than a new hand..."

"I was really too stupid, really..." put in Xianglin's Wife, raising her lacklustre eyes. "All I knew was that when it snowed and wild beasts up in the hills had nothing to eat, they might come to the villages. I didn't know that in spring they might come too. I got up at dawn and opened the door, filled a small basket with beans and told our Amao to sit on the doorstep and shell them. He was such a good boy; he always did as he was told, and out he went. Then I went to the back to chop wood and wash the rice, and when the rice was in the pan I wanted to steam the beans. I called Amao, but there was no answer. When I went out to look there were beans all over the ground but no Amao. He never went to the neighbours' houses to play; and, sure enough, though I asked everywhere he wasn't there. I got so worried, I begged people to help me find him. Not until that afternoon, after searching high and low, did they try the gully. There they saw one of his little shoes caught on a bramble. 'That's bad', they said. 'A wolf must have got him.' And sure enough, further on, there he was lying in the wolf's den, all his innards eaten away, still clutching that little basket tight in his hand...." At this point she broke down and could not go on.

My aunt had been undecided at first, but the rims of her eyes were rather red by the time Xianglin's Wife broke off. After a moment's thought she told her to take her things to the servant's quarters. Old Mrs. Wei heaved a sigh, as if a great weight had been lifted from her mind; and Xianglin's Wife, looking more relaxed than when first she came, went off quietly to put away her bedding without having to be told the way. So she started work again as a maid in Luzhen.

She was still known as Xianglin's Wife.

But now she was a very different woman. She had not worked there than two or three days before her mistress realized that she was not as quick as before. Her memory was much worse too, while her face, like a death-mask, never showed the least trace of a smile. Already my aunt was expressing herself as not too satisfied. Though my uncle had frowned as before when she first arrived, they always had such trouble finding servants that he raised no serious objections, simply warning his wife on the quiet that

对，只是暗暗地告诫四婶说，这种人虽然似乎很可怜，但是败坏风俗的，用她帮忙还可以，祭祀时候可用不着她沾手，一切饭菜，只好自己做，否则，不干不净，祖宗是不吃的。

四叔家里最重大的事件是祭祀，祥林嫂先前最忙的时候也就是祭祀，这回她却清闲了。桌子放在堂中央，系上桌帏，她还记得照旧的去分配酒杯和筷子。

“祥林嫂，你放着罢！我来摆。”四婶慌忙的说。

她讪讪的缩了手，又去职烛台。

“祥林嫂，你放着罢！我来拿。”四婶又慌忙的说。

她转了几个圆圈，终于没有事情做，只得疑惑的走开。她在这一天可做的事是不过坐在灶下烧火。

镇上的人们也仍然叫她祥林嫂，但音调和先前很不同；也还和她讲话，但笑容却冷冷的了。她全不理会那些事，只是直着眼睛，和大家讲她自己日夜不忘的故事：

“我真傻，真的，”她说。“我单知道雪天是野兽在深山里没有食吃，会到村里来；我不知道春天也会有。我一大早起来就开了门，拿小篮盛了一篮豆，叫我们的阿毛坐在门槛上剥豆去。他是很听话的孩子，我的话句句听；他就出去了。我就在屋后劈柴，淘米，米下了锅，打算蒸豆。我叫，‘阿毛！’没有应。出去一看，只见豆撒得满地，没有我们的阿毛了。各处去一问，都没有。我急了，央人去寻去。直到下半天，几个人寻到山坳里，看见刺柴上挂着一只他的小鞋。大家都说，完了，怕是遭了狼了。再进去；果然，他躺在草窠里，肚里的五脏已经都给吃空了，可怜他手里还紧紧的捏着那只小篮呢。……”她于是淌下眼泪来，声音也呜咽了。

这故事倒颇有效，男人听到这里，往往敛起笑容，没趣的走了开去；女人们却不独宽恕了她似的，脸上立刻改换了鄙薄的神气，还要陪出许多眼泪来。有些老女人没有在街头听到她的话，便特意寻来，要听她这一段悲惨的故事。直到她说到呜咽，她们也就一齐流下那停在眼角上的

while such people might seem very pathetic they exerted a bad moral influence. She could work for them but must have nothing to do with ancestral sacrifices. They would have to prepare all the dishes themselves. Otherwise they would be unclean and the ancestors would not accept them.

The most important events in my uncle's household were ancestral sacrifices, and formerly these had kept Xianglin's Wife espcially busy, but now she had virtually nothing to do. As soon as the table had been placed in the centre of the hall and a front curtain fastened around its legs, she started setting out the winecups and chopsticks in the way she still remembered.

"Put those down, Xianglin's Wife," cried my aunt hastily. "Leave that to me."

She drew back sheepishly then and went for the candlesticks.

"Put those down, Xianglin's Wife," cried my aunt again in haste. "I'll fetch them."

After walking round in the hall several times without finding anything to do, she moved doubtfully away. All she could do that day was to sit by the stove and feed the fire.

The townspeople still called her Xianglin's Wife, but in quite a different tone from before; and although they still talked to her, their manner was colder. Quite impervious to this, staring straight in front of her, she would tell everybody the story which night or day was never out of her mind.

"I was really too stupid, really," she would say. "All I knew was that when it snowed and the wild beasts up in the hills had nothing to eat, they might come to the villages. I didn't know that in spring they might come too. I got up at dawn and opened the door, filled a small basket with beans and told our Amao to sit on the doorstep and shell them. He was such a good boy; he always did as he was told, and out he went. Then I went to the back to chop wood and wash the rice, and when the rice was in the pan I wanted to steam the beans. I called Amao, but there was no answer. When I went out to look, there were beans all over the ground but no Amao. He never went to the neighbours' houses to play; and, sure enough, though I asked everywhere he wasn't there. I got so worried, I begged people to help me find him. Not until that afternoon, after searching high and low, did they try the gully. There they saw one of his little shoes caught on a bramble. 'That's bad,' they said. 'A wolf must have got him.' And sure enough, further on, there he was lying in the wolf's den, all his innards eaten away, still clutching that little basket tight in his hand...." At this point her voice would be choked with tears.

This story was so effective that men hearing it often stopped smiling and walked blankly away, while the women not only seemed to forgive her but wiped the contemptuous expression off their faces and added their tears to hers. Indeed, some old women who had not heard her in the street sought her out specially to hear her sad tale.

眼泪，叹息一番，满足的去了，一面还纷纷的评论着。

她就只是反复的向人说她悲惨的故事，常常引住了三五个人来听她。但不久，大家也都听得纯熟了，便是最慈悲的念佛的老太太们，眼里也再不见有一点泪的痕迹。后来全镇的人们几乎都能背诵她的话，一听到就烦厌得头痛。

"我真傻，真的，"她开首说。

"是的，你是单知道雪天野兽在深山里没有食吃，才会到村里来的。"他们立即打断她的话，走开去了。

她张着口怔怔的站着，直着眼睛看他们，接着也就走了，似乎自己也觉得没趣。但她还妄想，希图从别的事，如小篮，豆，别人的孩子上，引出她的阿毛的故事来。倘一看见两三岁的小孩子，她就说：

"唉唉，我们的阿毛如果还在，也就有这么大了。……"

孩子看见她的眼光就吃惊，牵着母亲的衣襟催她走。于是又只剩下她一个，终于没趣的也走了。后来大家又都知道了她的脾气，只要有孩子在眼前，便似笑非笑的先问她，道：

"祥林嫂，你们的阿毛如果还在，不是也就有这么大了么？"

她未必知道她的悲哀经大家咀嚼赏鉴了许多天，早已成为渣滓，只值得烦厌和唾弃；但从人们的笑影上，也仿佛觉得这又冷又尖，自己再没有开口的必要了。她单是一瞥他们，并不回答一句话。

鲁镇永远是过新年，腊月二十以后就忙起来了。四叔家里这回须雇男短工，还是忙不过来，另叫柳妈做帮手，杀鸡，宰鹅；然而柳妈是善女人，吃素，不杀生的，只肯洗器皿。祥林嫂除烧火之外，没有别的事，却闲着了，坐着只看柳妈洗器皿。微雪点点的下来了。

"唉唉，我真傻，"祥林嫂看了天空，叹息着，独语似的说。

"祥林嫂，你又来了。"柳妈不耐烦的看着她的脸，

And when she broke down, they too shed the tears which had gathered in their eyes, after which they sighted and went away satisfied, exchanging eager comments.

As for her, she asked nothing better than to tell her sad story over and over again, often gathering three or four hearers around her. But before long everybody knew it so well that no trace of a tear could be seen even in the eyes of the most kindly, Buddha-invoking old ladies. In the end, practically the whole town could recite it by heart and were bored and exasperated to hear it repeated.

"I was really too stupid, really," she would begin.

"Yes. All you knew was that in snowy weather, when the wild beasts in the mountains had nothing to eat, they might come down to the villages." Cutting short her recital abruptly, they walked away.

She would stand there open-mouthed, staring after them stupidly, and then wander off as if she too were bored by the story. But she still tried hopefully to lead up from other topics such as small baskets, and other people's children to the story of her Amao. At the sight of a child of two or three she would say, "Ah if my Amao were alive he'd be just that size...."

Children would take fright at the look in her eyes and clutch the hem of their mothers' clothes to tug them away. Left by herself again, she would eventually walk away. In the end everybody knew what she was like. If a child were present they would ask with a spurious smile, "If your Amao were alive, Xianglin's Wife, wouldn't he be just that size?"

She may not have realized that her tragedy, after being generally savoured for so many days, had long since grown so stale that it now aroused only revulsion and disgust. But she seemed to sense the cold mockery in their smiles, and the fact that there was no need for her to say any more. So she would simply look at them in silence.

New-Year preparations always start in Luzhen on the twentieth day of the twelfth lunar month. That year my uncle's household had to take on a temporary man-servant. And since there was more than he could do they asked Amah Liu to help by killing the chickens and geese; but being a devout vegetarian who would not kill living creatures, she would only wash the sacrificial vessels. Xianglin's Wife, with nothing to do but feed the fire, sat there at a loose end watching Amah Liu as she worked. A light snow began to fall.

"Ah, I was really too stupid," said Xianglin's Wife as if to herself, looking at the sky and sighing.

"There you go again, Xianglin's Wife." Amah Liu glanced with irritation at her face.

说。"我问你：你额角上的伤疤，不就是那时撞坏的么？"

"唔唔。"她含胡的回答。

"我问你：你那时怎么后来竟依了呢？"

"我么？……"

"你呀。我想：这总是你自己愿意了，不然……。"

"阿阿，你不知道他力气多么大呀。"

"我不信。我不信你这么大的力气，真会拗他不过。你后来一定是自己肯了，倒推说他力气大。"

"阿阿，你……你倒自己试试看。"她笑了。

柳妈的打皱的脸也笑起来，使她蹙缩得像一个核桃；干枯的小眼睛一看祥林嫂的额角，又钉住她的眼。祥林嫂似乎很局促了，立刻敛了笑容，旋转眼光，自去看雪花。

"祥林嫂，你实在不合算。"柳妈诡秘的说。"再一强，或者索性撞一个死，就好了。现在呢，你和你的第二个男人过活不到两年，倒落了一件大罪名。你想，你将来到阴司去，那两个死鬼的男人还要争，你给了谁好呢？阎罗大王只好把你锯开来，分给他们。我想，这真是…"

她脸上就显出恐怖的神色来，这是在山村里所未曾知道的。

"我想，你不如及早抵当。你到土地庙里去捐一条门槛，当做你的替身，给千人踏，万人跨，赎了这一世的罪名，免得死了去受苦。"

她当时并不回答什么话，但大约非常苦闷了，第二天早上起来的时候，两眼上便都围着大黑圈。早饭之后，她便到镇的西头的土地庙里去求捐门槛。庙祝起初执意不允许，直到她急得流泪，才勉强答应了。价目是大钱十二千。

她久已不和人们交口，因为阿毛的故事是早被大家厌弃了的；但自从和柳妈谈了天，似乎又即传扬开去，许多人都发生了新趣味，又来逗她说话了。至于题目，那自然是换了一个新样，专在她额上的伤疤。

"Tell me, wasn't that when you got that scar on your forehead?"

All the reply she received was a vague murmur.

"Tell me this: What made you willing after all?"

"Willing?"

"Yes. Seems to me you must have been willing. Otherwise...."

"Oh, you don't know how strong he was."

"I don't believe it. I don't believe he was so strong that you with your strength couldn't have kept him off. You must have ended up willing. That talk of his being so strong is just an excuse."

"Why... just try for yourself and see." She smiled.

Amah Liu's lined face broken into a smile too, wrinkling up like a walnut-shell. Her small beady eyes swept the other woman's forehead, then fastened on her eyes. At once Xianglin's Wife stopped smiling, as if embarrassed, and turned her eyes away to watch the snow.

"That was really a bad bargain you struck, Xianglin's Wife,"said Amah Liu mysteriously. "If you'd held out longer or knocked yourself to death outright, that would have been better. As it is, you're guilty of a great sin though you lived less than two years with your second husband. Just think: when you go down to the lower world, the ghosts of both men will start fighting over you. Which ought to have you? The King of Hell will have to saw you into two and divide you between them. I feel it really is...."

Xianglin's Wife's face registered terror then. This was something no one had told her up in the mountains.

"Better guard against that in good time, I say. Go to the Temple of the Tutelary God and buy a threshold to be trampled on instead of you by thousands of people. If you atone for your sins in this life you'll escape torment after death."

Xianglin's Wife said nothing at the time, but she must have taken this advice to heart, for when she got up the next morning there were dark rims round her eyes. After breakfast she went to the Temple of the Tutelary God at the west end of the town and asked to buy a threshold as an offering. At first the priest refused, only giving a grudging consent after she was reduced to tears of desperation. The price charged was twelve thousand cash.

She had long since given up talking to people after their contemptuous reception of Amao's story; but as word of her conversation with Amah Liu spread, many of the townsfolk took a fresh interest in her and came once more to provoke her into talking. The topic, of course, had changed to the scar on her forehead.

“祥林嫂，我问你：你那时怎么竟肯了？”一个说。

“唉，可惜，白撞了这一下。”一个看着她的疤，应和道。

她大约从他们的笑容和声调上，也知道是在嘲笑她，所以总是瞪着眼睛，不说一句话，后来连头也不回了。她整日紧闭了嘴唇，头上带着大家以为耻辱的记号的那伤痕，默默的跑街，扫地，洗菜，淘米。快够一年，她才从四婶手里支取了历来积存的工钱，换算了十二元鹰洋，请假到镇的西头去。但不到一顿饭时候，她便回来，神气很舒畅，眼光也分外有神，高兴似的对四婶说，自己已经在土地庙捐了门槛了。

冬至的祭祖时节，她做得更出力，看四婶装好祭品，和阿牛将桌子抬到堂屋中央，她便坦然的去拿酒杯和筷子。

“你放着罢，祥林嫂！”四婶慌忙大声说。

她像是受了炮烙似的缩手，脸色同时变作灰黑，也不再去取烛台，只是失神的站着。直到四叔上香的时候，教她走开，她才走开。这一回她的变化非常大，第二天，不但眼睛窈陷下去，连精神也更不济了。而且很胆怯，不独怕暗夜，怕黑影，即使看见人，虽是自己的主人，也总惴惴的，有如在白天出穴游行的小鼠；否则呆坐着，直是一个木偶人。不半年，头发也花白起来了，记性尤其坏，甚而至于常常忘却了去淘米。

“祥林嫂怎么这样了？倒不如那时不留她。”四婶有时当面就这样说，似乎是警告她。

然而她总如此，全不见有伶俐起来的希望。他们于是想打发她走了，教她回到卫老婆子那里去。但当我还在鲁镇的时候，不过单是这样说；看现在的情状，可见后来终于实行了。然而她是从四叔家出去就成了乞丐的呢，还是先到卫老婆子家然后再成乞丐的呢？那我可不知道。

我给那些因为在近旁而极响的爆竹声惊醒，看见豆

"Tell me, Xianglin's Wife, what made you willing in the end?" one would ask.

"What a waste, to have bashed yourself like that for nothing," another would chime in, looking at her scar.

She must have known from their smiles and tone of voice that they were mocking her, for she simply stared at them without a word and finally did not even turn her head. All day long she kept her lips tightly closed, bearing on her head the scar considered by everyone as a badge of shame, while she shopped, swept the floor, washed the vegetables and prepared the rice in silence. Nearly a year went by before she took her accumulated wages from my aunt, changed them for twelve silver dollars, and asked for leave to go to the west end of the town. In less time than it takes for a meal she was back again, looking much comforted. With an unaccustomed light in her eyes, she told my aunt contentedly that she had now offered up a threshold in the Temple of the Tutelary God.

When the time came for the ancestral sacrifice at the winter solstice she worked harder than ever, and as soon as my aunt took out the sacrificial vessels and helped Aniu to carry the table into the middle of the hall, she went confidently to fetch the winecups and chopsticks.

"Put those down, Xianglin's Wife!" my aunt called hastily.

She withdrew her hand as if scorched, her face turned ashen grey, and instead of fetching the candlesticks she just stood there in a daze until my uncle came in to burn some incense and told her to go away. This time the change in her was phenomenal: the next day her eyes were sunken, her spirit seemed broken. She took fright very easily too, afraid not only of the dark and of shadows, but of meeting anyone. Even the sight of her own master or mistress set her trembling like a mouse that had strayed out of its hole in broad daylight. The rest of the time she would sit stupidly as if carved out of wood. In less than half a year her hair had turned grey, and her memory had deteriorated so much that she often forgot to go and wash the rice.

"What come over Xianglin's Wife? We should never have taken her on again," my aunt would sometimes say in front of her, as if to warn her.

But there was not change in her, no sign that she would ever recover her wits. So they decided to get rid of her and tell her to go back to Old Mrs. Wei. That was what they were saying, at least, while I was there; and, judging by subsequent developments, this is evidently what they must have done. But whether she started begging as soon as she left my uncle's house, or whether she went first to Old Mrs. Wei and later became a beggar, I do not know.

I was woken up by the noisy explosion of crackers close at hand and, from the faint

一般大的黄色的灯火光，接着又听得毕毕剥剥的鞭炮，是四叔家正在“祝福”了；知道已是五更将近时候。我在蒙胧中，又隐约听到远处的爆竹声联绵不断，似乎合成一天音响的浓云，夹着团团飞舞的雪花，拥抱了全市镇。我在这繁响的拥抱中，也懒散而且舒适，从白天以至初夜的疑虑，全给祝福的空气一扫而空了，只觉得天地圣众歆享了牲醴和香烟，都醉醺醺的在空中蹒跚，豫备给鲁镇的人们以无限的幸福。

一九二四年二月七日。

glow shed by the yellow oil lamp and the bangs of fireworks as my uncle's household celebrated the sacrifice, I knew that it must be nearly dawn. Listening drowsily I heard vaguely the ceaseless explosion of crackers in the distance. It seemed to me that the whole town was enveloped by the dense cloud of noise in the sky, mingling with the whirling snowflakes. Enveloped in this medley of sound I relaxed; the doubt which had preyed on my mind from dawn till night was swept clean away by the festive atmosphere, and I felt only that the saints of heaven and earth had accepted the sacrifice and incense and were reeling with intoxication in the sky, preparing to give Luzhen's people boundless good fortune.

February 7, 1924

他满脸已经通红，似乎很有些醉，
但眼光却又消沉下去了。

His whole face was scarlet as if he were quite drunk,
but the gleam in his eyes had died down.

在酒楼上
In the Tavern

我从北地向东南旅行，绕道访了我的家乡，就到S城。这城离我的故乡不过三十里，坐了小船，小半天可到，我曾在这里的学校里当过一年的教员。深冬雪后，风景凄清，懒散和怀旧的心绪联结起来，我竟暂寓在S城的洛思旅馆里了；这旅馆是先前所没有的。城圈本不大，寻访了几个以为可以会见的旧同事，一个也不在，早不知散到那里去了；经过学校的门口，也改换了名称和模样，于我很生疏。不到两个时辰，我的意兴早已索然，颇悔此来为多事了。

我所住的旅馆是租房不卖饭的，饭菜必须另外叫来，但又无味，入口如嚼泥土。窗外只有渍痕斑驳的墙壁，帖着枯死的莓苔；上面是铅色的天，白皑皑的绝无精采，而且微雪又飞舞起来了。我午餐本没有饱，又没有可以消遣的事情，便很自然的想到先前有一家很熟识的小酒楼，叫一石居的，算来离旅馆并不远。我于是立即锁了房门，出街向那酒楼去。其实也无非想姑且逃避客中的无聊，并不专为买醉。一石居是在的，狭小阴湿的店面和破旧的招牌都依旧；但从掌柜以至堂倌却已没有一个熟人，我在这一石居中也完全成了生客。然而我终于跨上那走熟的屋角的扶梯去了，由此径到小楼上。上面也依然是五张小板桌；独有原是木棂的后窗却换嵌了玻璃。

“一斤绍酒。——菜？十个油豆腐，辣酱要多！”

我一面说给跟我上来的堂倌听，一面向后窗走，就在靠窗的一张桌旁坐下了。楼上“空空如也”，任我拣得最好的坐位：可以眺望楼下的废园。这园大概是不属于酒家的，我先前也曾眺望过许多回，有时也在雪天里。但现在从惯于北方的眼睛看来，却很值得惊异了：几株老梅竟斗雪开着满树的繁花，仿佛毫不以深冬为意；倒塌的亭子边还有一株山茶树，从暗绿的密叶里显出十几朵红花来，赫赫的在雪中明得如火，愤怒而且傲慢，如蔑视游人的甘心于远行。我这时又忽地想到这里积雪的滋润，著物不去，晶莹有光，不比朔雪的粉一般干，大风一吹，便飞得满空

During my travels from the north to the southeast I made a detour to my home and then went on to S— . This town, only thirty li from my native place, can be reached in less than half a day by a small boat. I had taught for a year in a school here. In the depth of winter after snow the landscape was bleak; but a combination of indolence and nostalgia made me put up briefly in the Luo Si Hotel, a new hotel since my time. The town was small. I looked for several old colleagues I thought I might find, but not one of them was there. They had long since gone their different ways. And when I passed the gate of the school that too had changed its name and appearance, making me feel quite a stranger. In less than two hours my enthusiasm had waned and I rather reproached myself for coming.

The hotel I was in let rooms but did not serve meals, which had to be ordered from outside, but these were about as unpalatable as mud. Outside the window was only a stained and spotted wall, covered with withered moss. Above was the leaden sky, a colourless dead white; moreover a flurry of snow had begun to fall. Since my lunch had been poor and I had nothing to do to while away the time, my thoughts turned quite naturally to a small tavern I had known well in the past called One Barrel House, which I reckoned could not be far from the hotel. I immediately locked my door and set out to find it. Actually, all I wanted was to escape the boredom of my stay, not to do any serious drinking. One Barrel House was still there, its narrow mouldering front and dilapidated signboard unchanged. But from the landlord down to the waiters there was not a soul I knew — in One Barrel House too I had become a complete strange. Still I climbed the familiar stairway in the corner to the little upper storey. The five small wooden tables up here were unchanged; only the window at the back, originally latticed, had been fitted with glass panes.

"A catty of yellow wine. To go with it? Ten pieces of fried beancurd with plenty of paprika sauce."

As I gave this order to the waiter who had come up with me I went and sat down at the table by the back window. The fact that the place was empty enabled me to pick the best seat, one with a view of the deserted garden below. Most likely this did not belong to the tavern. I had looked out at it many times in the past, sometimes too in snowy weather. But now, to eyes accustomed to the north, the sight was sufficiently striking. Several old plum trees in full bloom were braving the snow as if oblivious of the depth of winter; while among the thick dark green foliage of a camellia beside the crumbling pavilion a dozen crimson blossoms blazed bright as flame in the snow, indignant and arrogant, as if despising the wanderer's wanderlust. At this I suddenly remembered the moistness of the heaped snow here, clinging, glistening and shining, quite unlike the

如烟雾。……

“客人，酒。……”

堂倌懒懒的说着，放下杯，筷，酒壶和碗碟，酒到了。我转脸向了板桌，排好器具，斟出酒来。觉得北方固不是我的旧乡，但南来又只能算一个客子，无论那边的干雪怎样纷飞，这里的柔雪又怎样的依恋，于我都没有什么关系了。我略带些哀愁，然而很舒服的呷一口酒。酒味很纯正；油豆腐也煮得十分好；可惜辣酱太淡薄，本来S城人是不懂得吃辣的。

大概是因为正在下午的缘故罢，这虽说是酒楼，却毫无酒楼气，我已经喝下三杯酒去了，而我以外还是四张空板桌。我看着废园，渐渐的感到孤独，但又不愿有别的酒客上来。偶然听得楼梯上脚步响，便不由的有些懊恼，待到看见是堂倌，才又安心了，这样的又喝了两杯酒。

我想，这回定是酒客了，因为听得那脚步声比堂倌的要缓得多。约略料他走完了楼梯的时候，我便害怕似的抬头去看这无干的同伴，同时也就吃惊的站起来。我竟不料在这里意外的遇见朋友了，——假如他现在还许我称他为朋友。那上来的分明是我的旧同窗，也是做教员时代的旧同事，面貌虽然颇有些改变，但一见也就认识，独有行动却变得格外迂缓，很不像当年敏捷精悍的吕纬甫了。

“阿，——纬甫，是你么？我万想不到会在这里遇见你。”

“阿阿，是你？我也万想不到……”

我就邀他同坐，但他似乎略略踌躇之后，方才坐下来。我起先很以为奇，接着便有些悲伤，而且不快了。细看他相貌，也还是乱蓬蓬的须发；苍白的长方脸，然而衰瘦了。精神很沉静，或者却是颓唐；又浓又黑的眉毛底下的眼睛也失了精采，但当他缓缓的四顾的时候，却对废园忽地闪出我在学校时代常常看见的射人的光来。

“我们，”我高兴的，然而颇不自然的说，“我们这一别，怕有十年了罢。我早知道你在济南，可是实在懒得太难，终于没有写一封信。……”

dry northern snow which when a high wind blows will fly up to fill the sky like mist....

"Your wine, sir..." said the waiter carelessly, putting down my cup, chopsticks, winepot and dish. The wine had come. I turned to the table, set everything straight and filled my cup. I felt that the north was certainly not my home, yet when I came south I could only count as a stranger. The powdery dry snow which whirled through the air up there and the clinging soft snow here were equally a lien to me. In a slightly melancholy mood I took a leisurely sip of wine. The wine tasted pure and the fried beancurd was excellently cooked, only the paprika sauce was not hot enough; but then the people of S— had never understood pungent flavours.

Probalbly because it was the afternoon, the place had none of the atmosphere of a tavern. By the time I had drunk three cups, the four other tables were still unoccupied. A sense of loneliness stole over me as I stared at the deserted garden, yet I did not want other customers to come up. Thus I could not help being irritated by the occasional footsteps on the stairs, and was relieved to find it was only the waiter. And so I drank another two cups of wine.

"This time it must be a customer," I thought, at the sound of footsteps much slower than those of the waiter. When I judged that he must be at the top of the stairs, I raised my head rather apprehensively to look at this extraneous company and stood up with a start. It had never occurred to me that I might run into a friend here — if such he would still let me call him. The newcomer was an old classmate who had been my colleague when I was a teacher, and although he had changed a great deal I knew him at a glance. Only he had become very slow in his movements, quite unlike the spry dynamic Lü Weifu of the old days.

"Well, Weifu, is it you? Fancy meeting you here!"

"Well, well, is it you? Just fancy...."

I invited him to join me, but he seemed to hesitate before doing so. This struck me as strange, then felt rather hurt and annoyed. A closer look revearled that Lü had still the same unkempt hair and beard, but his pale lantern-jawed face was thin and wasted. He appeared very quiet if not dispirited, and his eyes beneath their thick black brows had lost their alertness; but while looking slowly around, at sight of the deserted garden they suddenly flashed with the same piercing light I had seen so often at school.

"Well," I said cheerfully but very awkwardly, "it must be ten years since last we saw each other. I heard long ago that you were at Jinan, but I was so wretchedly lazy I never wrote...."

“彼此都一样。可是现在我在太原了，已经两年多，和我的母亲。我回来接她的时候，知道你早搬走了，搬得很干净。”

“你在太原做什么呢？”我问。

“教书，在一个同乡的家里。”

“这以前呢？”

“这以前么？”他从衣袋里掏出一支烟卷来，点了火衔在嘴里，看着喷出的烟雾，沉思似的说，“无非做了些无聊的事情，等于什么也没有做。”

他也问我别后的景况；我一面告诉他一个大概，一面叫堂倌先取杯筷来，使他先喝着我的酒，然后再去添二斤。其间还点菜，我们先前原是毫不客气的，但此刻却推让起来了，终于说不清那一样是谁点的，就从堂倌的口头报告上指定了四样菜：茴香豆，冻肉，油豆腐，青鱼干。

“我一回来，就想到我可笑。”他一手擎着烟卷，一只手扶着酒杯，似笑非笑的向我说。“我在少年时，看见蜂子或蝇子停在一个地方，给什么来一吓，即刻飞去了，但是飞了一个小圈子，便又回来停在原地点，便以为这实在很可笑，也可怜。可不料现在我自己也飞回来了，不过绕了一点小圈子。又不料你也回来了。你不能飞得更远些么？”

“这难说，大约也不外乎绕点小圈子罢。”我也似笑非笑的说。“但是你为什么飞回来的呢？”

“也还是为了无聊的事。”他一口喝干了一杯酒，吸几口烟，眼睛略为张大了。“无聊的。——但是我们就谈谈罢。”

堂倌搬上新添的酒菜来，排满了一桌，楼上又添了烟气和油豆腐的热气，仿佛热闹起来了；楼外的雪也越加纷纷的下。

“你也许本来知道，”他接着说，“我曾经有一个小兄弟，是三岁上死掉的，就葬在这乡下。我连他的模样都记不清楚了，但听母亲说，是一个很可爱念的孩子，和我也很相投，至今她提起来还似乎要下泪。今年春天，一个

"It was the same with me. I've been at Taiyuan for more than two years now with my mother. When I came back to fetch her I learned that you had already left, left for good and all."

"What are you doing at Taiyuan?" I asked.

"Teaching in the family of a fellow-provincial."

"And before that?"

"Before that?" He took a cigarette from his pocket, lit it and put it to his lips, then watching the smoke he puffed out said reflectively, "Just futile work, amounting to nothing at all."

He in turn asked what I had been doing all these years. I gave him a rough idea, at the same time calling the waiter to bring a cup and chopsticks in order that Lü could share my wine while we had another two catties heated. We also ordered dishes. In the past we had never stood on ceremony, but now we began deferring to each other so that finally we fixed on four dishes suggested by the waiter: peas spiced with aniseed, jellied pork, fried beancurd and salted mackerel.

"As soon as I came back I knew I was a fool." Holding his cigarette in one hand and the winecup in the other, he spoke with a bitter smile. "When I was young, I saw the way bees or flies stuck to one spot. If something frightened them they would buzz off, but after flying in a small circle they would come back to stop in the same place; and I thought this really ridiculous as well as pathetic. Little did I think I'd be flying back myself too after only describing a small circle. And I didn't think you'd come back either. Couldn't you have flown a little further?"

"That's difficult to say. Probably I too have simply described a small circle." I also spoke with a rather bitter smile. "But why did you fly back?"

"For something quite futile." In one gulp he emptied his cup, then took several pulls at his cigarette and his eyes widened a little. "Futile — but you may as well hear about it."

The waiter brought up the freshly heated wine and dishes and set them on the table. The smoke and the fragrance of fried beancurd seemed to make the upstairs room more cheerful, while outside the snow fell still more thickly.

"Perhaps you knew," he went on, "that I had a little brother who died when he was three and was buried in the country here. I can't even remember clearly what he looked like, but I've heard my mother say he was a very lovable child and very fond of me. Even now it brings tears to her eyes to speak of him. This spring an elder cousin wrote to tell us that the ground beside his grave was gradually being swamped, and he was

堂兄就来了一封信，说他的坟边已经渐渐的浸了水，不久怕要陷入河里去了，须得赶紧去设法。母亲一知道就很着急，几乎几夜睡不着，——她又自己能看信的。然而我能有什么法子呢？没有钱，没有工夫：当时什么法也没有。

“一直挨到现在，趁着年假的闲空，我才得回南给他来迁葬。”他又喝干一杯酒，看着窗外，说，“这在那边那里能如此呢？积雪里会有花，雪地下会不冻。就在前天，我在城里买了一口小棺材，——因为我豫料那地下的应该早已朽烂了，——带着棉絮和被褥，雇了四个土工，下乡迁葬去。我当时忽而很高兴，愿意掘一回坟，愿意一见我那曾经和我很亲睦的小兄弟的骨殖：这些事我生平都没有经历过。到得坟地，果然，河水只是咬进来，离坟已不到二尺远。可怜的坟，两年没有培土，也平下去了。我站在雪中，决然的指着他对土工说，‘掘开来！’我实在是一个庸人，我这时觉得我的声音有些希奇，这命令也是一个在我一生中最为伟大的命令。但土工们却毫不骇怪，就动手掘下去了。待到掘着圹穴，我便过去看，果然，棺木已经快要烂尽了，只剩下一堆木丝和小木片。我的心颤动着，自去拨开这些，很小心的，要看一看我的小兄弟。然而出乎意外！被褥，衣服，骨骼，什么也没有。我想，这些都消尽了，向来听说最难烂的是头发，也许还有罢。我便伏下去，在该是枕头所在的泥土里仔仔细细的看，也没有。踪影全无！”

我忽而看见他眼圈微红了，但立即知道是有了酒意。他总不很吃菜，单是把酒不停的喝，早喝了一斤多，神情和举动都活泼起来，渐近于先前所见的吕纬甫了。我叫堂倌再添二斤酒，然后回转身，也拿着酒杯，正对面默默的听着。

“其实，这本已可以不必再迁，只要平了土，卖掉棺材，就此完事了的。我去卖棺材虽然有些离奇，但只要价钱极便宜，原铺子就许要，至少总可以捞回几文酒钱来。但我不这样，我仍然铺好被褥，用棉花裹了些他先前身体

afraid before long it would slip into the river: we should go at once and do something about it. This upset my mother so much that she couldn't sleep for several nights — she can read letters herself, you know. But what could I do? I had no money, no time: there was nothing that could be done.

"Now at last, because I'm on holiday over New Year, I've been able to come south to move his grave." He tossed off another cup of wine and looking out of the window exclaimed, "Could you find anything like this up north? Blossom in thick snow, and the soil beneath the snow not frozen. So the day before yesterday I bought a small coffin in town — because I reckoned that the one under the ground must have rotted long ago — took cotton and bedding, hired four workmen, and went into the country to move his grave, I suddenly felt most elated, eager to dig up the grave, eager to see the bones of the little brother who had been so fond of me: this was a new experience for me. When we reached the grave, sure enough, the river was encroaching on it and the water was less than two feet away. The poor grave not having had any earth added to it for two years was subsiding. Standing there in the snow, I pointed to it firmly and ordered the workmen, 'Dig it up.'

"I really am a commonplace fellow. I felt that my voice at this juncture was rather unnatural, and that this order was the greatest I had given in all my life. But the workmen didn't find it strange in the least, and set to work to dig. When they reached the enclosure I had a look, and sure enough the coffin had rotted almost completely away: there was nothing left but a heap of splinters and chips of wood. My heart beat faster as I set these aside myself, very carefully, wanting to see my little brother. However, I was in for a surprise. Bedding, clothes, skeleton, all had gone!"

"I thought, 'These have all disappeared, but hair, I have always heard, is the last thing to rot. There may still be some hair.' So I bent down and search carefully in the mud where the pillow should have been, but there was none. Not a trace remained."

I suddenly noticed that the rims of his eyes were rather red, but immediately attributed this to the effect of the wine. He had scarcely touched the dishes but had been drinking incessantly and must have drunk more than a catty; his looks and gestures had become more animated, more like the Lü Weifu whom I had known. I called the waiter to heat two more catties of wine, then turned back to face my companion, my cup in my hand, as I listened to him in silence.

"Actually there was really no need to move it: I had only to level the ground, sell the coffin and make an end of the business. Although it might have seemed odd my going to sell the coffin, if the price were low enough the shop from which I bought it would have taken it, and I could at least have recouped a few cents for wine. But I didn't. I

所在的地方的泥土，包起来，装在新棺材里，运到我父亲埋着的坟地上，在他坟旁埋掉了。因为外面用砖墩，昨天又忙了我大半天：监工。但这样总算完结了一件事，足够去骗骗我的母亲，使她安心些。——阿阿，你这样的看我，你怪我何以和先前太不相同了么？是的，我也还记得我们同到城隍庙里去拔掉神像的胡子的时候，连日议论些改革中国的方法以至于打起来的时候。但我现在就是这样了，敷敷衍衍，模模胡胡。我有时自己也想到，倘若先前的朋友看见我，怕会不认我做朋友了。——然而我现在就是这样。”

他又掏出一支烟卷来，衔在嘴里，点了火。

“看你的神情，你似乎还有些期望我，——我现在自然麻木得多了，但是有些事也还看得出。这使我很感激，然而也使我很不安：怕我终于辜负了至今还对我怀着好意的老朋友。……”他忽而停住了，吸几口烟，才又慢慢的说，“正在今天，刚在我到这一石居来之前，也就做了一件无聊事，然而也是我自己愿意做的。我先前的东边的邻居叫长富，是一个船户。他有一个女儿叫阿顺，你那时到我家里来，也许见过的，但你一定没有留心，因为那时她还小。后来她也长得并不好看，不过是平常的瘦瘦的瓜子脸，黄脸皮；独有眼睛非常大，睫毛也很长，眼白又青得如夜的晴天，而且是北方的无风的晴天，这里的就没有那么明净了。她很能干，十多岁没了母亲，招呼两个小弟妹都靠她；又得服侍父亲，事事都周到；也经济，家计倒渐渐的稳当起来了。邻居几乎没有一个不夸奖她，连长富也时常说些感激的话。这一次我动身回来的时候，我的母亲又记得她了，老年人记性真长久。她说她曾经知道顺姑因为看见谁的头上戴着红的剪绒花，自己也想有一朵，弄不到，哭了，哭了小半夜，就挨了她父亲的一顿打，后来眼眶还红肿了两三天。这种剪绒花是外省的东西，S城里尚且买不出，她那里想得到手呢？趁我这一次回南的便，便叫我买两朵去送她。

still spread out the bedding, wrapped up in cotton some of the clay where his body had been, covered it up, put it in the new coffin, moved it to my father's grave and buried it beside him. And having a brick vault built kept me busy most of yesterday too, supervising the work. But in this way I can count the affair ended, at least enough to deceive my mother and set her mind at rest. Well, well, the look you're giving me shows you are wondering why I've changed so much. Yes, I still remember the time when we went together to the tutelary god's temple to pull off the idols' beards, and how for days on end we used to discuss methods of reforming China until we even came to blows. But this is how I am now, willing to let things slide and to compromise. Sometimes I think, if my old friends were to see me now, probably they would no longer acknowledge me as a friend. But this is what I am like now."

He took out another cigarette, put it to his lips and lit it.

"Judging by your expression, you still expect something of me. Naturally I am much more obtuse than before, but I'm not completely blind yet. This makes me grateful to you, at the same time rather uneasy. I'm afraid I've let down the old friends who even now still wish me well...." He stopped and took several puffs at his cigarette before going on slowly, "Only today, just before coming to this One Barrel House, I did something futile yet something I was glad to do. My former neighbour on the east side was called Changfu. He was a boatman and had a daughter named Ashun. When you came to my house in those days you may have seen her but you certainly wouldn't have paid any attention to her, because she was still small then. She didn't grow up to be pretty either, having just an ordinary thin oval face and pale skin. Only her eyes were unusually large with very long lashes and whites as clear as a cloudless night sky — I mean the cloudless sky of the north on a windless day; here it is not so clear. She was very capable. She lost her mother while in her teens, and had to look after a small brother and sister besides waiting on her father; and all this she did very competently. She was so economical too that the family gradually grew better off. There was scarcely a neighbour who didn't praise her, and even Changfu often expressed his appreciation. When I was setting off on my journey this time, my mother remembered her — old people's memories are so long. She recalled that once Ashun saw someone wearing red velvet flowers in her hair, and wanted a spray for herself. When she couldn't get one she cried nearly all night, so that her father beat her and her eyes remained red and swollen for two or three days. These red flowers came from another province and couldn't be bought even in S— , so how could she ever hope to have any? Since I was coming south this time, my mother told me to buy two sprays for her.

“我对于这差使倒并不以为烦厌，反而很喜欢；为阿顺，我实在还有些愿意出力的意思的。前年，我回来接我母亲的时候，有一天，长富正在家，不知怎的我和他闲谈起来了。他便要请我吃点心，荞麦粉，并且告诉我所加的是白糖。你想，家里能有白糖的船户，可见决不是一个穷船户了，所以他也吃得很阔绰。我被劝不过，答应了，但要求只要用小碗。他也很识世故，便嘱咐阿顺说，‘他们文人，是不会吃东西的。你就用小碗，多加糖！’然而等到调好端来的时候，仍然使我吃一吓，是一大碗，足够我吃一天。但是和长富吃的一碗比起来，我的也确乎算小碗。我生平没有吃过荞麦粉，这回一尝，实在不可口，却是非常甜。我漫然的吃了几口，就想不吃了，然而无意中，忽然间看见阿顺远远的站在屋角里，就使我立刻消失了放下碗筷的勇气。我看她的神情，是害怕而且希望，大约怕自己调得不好，愿我们吃得有味。我知道如果剩下大半碗来，一定要使她很失望，而且很抱歉。我于是同时决心，放开喉咙灌下去了，几乎吃得和长富一样快。我由此才知道硬吃的苦痛，我只记得还做孩子时候的吃尽一碗拌着驱除蛔虫药粉的沙糖才有这样难。然而我毫不抱怨，因为她过来收拾空碗时候的忍着的得意的笑容，已尽够赔偿我的苦痛而有余了。所以我这一夜虽然饱胀得睡不稳，又做了一大串恶梦，也还是祝赞她一生幸福，愿世界为她变好。然而这些意思也不过是我的那些旧日的梦的痕迹，即刻就自笑，接着也就忘却了。

“我先前并不知道她曾经为了一朵剪绒花挨打，但因为母亲一说起，便也记得了荞麦粉的事，意外的勤快起来了。我先在太原城里搜求了一遍，都没有；一直到济南……”

窗外沙沙的一阵声响，许多积雪从被他压弯了的一枝山茶树上滑下去了，树枝笔挺的伸直，更显出乌油油的肥叶和血红的花来。天空的铅色来得更浓；小鸟雀啾唧的叫着，大概黄昏将近，地面又全罩了雪，寻不出什么食粮，都赶早回巢来休息了。

"Far from feeling vexed at this commission, I was actually delighted, really glad of the chance to do something for Ashun. The year before last I came back to fetch my mother, and one day when Changfu was at home I dropped in for some reason to chat with him. By way of refreshment he offered me some buckwheat mush, remarking that they added white sugar to it. As you can see, a boatman who could afford white sugar was obviously not poor and must eat pretty well. I let myself be persuaded but begged them to give me only a a small bowl. He quite understood and instructed Ashun, 'These scholars have no appetite. Give him a small bowl, but add more sugar.' However, when she had prepared the concoction and brought it in it gave me quite a turn, because it was a large bowl, as much as I could eat in a whole day. Though compared with Changfu's bowl, admittedly, it was small. This was the first time I had eaten buckwheat mush, and I just could not stomach it though it was so sweet. I gulped down a few mouthfuls and decided to leave the rest when I happened to notice Ashun standing some distance away in one corner of the room, and I simply hadn't the heart to put down my chopsticks. In her face I saw both hope and fear — fear presumably that she had prepared it badly, and hope that we would find it to our liking. I knew that if I left most of my bowl she would feel very disappointed and sorry. I made up my mind to it and shovelled the stuff down, eating almost as fast as Changfu. That taught me how painful it is forcing oneself to eat; and I remembered experiencing the same difficulty as a child when I had to finish a bowl of worm-medicine mixed with brown sugar. I didn't hold it against her though, because her half-suppressed smile of satisfaction when she came to take away our empty bowls more than repaid me for all my discomfort. So that night, although indigestion kept me from sleeping well and I had a series of nightmares, I still wished her a lifetime of happiness and hoped that for her sake the world would change for the better. But such thoughts were only the residue of my old dreams. The next instant I laughed at myself, and promptly frogot them.

"I hadn't known before that she had been beaten on account of a spray of velvet flowers, but when my mother spoke of it I remembered the buckwheat mush incident and became unaccountably diligent. First I made a search in Taiyuan, but none of the shops had them. It was only when I went to Jinan...."

There was a rustle outside the window as a pile of snow slithered off the camellia which had been bending beneath its weight; then the branches of the tree straightened themselves. Flaunting their thick dark foliage and blood-red flowers even more clearly. The sky had grown even more leaden. Sparrows were twittering, no doubt because dusk was falling and finding nothing to eat on the snow-covered ground they were going back early to their nests to sleep.

“一直到了济南，”他向窗外看了一回，转身喝干一杯酒，又吸几口烟，接着说。“我才买到剪绒花。我也不知道使她挨打的是不是这一种，总之是绒做的罢了。我也不知道她喜欢深色还是浅色，就买了一朵大红的，一朵粉红的，都带到这里来。

“就是今天午后，我一吃完饭，便去看长富，我为此特地耽搁了一天。他的家倒还在，只是看去很有些晦气色了，但这恐怕不过是我自己的感觉。他的儿子和第二个女儿——阿昭，都站在门口，大了。阿昭长得全不像她姊姊，简直像一个鬼，但是看见我走向她家，便飞奔的逃进屋里去。我就问那小子，知道长富不在家。‘你的大姊呢？’他立刻瞪起眼睛，连声问我寻她什么事，而且恶狠狠的似乎就要扑过来，咬我。我支吾着退走了，我现在是敷敷衍衍……

“你不知道，我可是比先前更怕去访人了。因为我已经深知道自己之讨厌，连自己也讨厌，又何必明知故犯的去使人暗暗地不快呢？然而这回的差使是不能不办妥的，所以想了一想，终于回到就在斜对门的柴店里。店主的母亲，老发奶奶，倒也还在，而且也还认识我，居然将我邀进店里坐去了。我们寒暄几句之后，我就说明了回到S城和寻长富的缘故。不料她叹息说：

“‘可惜顺姑没有福气戴这剪绒花了。’

“她于是详细的告诉我，说是‘大约从去年春天以来，她就见得黄瘦，后来忽而常常下泪了，问她缘故又不说；有时还整夜的哭，哭得长富也忍不住生气，骂她年纪大了，发了疯。可是一到秋初，起先不过小伤风，终于躺倒了，从此就起不来。直到咽气的前几天，才肯对长富说，她早就像她母亲一样，不时的吐红和流夜汗。但是瞒着，怕他因此要担心。有一夜，她的伯伯长庚又来硬借钱，——这是常有的事，——她不给，长庚就冷笑着说：你不要骄气，你的男人比我还不如！她从此就发了愁，又怕羞，不好问，只好哭。长富赶紧将她的男人怎样的挣气

"It was only when I went to Jinan...." He glanced out of the window, then turned back, drained a cup of wine, took several puffs at his cigarette and went on, "Only then did I buy the artificial flowers. I didn't know whether they were the same as those she had been beaten for, but at least they were made of velvet. And not knowing whether she liked deep or light colours, I bought one spray of red, one spray of red, one spray of pink, and brought them both here.

"This afternoon straight after lunch I went to see Changfu, having stayed on an extra day just for this. Though his house was still there it seemed to me rather gloomy, but perhaps that was simply my imagination. His son and second daughter Azhao were standing at the gate. Both of them had grown. Azhao is quite unlike her sister, she looks simply ghastly; but at my approach she rushed into the house. I learned from the boy that Changfu was not at home. 'And your elder sister?' I asked. At that he glared at me and demanded what my business with her was. He looked fierce enough to fling himself at me and bite me. I dithered, then walked away. Nowadays I just let things slide....

You can have no idea how I dread calling on people, much more so than in the old days. Because I know what a nuisance I am, I am even sick of myself; so, knowing this, why inflict myself on others? But since this commission had to be carried out, after some reflection I went back to the firewood shop almost opposite their house. The proprietor's mother old Mrs. Fa was still there and, what's more, still recognized me. She actually asked me into the shop to sit down. After the usual polite preliminaries I told her why I had come back to S— and was looking for Changfu. I was taken aback when she sighed:

"'What a pity Ashun hadn't the luck to wear these velvet flowers.'

"Then she told me the whole story. 'It was probably last spring that Ashun began to look pale and thin. Later she had fits of crying, but if asked why she wouldn't say. Sometimes she even cried all night until Changfu couldn't help losing his temper and swearing at her for carrying on like a crazy old maid. But when autumn came she caught a chill, then she took to her bed and never got up again. Only a few days before she died she confessed to Changfu that she had long ago started spitting blood and perspiring at night like her mother. But she hadn't told him for fear of worrying him. One evening her uncle Changgeng came to demand a loan — he was always sponging on them — and when she wouldn't give him any money he sneered, "Don't give yourself airs; your man isn't even up to me!" That upset her, but she was too shy to ask any questions and could only cry. As soon as Changfu knew this, he told her what a decent fellow the man chosen for her was; but it was too late. Besides, she didn't

的话说给她听，那里还来得及？况且她也不信，反而说；好在我已经这样，什么也不要紧了。’

“她还说，‘如果她的男人真比长庚不如，那就真可怕呵！比不上一个偷鸡贼，那是什么东西呢？然而他来送殓的时候，我是亲眼看见他的，衣服很干净，人也体面；还眼泪汪汪的说，自己撑了半世小船，苦熬苦省的积起钱来聘了一个女人，偏偏又死掉了。可见他实在是一个好人，长庚说的全是诳。只可惜顺姑竟会相信那样的贼骨头的诳话，白送了性命。——但这也不能去怪谁，只能怪顺姑自己没有这一份好福气。’

“那倒也罢，我的事情又完了。但是带在身边的两朵剪绒花怎么办呢？好，我就托她送了阿昭。这阿昭一见我就飞跑，大约将我当做一只狼或是什么，我实在不愿意去送她。——但是我也就送她了，对母亲只要说阿顺见了喜欢的了不得就是。这些无聊的事算什么？只要模模胡胡。模模胡胡的过了新年，仍旧教我的‘子曰诗云’去。”

“你教的是‘子曰诗云’么？”我觉得奇异，便问。

“自然。你还以为教的是ABCD么？我先是两个学生，一个读《诗经》，一个读《孟子》。新近又添了一个，女的，读《女儿经》。连算学也不教，不是我不教，他们不要教。”

“我实在料不到你倒去教这类的书，……”

“他们的老子要他们读这些；我是别人，无乎不可的。这些无聊的事算什么？只要随随便便，……”

他满脸已经通红，似乎很有些醉，但眼光却又消沉下去了。我微微的叹息，一时没有话可说。楼梯上一阵乱响，拥上几个酒客来：当头的是矮子，臃肿的圆脸；第二个是长的，在脸上很惹眼的显出一个红鼻子；此后还有人，一叠连的走得小楼都发抖。我转眼去看吕纬甫，他也正转眼来看我，我就叫堂倌算酒账。

“你借此还可以支持生活么？”我一面准备走，一面问。

“是的。——我每月有二十元，也不大能够敷衍。”

1. A book decribing the feudal standard of behaviour for girls and the virtues they should cultivate.

believe him. "It's a good thing I'm already this way," she said. "Now nothing matters any more."'

"Old Mrs. Fa also said, 'If her man really hadn't been up to Changgeng, that would have been truly frightful. Not up to a chicken thief — what sort of creature would that be? But I saw him with my own eyes at the funeral: dressed in clean clothes and quite presentable. And he said with tears in his eyes that he'd worked hard all those years on the boat to save up money to marry, but now the girl was dead. Obviously he was really a good sort, and Changgeng had been lying. It was too bad that Ashun believed such a rascally liar and died for nothing. Still, we can't blame anyone else: this was Ashun's fate.'

"Since that was the case, my business was finished too. But what about the two sprays of artificial flowers I had brought with me? Well, I asked her to give them to Azhao. This Azhao had fled at the sight of me as if I were a wolf or monster; I really didn't want to give them to her. However, give them I did, and I have only to tell my mother that Ashun was delighted with them and that will be that. Who cares about such futile affairs anyway? One only wants to muddle through them somehow. When I have muddled through New Year I shall go back to teaching the Confucian classics."

"Is that what you're teaching?" I asked in astonishment.

"Of course. Did you think I was teaching English? First I had two pupils, one studying the *Book of Songs*, the other *Mencius*. Recently I have got another, a girl, who is studying the *Canon for Girls*.[1] I don't even teach mathematics; not that I wouldn't teach it, but they don't want it taught."

"I could really never have guessed that you would be teaching such books."

"Their father wants them to study these. I'm an outsider, it's all the same to me. Who cares about such futile affairs anyway? There's no need to take them seriously...."

His whole face was scarlet as if he were quite drunk, but the gleam in his eyes had died down. I gave a slight sigh, not knowing what to say. There was a clatter on the stairs as several customers came up. The first was short, with a round bloated face; the second was tall, with a conspicuous red nose. Behind them followed others, and as they walked up the small upper floor shook. I turned to Lü Weifu who was trying to catch my eye, then called for the bill.

"Is your salary enough to live on?" I asked as we prepared to leave.

"I have twenty dollars a month, not quite enough to manage on."

"那么，你以后豫备怎么办呢？"

"以后？——我不知道。你看我们那时豫想的事可有一件如意？我现在什么也不知道，连明天怎样也不知道，连后一分……"

堂倌送上账来，交给我；他也不像初到时候的谦虚了，只向我看了一眼，便吸烟，听凭我付了账。

我们一同走出店门，他所住的旅馆和我的方向正相反，就在门口分别了。我独自向着自己的旅馆走，寒风和雪片扑在脸上，倒觉得很爽快。见天色已是黄昏，和屋宇和街道都织在密雪的纯白而不定的罗网里。

一九二四年二月一六日。

"What are your future plans then?"

"Future plans?" I don't know. Just think: Has any single thing turned out as we hoped of all we planned in the past? I'm not sure of anything now, not even of what tomorrow will bring, not even of the next minute...."

The waiter brought up the bill and handed it to me. Lü Weifu had abandoned his earlier formality. He just glanced at me, went on smoking, and allowed me to pay.

We left the tavern together, parting at the door because our hotels lay in opposite directions. As I walked back alone to my hotel, the cold wind buffeted my face with snowflakes, but I found this thoroughly refreshing. I saw that the sky, already dark, had interwoven with the houses and streets in the white, shifting web of thick snow.

February 16, 1924

他觉得胃里有点空虚了，放下笔，用两只手支着头，
教自己的头像地球仪似的在两个柱子间挂着。

Becoming aware of a hollow feeling in his stomach,
he put down the pen and rested his head on his hands,
like a globe supported by two axles.

幸福的家庭
——拟许钦文

A Happy Family[1]
— After the style of Xu Qinwen

“……做不做全由自己的便；那作品，像太阳的光一样，从无量的光源中涌出来，不像石火，用铁和石敲出来，这才是真艺术。那作者，也才是真的艺术家。——而我，……这算是什么？……”他想到这里，忽然从床上跳起来了。以先他早已想过，须得捞几文稿费维持生活了；投稿的地方，先定为幸福月报社，因为润笔似乎比较的丰。但作品就须有范围，否则，恐怕要不收的。范围就范围，……现在的青年的脑里的大问题是？……大概很不少，或者有许多是恋爱，婚姻，家庭之类的罢。……是的，他们确有许多人烦闷着，正在讨论这些事。那么，就来做家庭。然而怎么做做呢？……否则，恐怕要不收的，何必说些背时的话，然而……。他跳下卧床之后，四五步就走到书桌面前，坐下去，抽出一张绿格纸，毫不迟疑，但又自暴自弃似的写下一行题目道：《幸福的家庭》。

他的笔立刻停滞了；他仰了头，两眼瞪着房顶，正在安排那安置这“幸福的家庭”的地方。他想：“北京？不行，死气沉沉，连空气也是死的。假如在这家庭的周围筑一道高墙，难道空气也就隔断了么？简直不行！江苏浙江天天防要开仗；福建更无须说。四川，广东？都正在打。山东河南之类？——阿阿，要绑票的，倘使绑去一个，那就成为不幸的家庭了。上海天津的租界上房租贵；……假如在外国，笑话。云南贵州不知道怎样，但交通也太不便……。”他想来想去，想不出好地方，便要假定为A了，但又想，“现有不少的人是反对用西洋字母来代人地名的，说是要减少读者的兴味。我这回的投稿，似乎也不如不用，安全些。那么，在那里好呢？——湖南也打仗；大连仍然房租贵；察哈尔，吉林，黑龙江罢，——听说有马贼，也不行！……”他又想来想去，又想不出好地方，于是终于决心，假定这“幸福的家庭”所在的地方叫作A。

“总之，这幸福的家庭一定须在A，无可磋商。家庭

1. A novelist contemporary with Lu Xun. The author declared that he modelled this story on Xu's "An Ideal Companion."

2. During this period there was civil war between warlords in many parts of China.

"... One writes simply as one feels: such a work is like sunlight, radiating from a source of infinite brightness, not like a spark from a flint struck on iron or stone. This alone is true art. And such a writer alone is true artist.... But I... what do I rank as?"

Having thought so far he suddenly jumped out of bed. It had occurred to him that he must make some money by writing to support his family, and he had already decided to send his manuscripts to the *Happy Monthly* publishers, because the remuneration appeared to be comparatively generous. But in that case the choice of subjects would be limited, otherwise the work would probably not be accepted. All right, let it be limited. What were the chief problems occupying the minds of the younger generation?... Undoubtedly there must be not a few, perhaps a great many, concerning love, marriage, the family.... Yes, there were certainly many people perplexed by such questions, even now discussing them. In that case, write about the family! But how to write?... Otherwise it would probably not be accepted. Why predict anything unlucky? Still....

Jumping out of bed, in four or five steps he reached the desk, sat down, took out a piece of paper with green lines, and promptly yet resignedly wrote the title: A Happy Family.

His pen immediately came to a standstill. He raised his head, his two eyes fixed on the ceiling, trying to decide on an environment for this Happy Family.

"Beijing?" he thought. "That won't do; it's too dead, even the atmosphere is dead. Even if a high wall were built round this family, still the air could scarcely be kept separate. No, that would never do! Jiangsu and Zhejiang may start fighting any day, and Fujian is even more out of the question. Sichuan? Guangdong? They are in the midst of fighting.[2] What about Shandong or Henan?...No, one of them might be kidnapped, and if that happened the happy family would become an unhappy one. The rents in the foreign concessions in Shanghai and Tianjin are too high.... Somewhere abroad? Ridiculous. I don't know what Yunnan and Guizhou are like, but communications are too poor...."

He racked his brains but, unable to think of a good place, decided to fix tentatively on A— .Then, however, he thought, "Nowadays many people object to the use of the Western alphabet to represent the names of people and places, saying it lessens the readers' interest. Probably I had better not use it in my story this time, to be on the safe side. In that case what would be a good place? There is fighting in Hunan too; the rents in Dalian have gone up again. In Chahar, Jilin and Heilongjiang I have heard there are brigands, so they won't do either!..."

Again he racked his brains to think of a good place, but in vain; so finally he made up his mind to fix tentatively on A— as the name of the place where his Happy Family should be.

"After all this Happy Family will have to be at A— . There can't be any question

中自然是两夫妇，就是主人和主妇，自由结婚的。他们订有四十多条条约，非常详细，所以非常平等，十分自由。而且受过高等教育，优美高尚……。东洋留学生已经不通行，——那么，假定为西洋留学生罢。主人始终穿洋服，硬领始终雪白；主妇是前头的头发始终烫得蓬蓬松松像一个麻雀窠，牙齿是始终雪白的露着，但衣服却是中国装，……”

“不行不行，那不行！二十五斤！”

他听得窗外一个男人的声音，不由的回过头去看，窗幔垂着，日光照着，明得眩目，他的眼睛昏花了；接着是小木片撒在地上的声响。“不相干，”他又回过头来想，“什么‘二十五斤’？——他们是优美高尚，很爱文艺的。但因为都从小生长在幸福里，所以不爱俄国的小说……。俄国小说多描写下等人，实在和这样的家庭也不合。‘二十五斤’？不管他。那么，他们看看什么书呢？——裴伦的诗？吉支的？不行，都不稳当。——哦，有了，他们都爱看《理想之良人》。我虽然没有见过这部书，但既然连大学教授也那么称赞他，想来他们也一定都爱看，你也看，我也看，——他们一人一本，这家庭里一共有两本，……”他觉得胃里有点空虚了，放下笔，用两只手支着头，教自己的头像地球仪似的在两个柱子间挂着。

“……他们两人正在用午餐，”他想，“桌上铺了雪白的布；厨子送上菜来，——中国菜。什么‘二十五斤’？不管他。为什么倒是中国菜？西洋人说，中国菜最进步，最好吃，最合于卫生：所以他们采用中国菜。送来的是第一碗，但这第一碗是什么呢？……”

“劈柴，……”

他吃惊的回过头去看，靠左肩，便立着他自己家里的主妇，两只阴凄凄的眼睛恰恰钉住他的脸。

“什么？”他以为她来搅扰了他的创作，颇有些愤怒了。

“劈柴，都用完了，今天买了些。前一回还是十斤两吊四，今天就要两吊六。我想给他两吊五，好不好？”

about that. The family naturally consists of a husband and wife — the master and mistress — who married for love. Their marriage contract contains over forty terms going into great detail, so that they have extraordinary equality and absolute freedom. Moreover they have both had a higher education and belong to the cultured elite.... Japanese-returned students are no longer the fashion, so let them be Western-returned students. The master of the house always wears a foreign suit, his collar is always snowy white. His wife's hair is always curled up like a sparrow's nest in front, her pearly white teeth are always peeping out, but she wears Chinese dress...."

"That won't do, that won't do! Twenty-five catties!"

Hearing a man's voice outside the window he involuntarily turned his head to look. The sun shone through the curtains hanging by the window, dazzling his eyes, while he heard a sound like small bundles of wood being thrown down. "It doesn't matter," he thought, turning back again. "'Twenty-five catties' of what?... They are the cultured elite, devoted to the arts. But because they have both grown up in happy surroundings, they don't like Russian novels. Most Russian novels describe the lower classes, so they are really quite out of keeping with such a family. 'Twenty-five catties'? Never mind. In that case, what books do they read?... Byron's poetry? Keats? That won't do, neither of them are safe.... Ah, I have it: they both like reading *An Ideal Husband*. Although I haven't read the book myself, even university professors praise it so highly that I am sure this couple must enjoy it too. You read it, I read it — they have a copy each, two copies altogether in the family...."

Becoming aware of a hollow feeling in his stomach, he put down the pen and rested his head on his hands, like a globe supported by two axles.

"...The two of them are just having lunch," he thought. "The table is spread with a snowy white table cloth, and the cook brings in the dishes — Chinese food. 'Twenty-five catties.' Of what? Never mind. Why should it be Chinese food? Westerners say Chinese cooking is the most progressive, the best to eat, the most hygienic; so they eat Chinese food. The first dish is brought in, but what is this first dish?..."

"Firewood...."

He turned his head with a start, to see standing on his left the mistress of his own family, her two gloomy eyes fastened on his face.

"What?" He spoke rather indignantly, feeling that her coming disturbed his work.

"The firewood is all used up, so today I have bought some more. Last time it was still two hundred and forty cash for ten catties, but today he wants two hundred and sixty. Suppose I give him two hundred and fifty?"

“好好，就是两吊五。”

“称得太吃亏了。他一定只肯算二十四斤半；我想就算他二十三斤半，好不好？”

“好好，就算他二十三斤半。”

“那么，五五二十五，三五一十五，……”

“唔唔，五五二十五，三五一十五，……”他也说不下去了，停了一会，忽而奋然的抓起笔来，就在写着一行“幸福的家庭”的绿格纸上起算草，起了好久，这才仰起头来说道：

“五吊八！”

“那是，我这里不够了，还差八九个……。”

他抽开书桌的抽屉，一把抓起所有的铜元，不下二三十，放在她摊开的手掌上，看她出了房，才又回过头来向书桌。他觉得头里面很胀满，似乎椏椏叉叉的全被木柴填满了，五五二十五，脑皮质上还印着许多散乱的亚剌伯数目字。他很深的吸一口气，又用力的呼出，仿佛要借此赶出脑里的劈柴，五五二十五和亚剌伯数字来。果然，吁气之后；心地也就轻松不少了，于是仍复恍恍忽忽的想——

“什么菜？菜倒不妨奇特点。滑溜里脊，虾子海参，实在太凡庸。我偏要说他们吃的是‘龙虎斗’。但‘龙虎斗’又是什么呢？有人说是蛇和猫，是广东的贵重菜，非大宴会不吃的。但我在江苏饭馆的菜单上就见过这名目，江苏人似乎不吃蛇和猫，恐怕就如谁所说，是蛙和鳝鱼了。现在假定这主人和主妇为那里人呢？——不管他。总而言之，无论那里人吃一碗蛇和猫或者蛙和鳝鱼，于幸福的家庭是决不会有损伤的。总之这第一碗一定是‘龙虎斗’，无可磋商。

“于是一碗‘龙虎斗’摆在桌子中央了，他们两人同时捏起筷子，指着碗沿，笑迷迷的你看我，我看你……。

“‘My dear, please.’

“‘Please you eat first, my dear.’

“‘Oh no, please you！’

"All right, two hundred and fifty, let it be."

"He has weighted it very unfairly. He insists that there are twenty-four and a half catties, but suppose I count it as twenty-three and a half?"

"All right. Count it as twenty-three and a half catties."

"Then, five fives are twenty-fives, three fives are fifteen...."

"Oh, five fives are twenty-five, three fives are fifteen...." He could get no further either, but after stopping for a moment suddenly took up his pen and started working out a sum on the lined paper on which he had written "A Happy Family." After working at it for some time he raised his head to say:

"Five hundred and eighty cash."

"In that case I haven't got enough here; I am still eighty or ninety short...."

He pulled open the drawer of the desk, took out all the money in it — somewhere between twenty and thirty coppers — and put it in her outstretched hand. Then he watched her go out, and finally turned back to the desk. His head seemed to be bursting as if filled to the brim with sharp faggots. Five fives are twenty-five — scattered Arabic numerals were still imprinted on his brain. He gave a long sigh and breathed out again deeply, as if by this means he might expel the firewood, the "five fives are twenty-five," and the Arabic numerals which had stuck in his head. Sure enough, after breathing out his heart seemed much lighter, whereupon he started thinking vaguely again:

"What dish? It doesn't matter, so long as it is something out of the way. Fried pork or prawns' roe and sea-slugs are really too common. I must have them eating 'Dragon and Tiger.' But what is that exactly? Some people say it's made of snakes and cats, and is an upper-class Guangdong dish, only eaten at big feasts. But I've seen the name on the menu in a Jiangsu restaurant; still, Jiangsu people aren't supposed to eat snakes or cats, so it must be, as someone else said, made of frogs and eels. Now what part of the country shall this couple be from? Never mind. After all, people from any part of the country can eat a dish of snake and cat (or frog and eel), without injuring their Happy Family. At any rate, this first dish is to be 'Dragon and Tiger'; there can be no question about that.

"Now that this bowl of 'Dragon and Tiger' is placed in the middle of the table, they take up their chopsticks simultaneously, point to the dish, smile sweetly at each other and say, in a foreign tongue:

"'Chérie, s'il vous plaît!'

"'Voulez-vous commencer, chéri!'

"'Mais non, après vous!'

“于是他们同时伸下筷子去，同时夹出一块蛇肉来，——不不，蛇肉究竟太奇怪，还不如说是鳝鱼罢。那么，这碗‘龙虎斗’是蛙和鳝鱼所做的了。他们同时夹出一块鳝鱼来，一样大小，五五二十五，三五……不管他，同时放进嘴里去，……”他不能自制的只想回过头去看，因为他觉得背后很热闹，有人来来往往的走了两三回。但他还熬着，乱嘈嘈的接着想，“这似乎有点肉麻，那有这样的家庭？唉唉，我的思路怎么会这样乱，这好题目怕是做不完篇的了。——或者不必定用留学生，就在国内受了高等教育的也可以。他们都是大学毕业的，高尚优美，高尚……。男的是文学家；女的也是文学家，或者文学崇拜家。或者女的是诗人；男的是诗人崇拜者，女性尊重者。或者……”他终于忍耐不住，回过头去了。

就在他背后的书架的旁边，已经出现了一座白菜堆，下层三株，中层两株，顶上一株，向他叠成一个很大的A字。

“唉唉！”他吃惊的叹息，同时觉得脸上骤然发热了，脊梁上还有许多针轻轻的刺着。“吁……。”他很长的嘘一口气，先斥退了脊梁上的针，仍然想，“幸福的家庭的房子要宽绰。有一间堆积房，白菜之类都到那边去。主人的书房另一间，靠壁满排着书架，那旁边自然决没有什么白菜堆；架上满是中国书，外国书，《理想之良人》自然也在内，——一共有两部。卧室又一间；黄铜床，或者质朴点，第一监狱工场做的榆木床也就够，床底下很干净，……”他当即一瞥自己的床下，劈柴已经用完了，只有一条稻草绳，却还死蛇似的懒懒的躺着。

“二十三斤半，……”他觉得劈柴就要向床下“川流不息”的进来，头里面又有些桠桠叉叉了，便急忙起立，走向门口去想关门。但两手刚触着门，却又觉得未免太暴躁了，就歇了手，只放下那积着许多灰尘的门幕。他一面想，这既无闭关自守之操切，也没有开放门户之不安：是很合于“中庸之道”的。

3. A Confucian classic advocating the principle of moderation in all things.

"Then they reach out their chopsticks simultaneously, and simultaneously take a morsel of snake — no, no, snake's flesh really sounds too peculiar; it would be better after all to say a morsel of eel. It is settled then that 'Dragon and Tiger' is made of frogs and eels. They pick out two morsels of eel simultaneously, exactly the same size. Five fives are twenty-five, three fives.... Never mind. And simultaneously put them in their mouths...." Against his will he wanted to turn round, because he was conscious of a good deal of excitement behind him, and considerable coming and going. But he persevered, and pursued his train of thought distractedly:

"This seems rather sentimental; no family would behave like this. Whatever makes me so woolly-minded? I'm afraid this good subject will never be written up.... Or perhaps there is no need to have returned students; people who have received higher education in China would do just as well. They are both university graduates, the cultured elite, the elite..." The man is a writer; the woman is also a writer, or else a lover of literature. Or else the woman is a poetess; the man is a lover of poetry, a respecter of womanhood. Or else...."

Finally he could contain himself no longer, and turned round.

Beside the bookcase behind him had appeared a mound of cabbages, three at the bottom, two above, and one at the top, confronting him like a large letter A.

"Oh!" He started and gave a sigh, feeling his cheeks burn, while prickles ran up and down his spine. "Ah!" He took a very deep breath to get rid of the prickly feeling in his spine, then went on thinking, "The house of the Happy Family must have plenty of rooms. There is a store-room where things like cabbages are put. The master's study is apart, its walls lined with bookshelves; there are naturally no cabbages there. The shelves are filled with Chinese books and foreign books, including of course *An Ideal Husband* — two copies altogether. There is a separate bedroom, a brass bedstead, or something simpler like one of the elmwood beds made by the convicts of Number One Prison would do equally well. Beneath the bed is very clean...." He glanced beneath his own bed; the firewood had all been used up, and there was only a piece of straw rope left, still coiling there like a dead snake.

"Twenty-three and a half catties...." He felt that the firewood was just about to pour in in a never-ending stream under his bed, and his head ached again, so he got up quickly and went to the door to close it. But he had scarcely put his hand on the door when he felt that this was overhasty and let it go instead, dropping the door curtain that was thick with dust. At the same time he thought, "This method avoids the severity of shutting oneself in, as well as the discomfort of keeping the door open; it is quite in keeping with the *Doctrine of the Mean*.[3]

"……所以主人的书房门永远是关起来的。"他走回来，坐下，想，"有事要商量先敲门，得了许可才能进来，这办法实在对。现在假如主人坐在自己的书房里，主妇来谈文艺了，也就先敲门。——这可以放心，她必不至于捧着白菜的。

"'Come in, please, my dear.'

"然而主人没有工夫谈文艺的时候怎么办呢？那么，不理她，听她站在外面老是剥剥的敲？这大约不行罢。或者《理想之良人》里面都写着，——那恐怕确是一部好小说，我如果有了稿费，也得去买他一部来看看……。"

拍!

他腰骨笔直了，因为他根据经验，知道这一声"拍"是主妇的手掌打在他们的三岁的女儿的头上的声音。

"幸福的家庭，……"他听到孩子的呜咽了，但还是腰骨笔直的想，"孩子是生得迟的，生得迟。或者不如没有，两个人干干净净。——或者不如住在客店里，什么都包给他们，一个人干干……"他听得呜咽声高了起来，也就站了起来，钻过门幕，想着，"马克思在儿女的啼哭声中还会做《资本论》，所以他是伟人，……"走出外间，开了风门，闻得一阵煤油气。孩子就躺倒在门的右边，脸向着地，一见他，便"哇"的哭出来了。

"阿阿，好好，莫哭莫哭，我的好孩子。"他弯下腰去抱她。

他抱了她回转身，看见门左边还站着主妇，也是腰骨笔直，然而两手插腰，怒气冲冲的似乎豫备开始练体操。

"连你也来欺侮我！不会帮忙，只会捣乱，——连油灯也要翻了他。晚上点什么？……"

"阿阿，好好，莫哭莫哭，"他把那些发抖的声音放在脑后，抱她进房，摩着她的头，说，"我的好孩子。"于是放下她，拖开椅子，坐下去，使她站在两膝的中间，擎起手来道，"莫哭了呵，好孩子。爹爹做'猫洗脸'给你看。"他同时伸长颈子，伸出舌头，远远的对着手掌舔了两舔，就用这手掌向了自己的脸上画圆圈。

"... So the master's study door is always closed." He walked back, sat down and thought, "Anyone with business must first knock at the door, and have his permission to come in; that is really the only thing to be done. Now suppose the master is sitting in his study and the mistress comes to discuss literature, she knocks too.... At least of this one can be assured — she will not bring in any cabbages."

"'Entrez, chérie, s'il vous plaît!'"

"But what happens when the master has no time to discuss literature? Does he ignore her, hearing her stand outside tapping gently on the door? That probably wouldn't do. Maybe it is all described in *An Ideal Husband* — that must really be an excellent novel. If I get paid for this article I must buy a copy to read!"

Slap!

His back stiffened, because he knew from experience that this slapping sound was made by his wife's hand striking their three-year-old daughter's head.

"In a Happy Family..." he thought, his back still rigid, hearing the child sobbing, "children are born late, yes, born late. Or perhaps it would be better to have none at all, just two people without any ties.... Or it might be better to stay in a hotel and let them look after everything, a single man without...." Hearing the sound of sobbing increasing in volume, he stood up and brushed past the curtain, thinking, "Karl Marx wrote his *Das Kapital* while his children were crying around him. He must really have been a great man...." He walked out, opened the outer door, and was assailed by a strong smell of kerosene. The child was lying to the right of the door, face downwards. As soon as she saw him she started crying aloud.

"There, there, all right! Don't cry, don't cry! There's a good girl." He bent down to pick her up. Having picked her up he turned round to see his wife standing furiously to the left of the door, also with a rigid back, her hands on her hips as if she were preparing to start physical exercises.

"Even you have to come and bully me! You can't help, you only make trouble — even the kerosene lamp had to turn over. What shall we light this evening?..."

"There, there, all right! Don't cry, don't cry!" Ignoring his wife's trembling tones, he carried the child into the house, and stroked her head. "There's a good girl," he repeated. Then he put her down, pulled out a chair and sat down. Setting her between his knees, he raised his hand. "Don't cry, there's a good girl," he said. "Daddy will do 'Pussy Washing' for you." At the same time he craned his neck, licked his palms from a distance twice, then with them traced circles towards his face.

“呵呵呵，花儿。”她就笑起来了。

“是的是的，花儿。”他又连画上几个圆圈，这才歇了手，只见她还是笑迷迷的挂着眼泪对他看。他忽而觉得，她那可爱的天真的脸，正像五年前的她的母亲，通红的嘴唇尤其像，不过缩小了轮廓。那时也是晴朗的冬天，她听得他说决计反抗一切阻碍，为她牺牲的时候，也就这样笑迷迷的挂着眼泪对他看。他惘然的坐着，仿佛有些醉了。

“阿阿，可爱的嘴唇……”他想。

门幕忽然挂起。劈柴运进来了。

他也忽然惊醒，一定睛，只见孩子还是挂着眼泪，而且张开了通红的嘴唇对他看。“嘴唇……”他向旁边一瞥，劈柴正在进来，“……恐怕将来也就是五五二十五，九九八十一！……而且两只眼睛阴凄凄的……。”他想着，随即粗暴的抓起那写着一行题目和一堆算草的绿格纸来，揉了几揉，又展开来给她拭去了眼泪和鼻涕。“好孩子，自己玩去罢。”他一面推开她，说；一面就将纸团用力的掷在纸篓里。

但他又立刻觉得对于孩子有些抱歉了，重复回头，目送着她独自茕茕的出去；耳朵里听得木片声。他想要定一定神，便又回转头，闭了眼睛，息了杂念，平心静气的坐着。他看见眼前浮出一朵扁圆的乌花，橙黄心，从左眼的左角漂到右，消失了；接着一朵明绿花，墨绿色的心；接着一座六株的白菜堆，屹然的向他叠成一个很大的A字。

一九二四年二月一八日。

"Aha! Pussy!" She started laughing.

"That's right, that's right. Pussy." He traced several more circles, and then stopped, seeing her smiling at him with tears still in her eyes. It struck him suddenly that her sweet, innocent face was just like her mother's five years ago, especially her bright red lips, although the general outline was smaller. That had been another bright winter's day when she heard his decision to overcome all obstacles and sacrifice everything for her; when she too looked at him in the same way, smiling, with tears in her eyes. He sat down disconsolately, as if a little drunk.

"Ah, sweet lips," he thought.

The door curtain was suddenly fastened back and the firewood brought in.

Then, suddenly coming to himself again, he saw that the child, still with tears in her eyes, was looking at him with her bright red lips parted. "Lips...." He glanced sidewards to where the firewood was being brought in. "... Probably it will be nothing but five fives are twenty-five, nine nines are eighty-one, all over again!... And two gloomy eyes...." So thinking he snatched up the green-lined paper with the heading and the figures written on it, crumpled it up and then unfolded it again to wipe her eyes and nose. "Good girl, run along and play by yourself." He pushed her away as he spoke, at the same time throwing the ball of paper into the waste-paper basket.

But at once he felt rather sorry for the child, and, turning his head, followed her with his eyes as she walked forlornly away, while his ears were filled with the sound of firewood. Determined to concentrate, he turned back again and closed his eyes to put a stop to all distracting thoughts, sitting there quietly and peacefully.

He saw passing before him a flat, round, blackfreckled flower with an orange centre, which floated from the left of his left eye right over to the opposite side where it disappeared; then a bright green flower, with a dark green centre; and finally a pipe of six cabbages which formed themselves before him into an enormous letter A.

February 18, 1924

他好容易曲曲折折的汇出手来，
手里就有一个小小的长方包，葵绿色的，
一径递给四太太。

By dint of twisting and turning he extracted his hand at last with
a small oblong package in it, which he handed to his wife.

肥皂
Soap

四铭太太正在斜日光中背着北窗和她八岁的女儿秀儿糊纸锭，忽听得又重又缓的布鞋底声响，知道四铭进来了，并不去看他，只是糊纸锭。但那布鞋底声却愈响愈逼近，觉得终于停在她的身边了，于是不免转过眼去看，只见四铭就在她面前耸肩曲背的狠命掏着布马挂底下的袍子的大襟后面的口袋。

他好容易曲曲折折的汇出手来，手里就有一个小小的长方包，葵绿色的，一径递给四太太。她刚接到手，就闻到一阵似橄揽非橄揽的说不清的香味，还看见葵绿色的纸包上有一个金光灿烂的印子和许多细簇簇的花纹。秀儿即刻跳过来要抢着看，四太太赶忙推开她。

“上了街？……”她一面看，一面问。

“唔唔。”他看着她手里的纸包，说。

于是这葵绿色的纸包被打开了，里面还有一层很薄的纸，也是葵绿色，揭开薄纸，才露出那东西的本身来，光滑坚致，也是葵绿色，上面还有细簇簇的花纹，而薄纸原来却是米色的，似橄揽非橄揽的说不清的香味也来得更浓了。

“唉唉，这实在是好肥皂。”她捧孩子似的将那葵绿色的东西送到鼻子下面去，嗅着说。

“唔唔，你以后就用这个……。”

她看见他嘴里这么说，眼光却射在她的脖子上，便觉得颧骨以下的脸上似乎有些热。她有时自己偶然摸到脖子上，尤其是耳朵后，指面上总感着些粗糙，本来早就知道是积年的老泥，但向来倒也并不很介意。现在在他的注视之下，对着这葵绿异香的洋肥皂，可不禁脸上有些发热了，而且这热又不绝的蔓延开去，即刻一径到耳根。她于是就决定晚饭后要用这肥皂来拼命的洗一洗。

“有些地方，本来单用皂荚子是洗不干净的。”她自对自的说。

“妈，这给我！”秀儿伸手来抢葵绿纸；在外面玩耍的小女儿招儿也跑到了。四太太赶忙推开她们，裹好薄纸，又照旧包上葵绿纸，欠过身去搁在洗脸台上最高的一

1. In many parts of China, honey locust pods were used for washing. They were cheaper than soap, but not so effective.

With her back to the north window in the slanting sunlight, Siming's wife was pasting paper coins for the dead with her eight-year-old daughter, Xiu'er, when she heard the slow, heavy footsteps of someone in cloth shoes and knew her husband was back. She paid no attention, though, simply went on pasting coins. But the tread of cloth shoes drew nearer and nearer, till it finally stopped beside her. Then she could not help looking up to see Siming before her, hunching his shoulders and stooping forward to fumble desperately under his cloth jacket in the inner pocket of his long gown.

By dint of twisting and turning he extracted his hand at last with a small oblong package in it, which he handed to his wife. As she took it, she smelt an indefinable fragrance rather reminiscent of olive. On the green paper wrapper was a bright golden seal with a network of tiny designs. Xiu'er bounded forward to seize this and look at it, but her mother promptly pushed her aside.

"Been shopping?..." she asked as she looked at it.

"Er — yes." He stared at the package in her hand.

The green paper wrapper was opened. Inside was a layer of tissue paper, also a palm-leaf-green, and not till this was unwrapped was the object itself exposed — glossy and hard, besides being palm-leaf-green, with another network of fine designs on it. The tissue paper was a cream colour, it appeared. The indefinable fragrance rather reminiscent of olive was stronger now.

"My, this is really good soap!"

She held the soap to her nose as gingerly as if it were a child, and sniffed at it as she spoke.

"Er — yes. Just use this in future...."

As he spoke, she noticed him eyeing her neck, and felt herself flushing up to her cheekbones. Sometimes when she rubbed her neck, especially behind the ears, her fingers detected a roughness; and though she knew this was the accumulated dirt of many years, she had never given it much thought. Now, under his scrutiny, she could not help blushing as she looked at this green, foreign soap with the curious scent, and this blush sprcad right to the tips of her ears. She mentally resolved to have a thorough wash with this soap after supper.

"There are places you can't wash clean just with honey locust pods,"[1] She muttered to herself.

"Ma, can I have this?" As Xiu'er reached out for the palm-leaf-green paper, Zhao'er, the younger daughter who had been playing outside, came running in too. Mrs. Siming promptly pushed them both aside, folded the tissue paper in place, wrapped the green paper round it as before, then leant over to put it on the highest shelf of the wash-

层格子上，看一看，翻身仍然糊纸锭。

“学程！”四铭记起了一件事似的，忽而拖长了声音叫，就在她对面的一把高背椅子上坐下了。

“学程！”她也帮着叫。

她停下糊纸锭，侧耳一听，什么响应也没有，又见他仰着头焦急的等着，不禁很有些抱歉了，便尽力提高了喉咙，尖利的叫：

“绘儿呀！”

这一叫确乎有效，就听到皮鞋声橐橐的近来，不一会，绘儿已站在她面前了，只穿短衣，肥胖的圆脸上亮晶晶的流着油汗。

“你在做什么？怎么爹叫也不听见？”她谴责的说。

“我刚在练八卦拳……。”他立即转身向了四铭，笔挺的站着，看着他，意思是问他什么事。

“学程，我就要问你：‘恶毒妇’是什么？”

“‘恶毒妇’？……那是，‘很凶的女人’罢？……

“胡说！胡闹！”四铭忽而怒得可观。“我是‘女人’么！？”

学程吓得倒退了两步，站得更挺了。他虽然有时觉得他走路很像上台的老生，却从没有将他当做女人看待，他知道自己答的很错了。

“‘恶毒妇’是‘很凶的女人’，我倒不懂，得来请教你？——这不是中国话，是鬼子话，我对你说。这是什么意思，你懂么？”

“我，……我不懂。”学程更加局促起来。

“吓，我白化钱送你进学堂，连这一点也不懂。亏煞你的学堂还夸什么‘口耳并重’，倒教得什么也没有。说这鬼话的人至多不过十四五岁，比你还小些呢，已经叽叽咕咕的能说了，你却连意思也说不出，还有这脸说‘我不懂’！——现在就给我去查出来！”

学程在喉咙底里答应了一声“是”，恭恭敬敬的退出去了。

2. In Chinese this means "vicious wife."

stand. After one final glance, she turned back to her paper coins.

"Xuecheng!" Siming seemed to have remembered something. He gave a long-drawn-out shout, sitting down on a high-backed chair opposite his wife.

"Xuecheng!" she helped him call.

She stopped pasting coins to listen, but not a sound could she hear. When she saw him with upturned head waiting so impatiently, she felt quite apologetic.

"Xuecheng!" she called shrilly at the top of her voice.

This call indeed proved effective, for they heard the tramp of leather shoes draw near, and Xuecheng was standing before her. He was in shirt sleeves, and his plump round face was shiny with perspiration.

"What were you doing?" she asked disapprovingly. "Why didn't you hear your father call?"

"I was practising Hexagram Boxing...." He turned at once to his father and straightened up, looking at him as if to ask what he wanted.

"Xuecheng, I want to ask you the meaning of *e-du-fu*."[2]

"*E-du-fu*?... Isn't it a very fierce woman?"

"What nonsense! The idea!" Siming was suddenly furious. "Am I a woman, pray?"

Xuecheng recoiled two steps, and stood straighter than ever. Though his father's gait sometimes remined him of the way old men walked in Beijing opera, he had never considered Siming as a woman. His answer, he saw now, had been a great mistake.

"As if I didn't know *e-du-fu* means a very fierce woman. Would I have to ask you that? — This isn't Chinese, it's foreign devils' language, I'm telling you. What does it mean, do you know."

"I... I don't know." Xuecheng felt even more uneasy.

"Pah! What use is it my spending all that money to send you to school if you don't even understand a little thing like this? Your school boasts that it lays equal stress on speech and comprehension, yet it hasn't taught you anything. The ones speaking this devils' language couldn't have been more than fourteen or fifteen, actually a little younger than you, yet they were chattering away in it, while you can't even tell me the meaning. And you have the face to answer 'I don't know.' Go and look it up for me at once!"

"Yes," answered Xuecheng deep down in his throat, then respectfully withdrew.

“这真叫作不成样子，”过了一会，四铭又慷慨的说，“现在的学生是。其实，在光绪年间，我就是最提倡开学堂的，可万料不到学堂的流弊竟至于如此之大：什么解放咧，自由咧，没有实学，只会胡闹。学程呢，为他化了的钱也不少了，都白化。好容易给他进了中西折中的学堂，英文又专是‘口耳并重’的，你以为这该好了罢，哼，可是读了一年，连‘恶毒妇’也不懂，大约仍然是念死书。吓，什么学堂，造就了些什么？我简直说：应该统统关掉！”

“对咧，真不如统统关掉的好。”四太太糊着纸锭，同情的说。

“秀儿她们也不必进什么学堂了。‘女孩子，念什么书？’九公公先前这样说，反对女学的时候，我还攻击他呢；可是现在看起来，究竟是老年人的话对。你想，女人一阵一阵的在街上走；已经很不雅观的了，她们却还要剪头发。我最恨的就是那些剪了头发的女学生，我简直说，军人土匪倒还情有可原，搅乱天下的就是她们，应该很严的办一办……。”

“对咧，男人都像了和尚还不够，女人又来学尼姑了。”

“学程！”

学程正捧着一本小而且厚的金边书快步进来，便呈给四铭，指着一处说：

“这倒有点像。这个……。”

四铭接来看时，知道是字典，但文字非常小，又是横行的。他眉头一皱，擎向窗口，细着眼睛，就学程所指的一行念过去：

“‘第十八世纪创立之共济讲社之称。——唔，不对。——这声音是怎么念的？”他指着前面的“鬼子”字，问。

“恶特拂罗斯（Odd fellows）。”

“不对，不对，不是这个。”四铭又忽而愤怒起来了。“我对你说：那是一句坏话，骂人的话，骂我这样的

3. I.e., 1875-1908.

4. English was taught in nearly all the new schools at that time, and learning to speak was considered as important as learning to read.

5. Monks and nuns in China shaved their heads. Hence, at the end of the Qing Dynasty and later, conservatives laughed at the men who cut their queues, claiming they looked like monks.

"I don't know what students today are coming to," declared Siming with emotion after a pause. "As a matter of fact, in the time of Guang Xu,[3] I was all in favour of opening schools; but I never foresaw how great the evils would be. What 'emancipation' and 'freedom' have we had? There is no true learning, nothing but absurdities. I've spent quite a bit of money on Xuecheng, all to no purpose. It wasn't easy to get him into this half-Western, half-Chinese school, where they claim they lay equal stress on 'speaking and comprehending English.'[4] You'd think all should be well. But — bah! — after one whole year of study he can't even understand *e-du-fu*! He must still be studying dead books. What use is such a school, I ask you? What I say is: Close the whole lot of them!"

"Yes, really, better close the whole lot of them," chimed in his wife sympathetically, pasting away at the paper money.

"There's no need for Xiu'er and her sister to attend any school. 'What the good of girls studying?' as Ninth Grandpa said. When he opposed girls' schools I attacked him for it; but now I see the old folk were right after all. Just think, it's already in very poor taste the way women wander up and down the streets, and now they want to cut their hair as well. Nothing digusts me so much as these short-haired schoolgirls. What I say is: There's some excuse for soldiers and bandits, but these girls are the ones who turn everything upside-down. They ought to be very severely dealt with indeed...."

"Yes, as if it wasn't enough for all men to look like monks, the women are imitating nuns."[5]

"Xuecheng!"

Xuecheng hurried in holding a small, fat, gilt-edged book, which he handed to his father.

"This looks like it," he said, pointing to one place. "Here...."

Siming took it and looked at it. He knew it was a dictionary, but the characters were very small and horizontally printed too. He turned frowning towards the window, and screwed up his eyes to read the passage Xuecheng had pointed out.

"'A society founded in the eighteenth century for mutual relief.' — No, that can't be it. — How do you pronounce this?" He pointed at the devils' word in front.

"Odd fellows."

"No, no, that wasn't it." Siming suddenly lost his temper again. "I told you it was bad language, a swear-word of some sort, to abuse someone of my type. Understand?

人的。懂了么？查去！”

学程看了他几眼，没有动。

“这是什么闷胡卢，没头没脑的？你也先得说说清，教他好用心的查去。”她看见学程为难，觉得可怜，便排解而且不满似的说。

“就是我在大街上广润祥买肥皂的时候，”四铭呼出了一口气，向她转过脸去，说。“店里又有三个学生在那里买东西。我呢，从他们看起来，自然也怕太噜苏一点了罢。我一气看了六七样，都要四角多，没有买；看一角一块的，又太坏，没有什么香。我想，不如中通的好，便挑定了那绿的一块，两角四分。伙计本来是势利鬼，眼睛生在额角上的，早就撅着狗嘴的了；可恨那学生这坏小子又都挤眉弄眼的说着鬼话笑。后来，我要打开来看一看才付钱：洋纸包着，怎么断得定货色的好坏呢。谁知道那势利鬼不但不依，还蛮不讲理，说了许多可恶的废话；坏小子们又附和着说笑。那一句是顶小的一个说的，而且眼睛看着我，他们就都笑起来了：可见一定是一句坏话。”他于是转脸对着学程道，“你只要在‘坏话类’里去查去！”

学程在喉咙底里答应了一声“是”，恭恭敬敬的退去了。

“他们还嚷什么‘新文化新文化’，‘化’到这样了，还不够？”他两眼钉着屋梁，尽自说下去。“学生也没有道德，社会上也没有道德，再不想点法子来挽救，中国这才真个要亡了。——你想，那多么可叹？……”

“什么？”她随口的问，并不惊奇。

“孝女。”他转眼对着她，郑重的说。“就在大街上，有两个讨饭的。一个是姑娘，看去该有十八九岁了。——其实这样的年纪，讨饭是很不相宜的了，可是她还讨饭。——和一个六七十岁的老的，白头发，眼睛是瞎的，坐在布店的檐下求乞。大家多说她是孝女，那老的是祖母。她只要讨得一点什么，便都献给祖母吃，自己情愿饿肚皮。可是这样的孝女，有人肯布施么？”他射出眼光

Go and look it up!"

Xuecheng glanced at him several times, but did not move.

"This is too puzzling. How can he make head or tail of it? You must explain things clearly to him first, before he can look it up properly." Seeing Xuecheng in a quandary, his mother felt sorry for him and intervened rather indignantly on his behalf.

"It was when I was buying soap at Guang Run Xiang on the main street," sighed Siming, turning to her. "There were three students shopping there too. Of course, to them I must have seemed a little pernickety. I looked at five or six kinds of soap all over forty cents, and turned them down. Then I looked at some priced ten cents a cake, but it was too poor, with no scent at all. Since I thought it best to strike a happy mean, I chose that green soap at twenty-four cents a cake. The assistant was one of these supercilious young fellows with eyes on the top of his head, so he pulled a long dog's face. At that those impudent students started winking at each other and talking devils' language. Then I wanted to unwrap the soap and look at it before paying — for with all that foreign paper round it, how could I tell whether it was good or bad? But that supercilious young fellow not only refused, but was very unreasonable and passed some offensive remarks, at which those whipper-snappers laughed. It was the youngest of the lot who said that, looking straight at me, and the rest of them started laughing. So it must have been some bad word." He turned back to Xuecheng. "Look for it in the section headed Bad Language!"

"Yes," answered Xuecheng deep down in his throat, then respectfully withdrew.

"Yet they still shout 'New Culture! New Culture!' when the world's in such a state! Isn't this bad enough?" His eyes on the rafters, he went on. "The students have no morals, society has no morals. Unless we find some panacea, China will really be finished. Look, how pathetic that was!"

"What?" asked his wife casually, not really curious.

"A filial daughter...." His eyes came round to her, and there was respect in his voice. "There were two beggars on the main street. One was a girl who looked eighteen or nineteen. Actually, it's most improper to beg at that age, but beg she did. She was with an old woman of about seventy, who had white hair and was blind. They were begging under the eaves of that clothes shop, and everybody said how filial she was. The old one was her grandmother. Whatever trifle the girl received, she gave it to her grandmother, choosing to go hungry herself. But do you think people would give alms to even such a filial daughter?"

来钉住她，似乎要试验她的识见。

她不答话，也只将眼光钉住他，似乎倒是专等他来说明。

“哼，没有。”他终于自己回答说。“我看了好半天，只见一个人给了一文小钱；其余的围了一大圈，倒反去打趣。还有两个光棍，竟肆无忌惮的说：‘阿发，你不要看得这货色脏。你只要去买两块肥皂来，咯支咯支遍身洗一洗，好得很哩！’哪，你想，这成什么话？”

“哼，”她低下头去了，久之，才又懒懒的问，“你给了钱么？”

“我么？——没有。一两个钱，是不好意思拿出去的。她不是平常的讨饭，总得……。”

“嗡。”她不等说完话，便慢慢地站起来，走到厨下去，昏黄只显得浓密，已经是晚饭时候了。

四铭也站起身，走出院子去。天色比屋子里还明亮，学程就在墙角落上练习八卦拳：这是他的“庭训”，利用昼夜之交的时间的经济法，学程奉行了将近大半年了。他赞许似的微微点一点头，便反背着两手在空院子里来回的踱方步。不多久，那惟一的盆景万年青的阔叶又已消失在昏暗中，破絮一般的白云间闪出星点，黑夜就从此开头。四铭当这时候，便也不由的感奋起来，仿佛就要大有所为，与周围的坏学生以及恶社会宣战。他意气渐渐勇猛，脚步愈跨愈大，布鞋底声也愈走愈响，吓得早已睡在笼子里的母鸡和小鸡也都唧唧足足的叫起来了。

堂前有了灯光，就是号召晚餐的烽火，合家的人们便都齐集在中央的桌子周围。灯在下横；上首是四铭一人居中，也是学程一般肥胖的圆脸，但多两撇细胡子，在菜汤的热气里，独据一面，很像庙里的财神。左横是四太太带着招儿；右横是学程和秀儿一列。碗筷声雨点似的响，虽然大家不言语，也就是很热闹的晚餐。

招儿带翻了饭碗了，菜汤流得小半桌。四铭尽量的睁大了细眼睛瞪着看得她要哭，这才收回眼光，伸筷自去夹

He fixed her with his eye, as if to test her intelligence.

She made no answer, but fixed him with *her* eye, as if waiting for him to elucidate.

"Bah — no!" He supplied the answer himself at last. "I watched for a long time, and saw one person only give her a copper. Plenty of others had gathered round, but only to jeer at them. There were two low types as well, one of whom had the impertinence to say:

"'Afa! Don't be put off by the dirt on this piece of goods. If you buy two cakes of soap and give her a good scrubbing, the result won't be bad at all!' Think, what a way to talk!"

She snorted and lowered her head. After quite a time, she asked rather casually, "Did *you* give her any money?"

"Did I ? — No. I'd have felt ashamed to give just one or two coins. She wasn't an ordinary beggar, you know...."

"Mm." Without waiting for him to finish she stood up slowly and walked to the kitchen. Dusk was gathering, and it was time for supper.

Siming stood up too, and walked into the courtyard. It was lighter out than in. Xuecheng was practising Hexagram Boxing in a corner by the wall. This constituted his "home education," and he used the economical method of employing the hour between day and night for this purpose. Xuecheng had been boxing now for about half a year. Siming nodded very slightly, as if in approval, then began to pace the courtyard with his hands behind his back. Before long, the broad leaves of the evergreen which was the only potted plant they had were swallowed up in the darkness, and stars twinkled between white clouds which looked like torn cotton. Night had fallen. Siming could not repress his growing indignation. He felt called on to do great deeds, to declare war on all the bad students around and on this wicked society. By degrees he grew bolder and bolder, his steps became longer and longer, and the thud of his cloth soles grew louder and louder, waking the hen and her chicks in the coop so that they cheeped in alarm.

A light appeared in the hall — the signal that supper was ready — and the whole household gathered round the table in the middle. The lamps stood at the lower end of the table, while Siming sat alone at the head. His plump, round face was like Xuecheng's, with the additon of two sparse whiskers. Seen through the hot vapour from the vegetable soup, he looked like the God of Wealth you find in temples. On the left sat Mrs. Siming and Zhao'er. On the right Xuecheng and Xiu'er. Chopsticks pattered like rain against the bowls. Though no one said a word, their supper table was very animated.

Zhao'er upset her bowl, spilling soup over half the table. Siming opened his narrow eyes as wide as he could. Only when he saw she was going to cry did he stop glaring at

那早先看中了的一个菜心去。可是菜心已经不见了，他左右一瞥，就发见学程刚刚夹着塞进他张得很大的嘴里去，他于是只好无聊的吃了一筷黄菜叶。

“学程，”他看着他的脸说，“那一句查出了没有？”

“那一句？——那还没有。”

“哼，你看，也没有学问，也不懂道理，单知道吃！学学那个孝女罢，做了乞丐，还是一味孝顺祖母，自己情愿饿肚子。但是你们这些学生那里知道这些，肆无忌惮，将来只好像那光棍……。”

“想倒想着了一个，但不知可是。——我想，他们说的也许是‘阿尔特肤尔’。”

“哦哦，是的！就是这个！他们说的就是这样一个声音：‘恶毒夫咧。’这是什么意思？你也就是他们这一党：你知道的。”

“意思，——意思我不很明白。”

“胡说！瞒我。你们都是坏种！”

“‘天不打吃饭人，’你今天怎么尽闹脾气，连吃饭时候也是打鸡骂狗的。他们小孩子们知道什么。”四太太忽而说。

“什么？”四铭正想发话，但一回头，看见她陷下的两颊已经鼓起，而且很变了颜色，三角形的眼里也发着可怕的光，便赶紧改口说，“我也没有闹什么脾气，我不过教学程应该懂事些。”

“他那里懂得你心里的事呢。”她可是更气忿了。“他如果能懂事，早就点了灯笼火把，寻了那孝女来了。好在你已经给她买好了一块肥皂在这里，只要再去买一块……”

“胡说！那话是那光棍说的。”

“不见得。只要再去买一块，给她咯支咯支的遍身洗一洗，供起来，天下也就太平了。”

“什么话？那有什么相干？我因为记起了你没有肥皂……”

“怎么不相干？你是特诚买给孝女的，你咯支咯支的

6. Chinese transliteration of "old fool."

her and reach out with his chopsticks for a tender morsel of cabbage he had spotted. But the tender morsel had disappeared. He looked right and left, and discovered Xuecheng on the point of stuffing it into his wide-open mouth. Disappointed, he ate a mouthful of yellowish leaves instead.

"Xuecheng!" He looked at his son. "Have you found that phrase or not?"

"Which phrase? — No, not yet!"

"Pah! Look at you, not a good student and with no sense either — all you can do is eat! You should learn from that filial daughter: although she's a beggar, she still treats her grandmother very respectfully, even if it means going hungry herself. But what do you impudent students know of such things? You'll grow up like those low types...."

"I've thought of one possibility, but I don't know if it's right... I think, perhaps, they may have said *e-du-fu-la*."[6]

"That't right! That's it exactly! That's exactly the sound it was: *e-du-fu-la*. What does that mean? You belong to the same group: you must know."

"Mean? — I'm not sure what it means."

"Nonsense. Don't try to deceive me. You're all a bad lot."

"'Even thunder won't strike folk at a meal,'" burst out Mrs. Siming suddenly. "Why do you keep losing your temper today? Even at supper you can't stop hitting the hen while pointing at the dog. What do boys that age understand?"

"What?" Siming was on the point of answering back when he saw her sunken cheeks were quivering with anger, her colour had changed, and a fearful glint had come into her triangular eyes. He hastily changed his tune. "I've not been losing my temper. I'm just telling Xuecheng to learn a little sense."

"How can he understand what's in your mind?" She looked angrier than ever. "If he had any sense, he'd long since have lit a lantern or a torch and gone out to fetch that filial daughter. You've already bought her one cake of soap; all you have to do is buy another...."

"Nonsense! That's what that low type said."

"I'm not so sure. If you buy another cake and give her a good scrubbing, then worship her, the whole world will be at peace."

"How can you say such a thing? What connection is here? Because I remembered you'd no soap...."

"There's a connection all right. You bought it specially for the filial daughter; so go and

去洗去。我不配，我不要，我也不要沾孝女的光。”

“这真是什么话？你们女人……”四铭支吾着，脸上也像学程练了八卦拳之后似的流出油汗来，但大约大半也因为吃了太热的饭。

“我们女人怎么样？我们女人，比你们男人好得多。你们男人不是骂十八九岁的女学生，就是称赞十八九岁的女讨饭：都不是什么好心思。‘咯支咯支’，简直是不要脸！”

“我不是已经说过了？那是一个光棍……”

“四翁！”外面的暗中忽然起了极响的叫喊。

“道翁么？我就来！”四铭知道那是高声有名的何道统，便遇赦似的，也高兴的大声说。“学程，你快点灯照何老伯到书房去！”

学程点了烛，引着道统走进西边的厢房里，后面还跟着卜薇园。

“失迎失迎，对不起。”四铭还嚼着饭，出来拱一拱手，说。“就在舍间用便饭，何如？……”

“已经偏过了。”薇园迎上去，也拱一拱手，说。“我们连夜赶来，就为了那移风文社的第十八届征文题目，明天不是‘逢七’么？”

“哦！今天十六？”四铭恍然的说。

“你看，多么胡涂！”道统大嚷道。

“那么，就得连夜送到报馆去，要他明天一准登出来。”

“文题我已经拟下了。你看怎样，用得用不得？”道统说着，就从手巾包里挖出一张纸条来交给他。

四铭踱到烛台面前，展开纸条，一字一字的读下去：“‘恭拟全国人民合词吁请贵大总统特颁明令专重圣经崇祀孟母以挽颓风而存国粹文’。——好极好极。可是字数太多了罢？”

“不要紧的！”道统大声说。“我算过了，还无须乎多加广告费。但是诗题呢？”

“诗题么？”四铭忽而恭敬之状可掬了。“我倒有一个在这里：孝女行。那是实事，应该表彰表彰她。我今天

7. A woman famous for her virtue. According to tradition, she moved house three times to avoid undesirable companions for her son.

give her a good scrubbing. I don't deserve it. I don't want it. I don't want to share her glory."

"Really, how can you talk like that?" mumbled Siming. "You women...." His face was perspiring like Xuecheng's after Hexagram Boxing, probably mostly because the food had been so hot.

"What about us women? We women are much better than you men. If you men aren't cursing eighteen- or nineteen-year-old girl students, you're praising eighteen- or nineteen-year-old girl beggars: such dirty minds you have! Scrubbing, indeed! — Disgusting!"

"Didn't you hear? That was one of those low types...."

"Siming!" A thundering voice was heard from the darkness outside.

"Daotong? I'm coming!"

Siming knew this was He Daotong, famed for his powerful voice, and he shouted back as joyfully as a criminal newly reprieved.

"Xuecheng, hurry up and light the lamp to show Uncle He into the library!"

Xuecheng lit a candle, and ushered Daotong into a room on the west. They were followed by Bu Weiyuan.

"I'm sorry I didn't welcome you. Excuse me." With his mouth still full of rice, Siming came in and bowed with clasped hands in greeting. "Won't you join us at our simple meal?..."

"We've already eaten," Weiyuan stepped forward and greeted him. "We've hurried here at this time of night because of the eighteenth essay and poem contest of the Moral Rearmament Literary League. Isn't tomorrow the seventeenth?"

"What? Is it the sixteenth today?" asked Siming in surprise.

"See how absent-minded you are!" boomed Daotong.

"So we'll have to send something in tonight to the newspaper office, to make sure they print it tomorrow."

"I've already drafted the title of the essay. See whether you think it will do or not." As he was speaking, Daotong produced a slip of paper from his handkerchief and handed it to Siming.

Siming stepped up to the candle, unfolded the paper, and read it word by word, "'We humbly suggest an essay in the name of the whole nation to beg the President to issue an order for the promotion of the Confucian classics and the worship of the mother of Mencius,[7] in order to revive this moribund world and preserve our national character.' Very good. Very good. Isn't it a little long, though?"

"That doesn't matter," answered Daotong loudly. "I've worked it out, and it won't cost more to advertise. But what about the title for the poem?"

"The title for the poem?" Siming suddenly looked most respectful. "I've thought of one. How about 'The Filial Daughter'? It's a true story, and she deserves to be eulogized.

在大街上……”

“哦哦，那不行。”薇园连忙摇手，打断他的话。“那是我也看见的。她大概是‘外路人’，我不懂她的话，她也不懂我的话，不知道她究竟是那里人。大家倒都说她是孝女；然而我问她可能做诗，她摇摇头。要是能做诗，那就好了。”

“然而忠孝是大节，不会做诗也可以将就……。”

“那倒不然，而孰知不然！”薇园摊开手掌，向四铭连摇带推的奔过去，力争说。“要会做诗，然后有趣。”

“我们，”四铭推开他，“就用这个题目，加上说明，登报去。一来可以表彰表彰她；二来可以借此针砭社会。现在的社会还成个什么样子，我从旁考察了好半天，竟不见有什么人给一个钱，这岂不是全无心肝……”

“阿呀，四翁！”薇园又奔过来，“你简直是在‘对着和尚骂贼秃’了。我就没有给钱，我那时恰恰身边没有带着。”

“不要多心，薇翁。”四铭又推开他，“你自然在外，又作别论。你听我讲下去：她们面前围了一大群人，毫无敬意，只是打趣。还有两个光棍，那是更其肆无忌惮了，有一个简直说，‘阿发，你去买两块肥皂来，咯支咯支遍身洗一洗，好得很哩。’你想，这……”

“哈哈哈！两块肥皂！”道统的响亮的笑声突然发作了，震得人耳朵嗡嗡的叫。“你买，哈哈，哈哈！”

“道翁，道翁，你不要这么嚷。”四铭吃了一惊，慌张的说。

“咯支咯支，哈哈！”

“道翁！”四铭沉下脸来了，“我们讲正经事，你怎么只胡闹，闹得人头昏。你听，我们就用这两个题目，即刻送到报馆去，要他明天一准登出来。这事只好偏劳你们两位了。”

“可以可以，那自然。薇园极口应承说。

“呵呵，洗一洗，咯支……唏唏……”

“道翁！！！”四铭愤愤的叫。

8. In old China, it was considered romantic for women to exchange ideas with men through the medium of poems.

One the main street today...."

"Oh, no, that won't do," put in Weiyuan hastily, waving his hand to stop Siming. "I saw her too, She isn't from these parts, and I couldn't understand her dialect, nor she mine. I don't know where she's from. Everyone says she's filial; but when I asked her if she could write poems, she shook her head. If she could, that would be fine."[8]

"But since loyalty and filial piety are so important, it doesn't matter too much if she can't write poems...."

"That isn't true. Quite otherwise." Weiyuan raised his hands and rushed towards Siming, to shake and push him. "She'd only be interesting if she could write poems."

"Let's use this title." Siming pushed him aside. "Add an explanation and print it. In the first place, it will serve to eulogize her; in the second, we can use this to criticize society. What is the world coming to anyway? I watched for some time, and didn't see anybody give her a cent — aren't people utterly heartless?"

"*Aiya*, Siming!" Weiyuan rushed over again. "You're cursing baldheads to a monk. I didn't give her anything because I didn't happen to have any money on me."

"Don't be so sensitive, Weiyuan," Siming pushed him aside again. "Of course you're an exception. Let me finish. There was quite a crowd around them, showing no respect, just jeering. There were two low types as well, who were even more impertinent. One of them said, 'Afa! If you buy two cakes of soap and give her a good scrubbing, the result won't be bad at all!' Just think...."

"Daotong! Daotong! Don't make such a noise!" Siming gave a start, panic-stricken.

"A good scrubbing! Ho, ho, ho!"

"Daotong!" Siming looked stern. "We're discussing serious matters. Why should you make such a noise, nearly deafening everyone? Listen to me: we'll use both these titles, and send them straight to the newspaper office so that they come out without fail tomorrow. I'll have to trouble you both to take them there."

"All right, all right. Of course," agreed Weiyuan readily.

"Ha, ha! A good scrubbing! Ho, ho!"

"Daotong!" shouted Siming, furious.

道统给这一喝，不笑了。他们拟好了说明，薇园誊在信笺上，就和道统跑往报馆去。四铭拿着烛台，送出门口，回到堂屋的外面，心里就有些不安逸，但略一踌躕，也终于跨进门槛去了。他一进门，迎头就看见中央的方桌中间放着那肥皂的葵绿色的小小的长方包，包中央的金印子在灯光下明晃晃的发闪，周围还有细小的花纹。

秀儿和招儿都蹲在桌子下横的地上玩；学程坐在右横查字典。最后在离灯最远的阴影里的高背椅子上发见了四太太，灯光照处，见她死板板的脸上并不显出什么喜怒，眼睛也并不看着什么东西。

“咯支咯支，不要脸不要脸……”

四铭微微的听得秀儿在他背后说，回头看时，什么动作也没有了，只有招儿还用了她两只小手的指头在自己脸上抓。

他觉得存身不住，便熄了烛，踱出院子去。他来回的踱，一不小心，母鸡和小鸡又唧唧足足的叫了起来，他立即放轻脚步，并且走远些。经过许多时，堂屋里的灯移到卧室里去了。他看见一地月光，仿佛满铺了无缝的白纱，玉盘似的月亮现在白云间，看不出一点缺。

他很有些悲伤，似乎也像孝女一样，成了“无告之民”，孤苦零丁了。他这一夜睡得非常晚。

但到第二天的早晨，肥皂就被录用了。这日他比平日起得迟，看见她已经伏在洗脸台上擦脖子，肥皂的泡沫就如大螃蟹嘴上的水泡一般，高高的堆在两个耳朵后，比起先前用皂荚时候的只有一层极薄的白沫来，那高低真有霄壤之别了。从此之后，四太太的身上便总带着些似橄揽非橄揽的说不清的香味；几乎小半年，这才忽而换了样，凡有闻到的都说那可似乎是檀香。

一九二四年三月二二日。

"This shout made Daotong stop laughing. After they had drawn up the explanation, Weiyuan copied it on the paper and left with Daotong for the newspaper office. Siming carried the candle to see them out, then walked back to the door of the hall feeling rather apprehensive. After some hesitation, though, he finally crossed the threshold. As he went in, his eyes fell on the small, green, oblong package of soap in the middle of the central table, the gold characters on it glittering in the lamplight, with fine designs around them.

Xiu'er and Zhao'er were playing on the floor at the lower end of the table, while Xuecheng sat on the right side looking up something in his dictionary. Last of all, on the high-backed chair in the shadows far from the lamp, Siming discovered his wife. Her impassive face showed neither joy nor anger, and she was staring at nothing.

"A good scrubbing indeed! Disgusting!"

Faintly, Siming heard Xiu'er's voice behind him. He turned, but she was not moving. Only Zhao'er had put both small hands to her face as if to shame somebody.

"This was no place for him. He blew out the candle, and went into the yard to pace up and down. And, because he forgot to be quiet, the mother hen and her chicks started cheeping again. At once he walked more lightly, moving further away. After a long time, the lamp in the hall was transferred to the bedroom. The moonlight on the ground was like seamless white gauze, and the moon — quite full — seemed a jade disc among the bright clouds.

He felt not a little depressed, as if he, like the filial daughter, was "utterly forlorn and alone." That night he slept very late.

By the next morning, however, the soap was being honoured by being used. Getting up latter than usual, he saw his wife leaning over the wash-stand rubbing her neck, with bubbles like those emitted by great crabs heaped up over both her ears. The difference between these and the small white bubbles produced by honey locust pods was like that between heaven and earth. After this, an indefinable fragrance rather reminiscent of olive always emanated from Mrs. Siming. Not for nearly half a year did this suddenly give place to another scent, which all who smelt it averred was like sandalwood.

March 22, 1924

本来对了庙门立着的他，也转过脸来对他们看。

He had been standing in front of the temple gate,
but now he turned to regard them over his shoulder.

长明灯
The Lamp That Was Kept Alight

春阴的下午，吉光屯唯一的茶馆子里的空气又有些紧张了，人们的耳朵里，仿佛还留着一种微细沉实的声息——

“熄掉他罢！”

但当然并不是全屯的人们都如此。这屯上的居民是不大出行的，动一动就须查黄历，看那上面是否写着“不宜出行”；倘没有写，出去也须先走喜神方，迎吉利。不拘禁忌地坐在茶馆里的不过几个以豁达自居的青年人，但在蛰居人的意中却以为个个都是败家子。

现在也无非就是这茶馆里的空气有些紧张。

“还是这样么？”三角脸的拿起茶碗，问。

“听说，还是这样，”方头说，“还是尽说‘熄掉他熄掉他’。眼光也越加发闪了。见鬼！这是我们屯上的一个大害，你不要看得微细。我们倒应该想个法子来除掉他！”

“除掉他，算什么一回事。他不过是一个……。什么东西！造庙的时候，他的祖宗就捐过钱，现在他却要来吹熄长明灯。这不是不肖子孙？我们上县去，送他忤逆！”阔亭捏了拳头，在桌上一击，慷慨地说。一只斜盖着的茶碗盖子也噫的一声，翻了身。

“不成。要送忤逆，须是他的父母，母舅……”方头说。

“可惜他只有一个伯父……”阔亭立刻颓唐了。

“阔亭！”方头突然叫道。“你昨天的牌风可好？”

阔亭睁着眼看了他一会，没有便答；胖脸的庄七光已经放开喉咙嚷起来了：

“吹熄了灯，我们的吉光屯还成什么吉光屯，不就完了么？老年人不都说么：这灯还是梁武帝点起的，一直传下来，没有熄过；连长毛造反的时候也没有熄过……。你看，啧，那火光不是绿莹莹的么？外路人经过这里的都要看一看，都称赞……。啧，多么好……。他现在这么胡闹，什么意思？……”

“他不是发了疯么？你还没有知道？”方头带些藐视的神气说。

1. The Taiping revolutionaries of the mid-nineteenth century, who wore their hair loose as a protest against the queues imposed by the Qing rulers.

One overcast spring afternoon the atmosphere was somewhat tense in the one and only tea-house of Lucky Light Village, for in the customers' ears lingered the faint yet earnest cry:

"Put it out!"

This was not true of everyone in the village, of course. The villagers here were a stay-at-home lot, who before stirring abroad would look up the almanac to see whether that day was "propitious for a journey" or not. If it was, before setting out they would step in the direction of the God of Luck to be sure of meeting with good fortune. Sitting here so free from constraint in the tea-house were merely a few youths who prided themselves on their broad-mindedness, although in conservative eyes each mother's son among them was bound to be the ruin of his family.

The atmosphere was somewhat tense now in this tea-house.

"Still no change?" asked Triangle Face, picking up his bowl of tea.

"Still no change, they say," replied Square Head. "He keeps repeating, 'Put it out, put it out!' His eyes are flashing worse than ever. The devil! Don't think it's a joke — the fellow's a menace to our village. Fact is, we ought to find some way to get rid of him!"

"Get rid of him, by all means. He's nothing but a dirty bastard. When the temple was built his ancestors paid their share, yet now he wants to blow out the temple light! Is that unfilial or isn't it? Let's send him to the county court as an unfilial son!" Kuoting ended with a flourish, smashing his fist on the table. The tilted lid of one bowl fell off with a clatter."

"That won't do. Only parents or maternal uncles can charge an undutiful son..." objected Square Head.

"Pity all he has is a paternal uncle...." Kuoting's spirits immediately sank.

"Kuothing!" cried Square Head suddenly. "Did you have much luck in you game yesterday?"

Kuotitng stared at him round-eyed but did not answer. Fatfaced Zhuang Qiguang was already bellowing:

"If he puts out the lamp that'll be the end of Lucky Light Village, won't it? Don't all the old folk say this lamp was lit by Emperor Wu of Liang, and it's been burning ever since? Not even the Long Hairs[1].... Just look, ha! At that splendid green light it sheds! Folk from other parts passing this way always ask to see it and admire it.... It's something to be proud of.... What does he mean by carrying on like this?..."

"He's crazy. Didn't you know?" Square Head spoke scornfully. "Bah, you're so clever!" Zhuang's fat face glistened with sweat.

“哼，你聪明！”庄七光的脸上就走了油。

“我想：还不如用老法子骗他一骗，”灰五婶，本店的主人兼工人，本来是旁听着的，看见形势有些离了她专注的本题了，便赶忙来岔开纷争，拉到正经事上去。

“什么老法子？”庄七光诧异地问。

“他不是先就发过一回疯么：和现在一模一样。那时他的父亲还在，骗了他一骗，就治好了。”

“怎么骗？我怎么不知道？”庄七光更其诧异地问。

“你怎么会知道？那时你们都还是小把戏呢，单知道喝奶拉矢。便是我，那时也不这样。你看我那时的一双手呵，真是粉嫩粉嫩……”

“你现在也还是粉嫩粉嫩……”方头说。

“放你妈的屁！”灰五婶怒目地笑了起来，“莫胡说了。我们讲正经话。他那时也还年青哩；他的老子也就有些疯的。听说：有一天他的祖父带他进社庙去，教他拜社老爷，瘟将军，王灵官老爷，他就害怕了，硬不拜，跑了出来，从此便有些怪。后来就像现在一样，一见人总和他们商量吹熄正殿上的长明灯。他说熄了便再不会有蝗虫和病痛，真是像一件天大的正事似的。大约那是邪祟附了体，怕见正路神道了。要是我们，会怕见社老爷么？你们的茶不冷了么？对一点热水罢。好，他后来就自己闯进去，要去吹。他的老子又太疼爱他，不肯将他锁起来。呵，后来不是全屯动了公愤，和他老子去吵闹了么？可是，没有办法，——幸亏我家的死鬼那时还在，给想了一个法：将长明灯用厚棉被一围，漆漆黑黑地，领他去看，说是已经吹熄了。”

“唉唉，这真亏他想得出。”三角脸吐一口气，说，不胜感服之至似的。

“费什么这样的手脚，”阔亭愤愤地说，“这祥的东西，打死了就完了，吓！”

“那怎么行？”她吃惊地看着他，连忙摇手道，“那怎么行！他的祖父不是捏过印靶子的么？”

阔亭们立刻面面相觑，觉得除了“死鬼”的妙法以外，也委实无法可想了。

“后来就好了的！”她又用手背抹去一些嘴角上的白

"I say, trick him again in the old way." Huiwu's wife, proprietor-cum-waitress of this tea-house, had been no more than a listener hitherto; but at this digression from a topic which enthralled her she hastily intervened to prevent a quarrel and lead them back to the subject.

"What old way?" asked Zhuang in surprise.

"Didn't he go crazy, just like this, once before? That was in his father's time. After being tricked, he recovered."

"Tricked — how? Why did I never hear of it?" asked Zhuang in even greater surprise.

"How could you? You were just brats at the time, guzzling your mammy's milk. I wasn't like this either, I'd have you know. You should have seen my hands in those days, so smooth and soft and white...."

"You're still smooth and soft and white..." interposed Square Head.

"Get away with you!"Her glare turned into a smile. "Enough of your nonsense! Let's be serious. He was young then and his father was little crazy too. They say one day his grandfather took him to the temple and told him to bow to Old Man Earth, General Plague and Guardian Angel Wang, but instead he ran off in a fright and he's been odd ever since, just the way he is now. He talks to everyone he meets about blowing out the lamp that's always kept alight in the main hall. Once it's blown out there'll be no more locusts or plagues, he says, as if that would be such a wonderful thing. Most likely he's possessed by some devil that's afraid of seeing true gods. Which of us is afraid of Old Man Earth? Is your tea cold? Let me add some hot water. There! Yes, after that he rushed in to blow it out. His father was too fond of him to lock him up. But that provoked the whole village, and folk kept after his father, Still no one knew what to do. Thank goodness my old man was still alive in those days to work out a plan. He blacked out the lamp with a cotton quilt, then took him to see it and told him it had been put out!"

"My, my! That took some thinking out!" Triangle Face heaved an admiring sigh.

"Why go to all that trouble?" growled Kuoting. "A bastard like that should be beaten to death — good riddance!"

"What an idea!" Staring at him in horror, she made a sign of dissent. "The idea! Didn't his grandfather hold an official rank?"

Kuoting and the rest eyed each other, unable to improve on her old man's plan.

"That cured him!" Brushing the spittle from her mouth with the back of one hand,

沫，更快地说，“后来全好了的！他从此也就不再走进庙门去，也不再提起什么来，许多年。不知道怎么这回看了赛会之后不多几天，又疯了起来了。哦，同先前一模一样。午后他就走过这里，一定又上庙里去了。你们和四爷商量商量去，还是再骗他一骗好。那灯不是梁五弟点起来的么？不是说，那灯一灭，这里就要变海，我们就都要变泥鳅么？你们快去和四爷商量商量罢，要不……”

“我们还是先到庙前去看一看，”方头说着，便轩昂地出了门。

阔亭和庄七光也跟着出去了。三角脸走得最后，将到门口，回过头来说道：

“这回就记了我的账！入他……。”

灰五婶答应着，走到东墙下拾起一块木炭来，就在墙上画有一个小三角形和一串短短的细线的下面，划添了两条线。

他们望见社庙的时候，果然一并看到了几个人：一个正是他，两个是闲看的，三个是孩子。

但庙门却紧紧地关着。

“好！庙门还关着。”阔亭高兴地说。

他们一走近，孩子们似乎也都胆壮，围近去了。本来对了庙门立着的他，也转过脸来对他们看。

他也还如平常一样，黄的方脸和蓝布破大衫，只在浓眉底下的大而且长的眼睛中，略带些异样的光闪，看人就许多工夫不眨眼，并且总含着悲愤疑惧的神情。短的头发上粘着两片稻草叶，那该是孩子暗暗地从背后给他放上去的，因为他们向他头上一看之后，就都缩了颈子，笑着将舌头很快地一伸。

他们站定了，各人都互看着别个的脸。

"你干什么？”但三角脸终于走上一步，诘问了。

“我叫老黑开门，”他低声，温和地说。“就因为那一盏灯必须吹熄。你看，三头六臂的蓝脸，三只眼睛，长帽，半个的头，牛头和猪牙齿，都应该吹熄……吹熄。吹

she went on even faster. "That cured him completely! He's never crossed the temple threshold again or said a word about the lamp all these years. I don't know what sent him off his head again a few days after the last temple fair. It's exactly the same as last time, that I know. Soon after noon he passed this way, going to the temple no doubt. Go and talk it over with Fourth Master and see if you can't trick him again. Wasn't that lamp lit by Emperor Wu of Liang? Don't they say that if it goes out this village will become a sea and we'll change into eels? Do go on and talk it over with Fourth Master...."

"We'd better have a look at the temple first," said Square Head striding out.

Kuoting and Zhuang Qiguang followed him. Triangle Face, the last, turned at the door to say:

"Score it up to me today, dammit!..."

Huiwu's wife, assenting, picked up a piece of charcoal from the floor. On the east wall, under a small triangle with a cluster of short lines beneath it, she drew two more lines.

Looking towards the temple, sure enough, they saw a small group gathered: the fellow himself, two onlookers, three children.

But the temple gate was shut tight.

"Good! The temple gate's still closed," said Kuoting approvingly.

Their approach apparently gave the children courage, for they closed in. He had been standing in front of the temple gate, but now he turned to regard them over his shoulder.

He seemed the same as usual with his sallow, square face and shabby blue cotton gown, except that his large, almond eyes shone under their shaggy brows with a strange light and he stared at them unwinking for some moments, grief, suspicion and fear in his gaze. Two straws were sticking to his short hair, no doubt thrown by the children behind his back, for each time they looked at his head they hunched their shoulders and grinned, sticking out their tongues.

They all stood still, eyeing each other.

"What are you up to?" It was Triangle Face who finally stepped forward to put this question.

"I've asked Old Hei to open the gate," his voice was low and gentle. "Because that lamp has got to be blown out. You see, they should all be put out: Blue Face with his three heads and six arms, Three Eyes, Long Hat, Half Head, Ox Head and Swine

熄，我们就不会有蝗虫，不会有猪嘴瘟……。”

“唏唏，胡闹！”阔亭轻蔑地笑了出来，“你吹熄了灯，蝗虫会还要多，你就要生猪嘴瘟！”

“唏唏！”庄七光也陪着笑。

一个赤膊孩子擎起他玩弄着的苇子，对他瞄准着，将樱桃似的小口一张，道：

“吧！”

“你还是回去罢！倘不，你的伯伯会打断你的骨头！灯么，我替你吹。你过几天来看就知道。”阔亭大声说。

他两眼更发出闪闪的光来，钉一般看定阔亭的眼，使阔亭的眼光赶紧辟易了。

“你吹？”他嘲笑似的微笑，但接着就坚定地说，“不能！不要你们。我自己去熄，此刻去熄！”

阔亭便立刻颓唐得酒醒之后似的无力；方头却已站上去了，慢慢地说道：

“你是一向懂事的，这一回可是太胡涂了。让我来开导你罢，你也许能够明白。就是吹熄了灯，那些东西不是还在么？不要这么傻头傻脑了，还是回去！睡觉去！”

“我知道的，熄了也还在。”他忽又现出阴鸷的笑容，但是立即收敛了，沉实地说道，“然而我只能姑且这么办。我先来这么办，容易些。我就要吹熄他，自己熄！”他说着，一面就转过身去竭力地推庙门。

“喂！”阔亭生气了，“你不是这里的人么？你一定要我们大家变泥鳅么？回去！你推不开的，你没有法子开的！吹不熄的！还是回去好！”

“我不回去！我要吹熄他！”

“不成！你没法开！”

“…………”

“你没法开！”

“那么，就用别的法子来。”他转脸向他们一瞥，沉静地说。

“哼，看你有什么别的法。”

“…………”

Tusk.... Out with the lot of them! When they're out we shall have no more locusts, no more plague...."

"Hee-hee! Nonsense!" Kuoting tittered scornfully. "If you blow out that lamp there'll be even more locusts, you'll catch the plague yourself!"

"Hee-hee!" tittered Zhuang Qiguang.

A child, clothed only in a pair of pants, held up the reed he was playing with and aimed it at him, parting small cherry lips to cry:

"Bang!"

"Go on home now!" said Kuoting loudly. "If you don't your uncle will break you bones! We'll blow out the lamp for you. You can come back in a few days and see for yourself."

His gaze glittered even more brightly as he looked Kuoting in the eye, forcing Kuoting to turn his eyes away.

"*You'll* blow it out?" With a contemptuous smile he went on firmly, "Not you! I don't need any of you. I'll do it myself. I'm going to blow it out now!"

Kuoting was promptly reduced to the state of collapse that follows a bout of drinking. But Square Head had stepped forward to say slowly:

"You're always shown yourself an intelligent man, but this is ridiculous! Let me tell you something you should be able to grasp. Even if the lamp's blown out, those creatures will still be there, won't they? Stop playing the fool and go home! Go and have some sleep!"

"I know they'll still be there if it's blown out." He flashed them another grim smile before regaining his gravity and proceeding earnestly, "I shall just be doing the best I can. I'm tackling this first because it's easiest. I'm going to blow it out now, I'll do it myself! He turned back to batter at the temple gate.

"Hey!" Kuoting was angry. "Don't you belong to this village? Do you want us all to turn into eels? Go home! You can't push that door open, you've no way of opening it! You can't blow out the lamp — go on home!"

"I'm not going home. I'm going to blow it out."

"Not you! You can't get in!"

"......"

"You can't get in!"

"I'll think of some other way then,"he said gravely, turning to eye them intently.

"Ha, let's see what other way you have."

"...."

“看你有什么别的法！”

“我放火。”

“什么？”阔亭疑心自己没有听清楚。

“我放火！”

沉默像一声清磬，摇曳着尾声，周围的活物都在其中凝结了。但不一会，就有几个人交头接耳，不一会，又都退了开去；两三人又在略远的地方站住了。庙后门的墙外就有庄七光的声音喊道：

“老黑呀，不对了！你庙门要关得紧！老黑呀，你听清了么？关得紧！我们去想了法子就来！”

但他似乎并不留心别的事，只闪烁着狂热的眼光，在地上，在空中，在人身上，迅速地搜查，仿佛想要寻火种。

方头和阔亭在几家的大门里穿梭一般出入了一通之后，吉光屯全局顿然扰动了。许多人们的耳朵里，心里，都有了一个可怕的声音：“放火！”但自然还有多少更深的蛰居人的耳朵里心里是全没有。然而全屯的空气也就紧张起来，凡有感得这紧张的人们，都很不安，仿佛自己就要变成泥鳅，天下从此毁灭。他们自然也隐约知道毁灭的不过是吉光屯，但也觉得吉光屯似乎就是天下。

这事件的中枢，不久就凑在四爷的客厅上了。坐在首座上的是年高德劭的郭老娃，脸上已经皱得如风干的香橙，还要用手捋着下颏上的白胡须，似乎想将他们拔下。

“上半天，”他放松了胡子，慢慢地说，“西头，老富的中风，他的儿子，就说是：因为，社神不安，之故。这样一来，将来，万一有，什么，鸡犬不宁，的事，就难免要到，府上……是的，都要来到府上，麻烦。”

“是么，”四爷也捋着上唇的花白的鲇鱼须，却悠悠然，仿佛全不在意模样，说，“这也是他父亲的报应呵。他自己在世的时候，不就是不相信菩萨么？我那时就和他不合，可是一点也奈何他不得。现在，叫我还有什么法？”

“我想，只有，一个。是的，有一个。明天，捆上城去，给他在那个，那个城隍庙里，搁一夜，是的，搁一

"Let's see what other way you have!"

"I'll set the place on fire."

"What?" Kuoting could hardly believe his ears.

"I'll set the place on fire!"

The silence was like a clear chime which died away so slowly that all living creatures near by were held motionless. But presently they started whispering together, and presently they withdrew. Two or three halted at a distance. Outside the back gate of the temple, Zhuang Qiguang shouted:

"Old Hei! Watch out! Keep the temple gates closed tight! Do you hear me, Old Hei? Close them tight. We'll come back when we've decided what to do!"

But he, seemingly oblivious of all else, flashed his blazing eyes as if searching the earth, the air and men's bodies for the wherewithal to kindle a fire.

After Square Head and Kuoting had shuttled to and fro between some of the larger houses, the whole of Lucky Light Village was plunged in confusion. Many ears and hearts were filled with that fearful word "Fire!" This was not true, of course, of quite a few more conservative ears and hearts. Still there was an air of tension throughout the village, and all conscious of this tension felt as acutely uneasy as if at any moment they were liable to change into eels and the whole world to perish. Although they were vaguely aware that only Lucky Light Village was to perish, to them Lucky Light Village was the world.

The centre of all this activity soon shifted to Fourth Master's reception room. In the place of honour sat old Guo, in the fullness of years and virtue, his face as wrinkled as a wind-dried orange, plucking at the white hairs on his chin as if eager to pull them out.

"This forenoon," he declared slowly, releasing his beard, "when Old Fu in the west end had a stroke, his son said it was because the God of the Earth was displeased. That being so, in future, if by any chance something disturbing should happen, it is almost sure to affect you. Yes, you — most unfortunate."

"True." Fourth Master tugged casually and absent-mindedly at his grizzled moustache. "This is a judgment on his father's sins. My brother never believed in Buddha, did he?... I didn't agree with him, but what could I do? What do you expect me to do now?"

"To my mind, there is one way only. Only one. Tomorrow, tie him up, send him to town, and leave him in the big temple for one night — yes, for one night — to exorcize

夜，赶一赶，邪祟。”

阔亭和方头以守护全屯的劳绩，不但第一次走进这一个不易瞻仰的客厅，并且还坐在老娃之下和四爷之上，而且还有茶喝。他们跟着老娃进来，报告之后，就只是喝茶，喝干之后，也不开口，但此时阔亭忽然发表意见了：

“这办法太慢！他们两个还管着呢。最要紧的是马上怎么办。如果真是烧将起来……”

郭老娃吓了一跳，下巴有些发抖。

“如果真是烧将起来……”方头抢着说。

“那么，”阔亭大声道，“就糟了！”

一个黄头发的女孩子又来冲上茶。阔亭便不再说话，立即拿起茶来喝。浑身一抖，放下了，伸出舌尖来舔了一舔上嘴唇，揭去碗盖嘘嘘地吹着。

“真是拖累煞人！”四爷将手在桌上轻轻一拍，“这种子孙，真该死呵！唉！”

“的确，该死的。”阔亭抬起头来了，“去年，连各庄就打死一个：这种子孙。大家一口咬定，说是同时同刻，大家一齐动手，分不出打第一下的是谁，后来什么事也没有。”

“那又是一回事。”方头说，“这回，他们管着呢。我们得赶紧想法子。我想……”

老娃和四爷都肃然地看着他的脸。

“我想：倒不如姑且将他关起来。”

“那倒也是一个妥当的办法。”四爷微微地点一点头。

“妥当！”阔亭说。

“那倒，确是，一个妥当的，办法。”老娃说，“我们，现在，就将他，拖到府上来。府上，就赶快，收拾出，一间屋子来。还，准备着，锁。”

“屋子？”四爷仰了脸，想了一会，说，“舍间可是没有这样的闲房。他也说不定什么时候才会好……”

“就用，他，自己的……”老娃说。

“我家的六顺，”四爷忽然严肃而且悲哀地说，声音也有些发抖了。“秋天就要娶亲……。你看，他年纪这么

this evil spirit."

This was not merely the first time Kuoting and Square Head had entered this normally inaccessible room in their capacity as champions of the village, they were actually sitting below Old Guo yet above Fourth Master, and moreover had been offered tea. Having entered with Old Guo, after making their report they had confined themselves to sipping tea, not even opening their mouths when the tea was finished. But now, without warning, Kuoting voiced his opinion:

"That would take too long! The two of them are still there watching him. The main thing is to decide on immediate action. If he really starts a fire...."

Old Guo jumped for fright and his jaw began to tremble.

"If he really starts a fire..." chimed in Square Head.

"Well," said Kuoting loudly, "that would be the end!"

A brown-haired girl came in to fill their bowls. Kuoting subsided into silence, picking up his bowl immediately to drink. With a convulsive start he set it down, licking his upper lip, then removed the lid and blew on the tea to cool it.

"I hate being involved like this." Fourth Master drummed softly on the table. "A son who's such a disgrace to his family would be better dead!" He sighed.

"That's true, he'd be better dead." Kuoting looked up. "Last year they killed one like him in Liange Village, a disgrace to his family. Everyone agreed to set on him together at the same instant, so that nobody could say who struck the first blow. And no trouble came of it."

"That was different," said Square Head. "This time the authorities are in charge. We must think quickly what to do. In my opinion...."

Old Guo and Fourth Master solemnly studied his face.

"In my opinion, we'd better lock him up."

"That's a good idea." Fourth Master nodded slowly.

"Good," agreed Kuoting.

"That certainly is good idea," drawled Old Guo. "We'll have him brought here now. We must make haste, here, to prepare a room. A padlock too."

"A room?" Fourth Master threw back his head to think. "I've no suitable room to spare here. Besides, we don't know how long he'll be in this state."

"Use his own..." suggested Old Guo.

"Our Liushun is marrying this autumn." Suddenly Fourth Master sounded both stern and grieved, and his voice was trembling. "...What a nephew, long since past the age to marry, yet instead of founding a family and settling down, all he can do is go

大了，单知道发疯，不肯成家立业。舍弟也做了一世人，虽然也不大安分，可是香火总归是绝不得的……。”

“那自然！”三个人异口同音地说。

“六顺生了儿子，我想第二个就可以过继给他。但是，——别人的儿子，可以白要的么？”

“那不能！”三个人异口同音地说。

“这一间破屋，和我是不相干；六顺也不在乎此。可是，将亲生的孩子白白给人，做母亲的怕不能就这么松爽罢？”

“那自然！”三个人异口同音地说。

四爷沉默了。三个人交互看着别人的脸。

“我是天天盼望他好起来，”四爷在暂时静穆之后，这才缓缓地说，“可是他总不好。也不是不好，是他自己不要好。无法可想，就照这一位所说似的关起来，免得害人，出他父亲的丑，也许倒反好，倒是对得起他的父亲……。”

“那自然，”阔亭感动的说，“可是，房子……”

“庙里就没有闲房？……”四爷慢腾腾地问道。

“有！”阔亭恍然道，“有！进大门的西边那一间就空着，又只有一个小方窗，粗木直栅的，决计挖不开。好极了！”

老娃和方头也顿然都显了欢喜的神色；阔亭吐一口气，尖着嘴唇就喝茶。

未到黄昏时分，天下已经泰平，或者竟是全都忘却了，人们的脸上不特已不紧张，并且早褪尽了先前的喜悦的痕迹。在庙前，人们的足迹自然比平日多，但不久也就稀少了。只因为关了几天门，孩子们不能进去玩，便觉得这一天在院子里格外玩得有趣，吃过了晚饭，还有几个跑到庙里去游戏，猜谜。

“你猜。”一个最大的说，“我再说一遍：

白篷船，红划楫，
摇到对岸歇一歇，
点心吃一些，
戏文唱一出”。

mad! My brother did his duty. He may not have been too good a citizen, but at least someone must continue the sacrifices to him...."

"Yes, indeed!" said the other three together.

"When Liushun has sons, I shall let him adopt the second. But can you take someone else's son for nothing?"

"No, indeed!" said the other three together.

"This tumble-down house means nothing to me, and Liushun doesn't care about such things either. But will the child's mother be willing to give away her own flesh and blood for no return?"

"No, indeed!" said the other three together.

Fourth Master fell silent. The other three looked at each other.

"Every day I've been hoping for his recovery," resumed Fourth Master slowly after a pause. "But he doesn't get any better. It's not that he can't, he won't. There's nothing for it but to lock him up as this gentleman suggests, to keep him out of mischief, lest he disgrace his father. This may be just as well, we owe it to his father...."

"Yes, of course," said Kuoting with emotion. "But what about a room?..."

"Aren't there spare rooms in the temple?" asked Fourth Master slowly.

"Yes!" Kuoting saw light. "There are!" That room to the west as you go in is empty, and there's only a small square window with thick bars — he'll never get out of that. Just the thing!

Old Guo and Square Head hastened to express their approval. Kuoting heaved a sigh and puckered his lips to sip tea.

Before dusk fell, peace reigned once more, or the matter was completely forgotten, for tense expressions had relaxed and the earlier signs of jubilation had vanished. Naturally there were more visitors to the temple than usual, but the number soon dwindled. Only the children who had been unable to play there for some days because the gates were closed found the temple yard a special attraction today. After supper several of them ran back there to play at riddles.

"You guess," said the biggest. "I'll say it once more:

> Red oars, a snow-white boat,
> I paddle across, then rest;
> I eat a snack, then sing;
> What am I — have you guessed?"

“那是什么呢？‘红划楫’的。”一个女孩说。

“我说出来罢，那是……”

“慢一慢！”生癞头疮的说，“我猜着了：航船。”

“航船。”赤膊的也道。

“哈，航船？”最大的道，“航船是摇橹的。他会唱戏文么？你们猜不着。我说出来罢……”

“慢一慢，”癞头疮还说。

“哼，你猜不着。我说出来罢，那是：鹅。”

“鹅！”女孩笑着说，“红划楫的。”

“怎么又是白篷船呢？”赤膊的问。

“我放火！”

孩子们都吃惊，立时记起他来，一齐注视西厢房，又看见一只手扳着木栅，一只手撕着木皮，其间有两只眼睛闪闪地发亮。

沉默只一瞬间，癞头疮忽而发一声喊，拔步就跑；其余的也都笑着嚷着跑出去了。赤膊的还将苇子向后一指，从喘吁吁的樱桃似的小嘴唇里吐出清脆的一声道：

“吧！”

从此完全静寂了，暮色下来，绿莹莹的长明灯更其分明地照出神殿，神龛，而且照到院子，照到木栅里的昏暗。

孩子们跑出庙外也就立定，牵着手，慢慢地向自己的家走去，都笑吟吟地，合唱着随口编派的歌：

“白篷船，对岸歇一歇。
此刻熄，自己熄。
戏文唱一出。
我放火！哈哈哈！
火火火，点心吃一些。
戏文唱一出。
……………
………
…”

一九二五年三月一日。

"Red oars — what are they?"asked one little girls.

"I'll tell you, it's a...."

"Wait a bit!" begged one with a scabby head. "I know: a boat!"

"A boat!" repeated the boy wearing nothing but pants.

"A boat, eh?" said the biggest. "A boat is paddled, but can it sing? You'll never guess. I'll tell you...."

"Wait a bit," begged Scabby Head.

"Bah, you'll never guess. I'll tell you. It's a goose."

"A goose!" The girl chuckled. "Red oars."

"Why a white boat?" asked the boy in nothing but pants.

"I'll set the place on fire!"

With a start the children remembered him and turned together to look at the west room, where they saw him clutching the window frame with one hand and tearing with the other at the bars, between which two bright eyes were flashing.

After a second's silence, Scabby Head rushed off with a shout, and laughing and shouting the others raced after him. The boy wearing nothing but pants pointed his reed over his shoulder and, parting his cherry lips, called out distinctly:

"Bang!"

Then all was utterly still. As the shades of night fell, the bright green altar lamp shone even more brightly on the gods on the dais and on the hall, shining into the yard and into the gloom behind the wooden bars.

After scampering out of the temple the children came to a halt. Holding hands, they sauntered slowly home, spluttering with laughter as they sang in chorus a song they had just made:

A white boat moors not far away.
I'll blow it out myself,
See if I don't !
Come on, come on and join our play!
I'm going to start a fire!
Oh, no, you won't!
Can you guess my riddle, pray?

March 1, 1925

刹时间，也就围满了大半圈的看客。

In a second, a semi-circle of onlookers gathered.

示众
A Public Example

首善之区的西城的一条马路上，这时候什么扰攘也没有。火焰焰的太阳虽然还未直照，但路上的沙土仿佛已是闪烁地生光；酷热满和在空气里面，到处发挥着盛夏的威力。许多狗都拖出舌头来，连树上的乌老鸦也张着嘴喘气，——但是，自然也有例外的。远处隐隐有两个铜盏相击的声音，使人忆起酸梅汤，依稀感到凉意，可是那懒懒的单调的金属音的间作，却使那寂静更其深远了。

只有脚步声，车夫默默地前奔，似乎想赶紧逃出头上的烈日。

"热的包子咧！刚出屉的……。"

十一二岁的胖孩子，细着眼睛，歪了嘴在路旁的店门前叫喊。声音已经嘶嗄了，还带些睡意，如给夏天的长日催眠。他旁边的破旧桌子上，就有二三十个馒头包子，毫无热气，冷冷地坐着。

"荷阿！馒头包子咧，热的……。"

像用力掷在墙上而反拨过来的皮球一般，他忽然飞在马路的那边了。在电杆旁，和他对面，正向着马路，其时也站定了两个人：一个是淡黄制服的挂刀的面黄肌瘦的巡警，手里牵着绳头，绳的那头就拴在别一个穿蓝布大衫上罩白背心的男人的臂膊上。这男人戴一顶新草帽，帽檐四面下垂，遮住了眼睛的一带。但胖孩子身体矮，仰起脸来看时，却正撞见这人的眼睛了。那眼睛也似乎正在看他的脑壳。他连忙顺下眼，去看白背心，只见背心上一行一行地写着些大大小小的什么字。

刹时间，也就围满了大半圈的看客。待到增加了秃头的老头子之后，空缺已经不多，而立刻又被一个赤膊的红鼻子胖大汉补满了。这胖子过于横阔，占了两人的地位，所以续到的便只能屈在第二层，从前面的两个脖子之间伸进脑袋去。

秃头站在白背心的略略正对面，弯了腰，去研究背心上的文字，终于读起来：

"嗡，都，哼，八，而，……"

胖孩子却看见那白背心正研究着这发亮的秃头，他也便跟着去研究，就只见满头光油油的，耳朵左近还有一片灰

1. A sarcastic reference to Beijing. According to the *Han History*, "To establish a model, a start must be made in the capital."

2. Used by vendors of wild-plum juice to attract customers.

In a street in the west city of the model region,[1] nothing was stirring. Although the blazing sun was not yet directly overhead, the dust on the road already seemed to be glinting and fierce heat pervaded the air, making the might of high summer felt everywhere. The dogs' tongues were lolling out, even the crows on the trees were panting for breath — but naturally there were exceptions. From far away came the faint clash of two copper blows,[2] turning people's thoughts to wild-plum juice and giving them a faint sensation of cool. However, the intervals between those lazy, monotonous clinks seemed to deepen the silence.

There was only the sound of footfalls as rickshaw men sped forward silently, as if in a hurry to escape the fierce sun overhend.

"Hot dumplings! Newly steamed..."

A fat boy of eleven or twelve, eyes narrowed, mouth crooked, was calling out in front of a roadside shop. His voice was already hoarse and rather drowsy, as if the long summer day had made him sleepy. On the rickety table beside him sat two dozen steamed buns and dumplings, not steaming hot but stone cold.

"Hey! Steamed buns and dumplings, piping hot...."

Suddenly, like a rubber ball rebounding from a wall, he flew across the road. By the telegraph pole opposite, facing the road, two men had halted. One, a scrawny policeman with a sallow face in a yellow uniform, had a sword at his waist. He was holding a rope, its other end tied round the arm of a man in a blue cotton gown and white sleeveless jerkin. His new straw hat, its brim turned down, covered his eyes. But Fat Boy was short, and when he looked up he met the prisoner's eyes. They seemed to be fixed on his head. He hastily lowered his eyes to look at the white jerkin, on which were lines of writing, large and small.

In a second, a semi-circle of onlookers gathered. After they were joined by an old bald-head, the little space left was promptly occupied by a bare-chested fat fellow with a red nose. Being outsize, he filled the place of two people, so that later arrivals could only form a second row to peer between the necks of those in front.

Baldy, standing almost directly opposite White Jerkin, stooped to study the characters written on his jerkin. Finally he read out:

"*Weng, du, heng, ba, er....*"

Fat Boy saw that White Jerkin was studying that glistening bald-head, so he followed suit, but saw nothing remarkable apart from an oily scalp with a tuft of grey-white hair to the left of his ear. But an amah behind, who was carrying a child, tried to seize

白色的头发，此外也不见得有怎样新奇。但是后面的一个抱着孩子的老妈子却想乘机挤进来了；秃头怕失了位置，连忙站直，文字虽然还未读完，然而无可奈何，只得另看白背心的脸：草帽檐下半个鼻子，一张嘴，尖下巴。

又像用了力掷在墙上而反拨过来的皮球一般，一个小学生飞奔上来，一手按住了自己头上的雪白的小布帽，向人丛中直钻进去。但他钻到第三——也许是第四——层，竟遇见一件不可动摇的伟大的东西了，抬头看时，蓝裤腰上面有一座赤条条的很阔的背脊，背脊上还有汗正在流下来。他知道无可措手，只得顺着裤腰右行，幸而在尽头发见了一条空处，透着光明。他刚刚低头要钻的时候，只听得一声“什么”，那裤腰以下的屁股向右一歪，空处立刻闭塞，光明也同时不见了。

但不多久，小学生却从巡警的刀旁边钻出来了。他诧异地四顾：外面围着一圈人，上首是穿白背心的，那对面是一个赤膊的胖小孩，胖小孩后面是一个赤膊的红鼻子胖大汉。他这时隐约悟出先前的伟大的障碍物的本体了，便惊奇而且佩服似的只望着红鼻子。胖小孩本是注视着小学生的脸的，于是也不禁依了他的眼光，回转头去了，在那里是一个很胖的奶子，奶头四近有几枝很长的毫毛。

“他，犯了什么事啦？……”

大家都愕然看时，是一个工人似的粗人，正在低声下气地请教那秃头老头子。

秃头不作声，单是睁起了眼睛看定他。他被看得顺下眼光去，过一会再看时，秃头还是睁起了眼睛看定他，而且别的人也似乎都睁了眼睛看定他。他于是仿佛自己就犯了罪似的局促起来，终至于慢慢退后，溜出去了。一个挟洋伞的长子就来补了缺；秃头也旋转脸去再看白背心。

长子弯了腰，要从垂下的草帽檐下去赏识白背心的脸，但不知道为什么忽又站直了。于是他背后的人们又须竭力伸长了脖子；有一个瘦子竟至于连嘴都张得很大，像一条死鲈鱼。

巡警，突然间，将脚一提，大家又愕然，赶紧都看他

this chance to squeeze in. For fear of losing his place Baldy promptly straightened up, though he had not finished reading, and this forced him to look instead at White Jerkin's face: half a nose, a mouth and a pointed chin under the projecting brim of the straw hat.

Again, like a rubber ball rebounding from a wall, a small schoolboy rushed up, one hand holding on his snow-white cotton cap, and shoved his way through the crowd. But when he had shoved past three or four rows, he came up against something immovable and massive. Looking up he saw, above a pair of blue pants, a broad, bare back running with sweat. Knowing that there was no coping with this, he edged to the right and there, luckily, was a crack letting through the light. But as he prepared to butt his way through, he heard an exclamation and the seat of the trousers swivelled to the right. At once the space was blocked, the light blotted out.

However, soon the schoolboy squeezed his way out beside the policeman's sword. He gazed round in astonishment. Encircled by people, the prisoner was wearing a white jerkin. In front of him was a barechested fat boy, behind whom stood a bare-chested fat fellow with a red nose. He vaguely identified him with the huge obstacle he had come up against, and fixed amazed, admiring eyes on that red nose. Fat Boy was staring at Schoolboy's face. Unable to stand this scrutiny he turned his head towards a bulging breast with a few long hairs round the nipple.

"Hey, what has he done wrong?..."

All stared in astonishment as a rough fellow, who looked like a workman, asked Baldy this question in a low, diffident voice.

Baldy made no answer, simply glaring at him till he lowered his eyes. When presently he looked again, Baldy was still glaring at him, and so were all the others apparently. So, as flustered as if he himself had committed some crime, he slowly backed out and left. His place was taken by a tall fellow with an umbrella. Baldy turned back to look at White Jerkin.

Longfellow stooped to appraise White Jerkin's face beneath the drooping hat brim, then for some reason straightened up abruptly. Thereupon the people behind him were forced to crane their necks hard again, one lean fellow even gaping like a dead perch.

All of a sudden, the policeman raised one foot. Immediately everyone stared in stupefaction; but when he set it down steadily again, they went on watching White

的脚；然而他又放稳了，于是又看白背心。长子忽又弯了腰，还要从垂下的草帽檐下去窥测，但即刻也就立直，擎起一只手来拼命搔头皮。

秃头不高兴了，因为他先觉得背后有些不太平，接着耳朵边就有唧咕唧咕的声响。他双眉一锁，回头看时，紧挨他右边，有一只黑手拿着半个大馒头正在塞进一个猫脸的人的嘴里去。他也就不说什么，自去看白背心的新草帽了。

忽然，就有暴雷似的一击，连横阔的胖大汉也不免向前一跄踉。同时，从他肩膊上伸出一只胖得不相上下的臂膊来，展开五指，拍的一声正打在胖孩子的脸颊上。

“好快活！你妈的……”同时，胖大汉后面就有一个弥勒佛似的更圆的胖脸这么说。

胖孩子也跄踉了四五步，但是没有倒，一手按着脸颊，旋转身，就想从胖大汉的腿旁的空隙间钻出去。胖大汉赶忙站稳，并且将屁股一歪，塞住了空隙，恨恨地问道：

“什么？”

胖孩子就像小鼠子落在捕机里似的，仓皇了一会，忽然向小学生那一面奔去，推开他，冲出去了。小学生也返身跟出去了。

“吓，这孩子……。”总有五六个人都这样说。

待到重归平静，胖大汉再看白背心的脸的时候，却见白背心正在仰面看他的胸脯；他慌忙低头也看自己的胸脯时，只见两乳之间的洼下的坑里有一片汗，他于是用手掌拂去了这些汗。

然而形势似乎总不甚太平了。抱着小孩的老妈子因为在骚扰时四顾，没有留意，头上梳着的喜鹊尾巴似的“苏州俏”便碰了站在旁边的车夫的鼻梁。车夫一推，却正推在孩子上；孩子就扭转身去，向着圈外，嚷着要回去了。老妈子先也略略一跄踉，但便即站定，旋转孩子来使他正对白背心，一手指点着，说道：

“阿，阿，看呀！多么好看哪！……”

空隙间忽而探进一个戴硬草帽的学生模样的头来，将一粒瓜子之类似的东西放在嘴里，下颚向上一磕，咬开，

Jerkin. Longfellow stooped abruptly again to peer beneath the drooping brim of the straw hat, but promptly straightened up once more, raising one hand to scratch his head furiously.

Baldy was annoyed, first becoming aware of a commotion behind him, then hearing a champing beside his ear. Scowling, he looked round. A grimy hand close to his right side was stuffing a bun half the size of his fist into the mouth of a feline face. He said nothing, turning to look at White Jerkin's new straw hat.

Without warning, a clap like a thunderbolt made even outsize Fat Fellow stagger forward. The same instant, over his shoulder stretched an arm almost as fat as his own, five fingers outspread, and slapped Fat Boy's cheeks.

"Larking about, eh! Dammit!..." An even rounder fat face, like that of a Maitreya Buddha, loomed behind Fat Fellow.

Fat Boy also staggered four or five steps, but did not fall. One hand pressed to his cheek, he turned, as if to squeeze out through the space by Fat Fellow's leg. Fat Fellow promptly stood firm, swivelling his bottom to block the space.

"What the hell!" he growled.

Fat Boy panicked, like a mouse caught in a trap, then bolted across to Schoolboy, pushed him aside and charged out. Schoolboy turned and followed.

"Bah, boys..." complained half a dozen people.

When quiet was restored and Fat Fellow looked back at White Jerkin's face, he found the latter was looking up at his chest. He hastily lowered his head to eye it himself, but all he saw was sweat in the cleft between his two breasts. He wiped this off with his hand.

Still, things did not seem too peaceful. Amah holding a child, having been busy looking round during the commotion, had carelessly bumped the nose of Rickshaw Man beside her with her Suzhou-style hair combed like the tail of a magpie. Rickshaw Man, trying to shove her away, shoved the child, which turned to face out and clamoured to go home. Amah lurched but then regained her balance, and turned the child round to face White Jerkin. Pointing at him she said:

"Hey, hey, look! Isn't that a fine sight!..."

Suddenly a stiff straw hat on the head of what seemed a student poked through a space. He was conveying to his mouth what seemed to be a sunflower seed. His lower jaw rose to crack it open, then he withdrew. His place was taken by the oval face of a

退出去了。这地方就补上了一个满头油汗而粘着灰土的椭圆脸。

挟洋伞的长子也已经生气，斜下了一边的肩膊，皱眉疾视着肩后的死鲈鱼。大约从这么大的大嘴里呼出来的热气，原也不易招架的，而况又在盛夏。秃头正仰视那电杆上钉着的红牌上的四个白字，仿佛很觉得有趣。胖大汉和巡警都斜了眼研究着老妈子的钩刀般的鞋尖。

"好！"

什么地方忽有几个人同声喝采。都知道该有什么事情起来了，一切头便全数回转去。连巡警和他牵着的犯人也都有些摇动了。

"刚出屉的包子咧！荷阿，热的……。"

路对面是胖孩子歪着头，磕睡似的长呼；路上是车夫们默默地前奔，似乎想赶紧逃出头上的烈日。大家都几乎失望了，幸而放出眼光去四处搜索，终于在相距十多家的路上，发见了一辆洋车停放着，一个车夫正在爬起来。

圆阵立刻散开，都错错落落地走过去。胖大汉走不到一半，就歇在路边的槐树下；长子比秃头和椭圆脸走得快，接近了。车上的坐客依然坐着，车夫已经完全爬起，但还在摩自己的膝髁。周围有五六个人笑嘻嘻地看他们。

"成么？"车夫要来拉车时，坐客便问。

他只点点头，拉了车就走；大家就惘惘然目送他。起先还知道那一辆是曾经跌倒的车，后来被别的车一混，知不清了。

马路上就很清闲，有几只狗伸出了舌头喘气；胖大汉就在槐阴下看那很快地一起一落的狗肚皮。

老妈子抱了孩子从屋檐阴下蹩过去了。胖孩子歪着头，挤细了眼睛，拖长声音，磕睡地叫喊——

"热的包子咧！荷阿！……刚出屉的……。"

一九二五年三月一八日。

sweaty head caked with dust.

Longfellow with the umbrella was angry too now. He lowered one shoulder to frown at Dead Perch behind it. Probably because the hot air exhaled from that huge mouth was hard to ward off, especially now that this was the height of summer. Baldy was looking up as if fascinated at the four big white characters on the red board nailed to the telegraph pole. Fat Fellow and the policeman, out of the corners of their eyes, were studying the upturned tips of Amah's slippers.

"Bravo!"

This sudden approving shout from several people somewhere made them realize that something must be up. All heads swivelled round several times. Even the policeman and the prisoner he had in tow also wavered.

"Freshly steamed dumplings! Hey, piping hot...."

Across the road Fat Boy, his head on one side, spun out his cry sleepily. On the road, rickshaw men were silently speeding forward, as if in a hurry to escape from the fierce sun overhead. There was a general sense of disappointment. Fortunately, their eyes searching the surroundings finally spotted a rickshaw, which had stopped on the road a dozen buildings away. The rickshaw man was just scrambling up from the ground.

At once the circular formation scattered. Higgledy-piggledy all made their way over. Halfway there Fat Fellow stopped to rest under a locust tree beside the road. Longfellow was nearly there, being faster than Baldy and Oval Face. The passenger was still seated in the rickshaw while the rickshaw man had now risen to his feet, but was still rubbing his knees. Five or six people had gathered round, grinning, to watch.

"All right?" asked the passenger, as the rickshaw man picked up the shafts.

The latter nodded and pulled the rickshaw off, followed by everyone's disconcerted eyes. They learned that this rickshaw had first upset, then become entangled with another, no one knew exactly how.

Now all was quiet on the road. A few dogs were panting, their tongues lolling out. Fat Fellow under the locust tree watched their rapidly heaving stomachs.

Amah carried over the child, flitting under the shade of the eaves. Fat Boy, his head on one side, narrowed his eyes and spun out his sleepy cry:

"Hot dumplings! Hey!... Freshly steamed...."

March 18, 1925

一枝夭斜的树枝横在他面前，
已被他的头撞得树叶都微微发抖。

A horizontal branch stretched in front of his face,
its leaves quivering from the collision with his head.

高老夫子
Master Gao

这一天，从早晨到午后，他的工夫全费在照镜，看《中国历史教科书》和查《袁了凡纲鉴》里；真所谓“人生识字忧患始”，顿觉得对于世事很有些不平之意了。而且这不平之意，是他从来没有经验过的。

首先就想到往常的父母实在太不将儿女放在心里。他还在孩子的时候，最喜欢爬上桑树去偷桑椹吃，但他们全不管，有一回竟跌下树来磕破了头，又不给好好地医治，至今左边的眉棱上还带着一个永不消灭的尖劈形的瘢痕。他现在虽然格外留长头发，左右分开，又斜梳下来，可以勉强遮住了，但究竟还看见尖劈的尖；也算得一个缺点，万一给女学生发见，大概是免不了要看不起的。他放下镜子，怨愤地吁一口气。

其次，是《中国历史教科书》的编纂者竟太不为教员设想。他的书虽然和《了凡纲鉴》也有些相合，但大段又很不相同，若即若离，令人不知道讲起来应该怎样拉在一处。但待到他瞥着那夹在教科书里的一张纸条，却又怨起中途辞职的历史教员来了，因为那纸条上写的是：

“从第八章《东晋之兴亡》起。”

如果那人不将三国的事情讲完，他的豫备就决不至于这么困苦。他最熟悉的就是三国，例如桃园三结义，孔明借箭，三气周喻，黄忠定军山斩夏侯渊以及其他种种，满肚子都是，一学期也许讲不完。到唐朝，则有秦琼卖马之类，便又较为擅长了，谁料偏偏是东晋。他又怨愤地吁一口气，再拉过《了凡纲鉴》来。

“哙，你怎么外面看看还不够，又要钻到里面去看了？”

一只手同时从他背后弯过来，一拨他的下巴。但他并不动，因为从声音和举动上，便知道是暗暗躄进来的打牌的老朋友黄三。他虽然是他的老朋友，一礼拜以前还一同打牌，看戏，喝酒，跟女人，但自从他在《大中日报》上发表了《论中华国民皆有整理国史之义务》这一篇烩炙人口的名文，接着又得了贤良女学校的聘书之后，就觉得这

1. An outline of history by a sixteenth-century historian.

2. A line from a poem by Su Shi of the Song Dynasty.

3. Episodes from the popular novel *Romance of the Three Kingdoms*.

4. A story from *Tales of the Tang*.

He spent the whole morning till after noon today looking at himself in the mirror, reading *A Textbook of Chinese History* and looking up *Yuan Liaofan's Outline*.[1] How true it is that "literacy is the start of men's grief."[2] He was suddenly struck by the injustice of life. And this sense of injustice was one he had never experienced before.

First he reflected how very little thought his father and mother had given to their children. As a small boy, what he liked best was climbing mulberry trees to steal mulberries to eat; but they paid no attention at all. Once, when he fell off a tree and cracked open his head, they hadn't given him the right medical treatment, so that to this day above his left eyebrow remained an indelible wedge-shaped scar. Though he now wore his hair extra long, parted in the middle and combed down in front to more or less cover the scar, its tip was still visible, and that was a blemish. If schoolgirls saw it, most likely they would despise him. He laid down the mirror and huffed with exasperation.

In the second place, whoever compiled *A Textbook of Chinese History* had shown too little consideration for teachers. Although this book corresponded to some extent with the *Outline*, whole passages were different, and this partial conformity made it impossible to know how to piece them together in a lecture. But when his eyes fell on the slip of paper inserted in the textbook, he transferred his resentment to the history teacher who had resigned in the middle of the term; because on it was written:

Start from Chapter 8, "The Rise and Fall of Eastern Jin."

If the fellow hadn't finished with the Three Kingdoms, it certainly wouldn't have been so difficult for him to prepare. The Three Kingdoms period was the one he knew best. For instance, the stories of how the three heroes became sworn brothers in the Peach Orchard, how Zhuge Liang borrowed an arrow, Zhou Yu was enraged three times, Huang Zhong killed Xia Houyuan at Mt. Dingjun,[3] and so on — he knew them all by heart. He might have held forth on these for a term or more. And when it came to the Tang Dynasty, such tales as that about Qin Qiong selling a horse[4] he also knew fairly well. How could he have foreseen that he would be landed with Eastern Jin of all periods? He gave another huff of exasperation, and once more pulled over the *Outline*.

"Hey, haven't you done enough reading outside, without burrowing in here to read?"

A hand had reached round from behind him to grab his chin. He did not move, however, knowing from the voice and action that it was his old friend Huang San, with whom he played mahjong, who had tiptoed in. But though Huang was his old friend, with whom a week before he had played mahjong, watched operas, drunk and chased after girls, ever since the *Dazhong Daily* had published his much acclaimed article "On the Duty of All Chinese to Revise the National History," after which he had received a

黄三一无所长，总有些下等相了。所以他并不回头，板着脸正正经经地回答道：

“不要胡说！我正在豫备功课……。”

“你不是亲口对老钵说的么：你要谋一个教员做，去看看女学生？”

“你不要相信老钵的狗屁！”

黄三就在他桌旁坐下，向桌面上一瞥，立刻在一面镜子和一堆乱书之间，发见了一个翻开着的大红纸的帖子。他一把抓来，瞪着眼睛一字一字地看下去；

> 今敦请
> 尔础高老夫子为本校历史教员每周授课四小时每
> 小时敬送修金大洋三角正按时间计算此约
> 贤良女学校校长何万淑贞敛衽谨订
> 中华民国十三年夏历菊月吉旦　立

“‘尔础高老夫子’？谁呢？你么？你改了名字了么？”黄三一看完，就性急地问。

但高老夫子只是高傲地一笑；他的确改了名字了。然而黄三只会打牌，到现在还没有留心新学问，新艺术。他既不知道有一个俄国大文豪高尔基，又怎么说得通这改名的深远的意义呢？所以他只是高傲地一笑，并不答复他。

“喂喂，老杆，你不要闹这些无聊的玩意儿了！”黄三放下聘书，说。“我们这里有了一个男学堂，风气已经闹得够坏了；他们还要开什么女学堂，将来真不知道要闹成什么样子才罢。你何苦也去闹，犯不上……。”

“这也不见得。况且何太太一定要请我，辞不掉……。”因为黄三毁谤了学校，又看手表上已经两点半，离上课时间只有半点了，所以他有些气忿，又很露出焦躁的神情。

“好！这且不谈。”黄三是乖觉的，即刻转帆，说，“我们说正经事罢：今天晚上我们有一个局面。毛家屯毛

5. Gorki's pen-name, *Gaoerji* in Chinese, is a surname. But Gao takes Erji to be his personal name, so gives himself the name Erchu.

6. "He" is her husband's surname.

contract from Xianliang Girls' School, he had considered Huang San a nonentity and rather contemptible. So without turning his head, he pulled a long face and answered seriously:

"Don't talk nonsense! I'm preparing a lesson...."

"Didn't you tell Old Bo you wanted to find a teaching post so as to see girl students?"

"You can't believe that farting dog Old Bo!"

Huang San sat down by his desk, glanced at it and promptly spotted, between the mirror and the clutter of books, a scarlet invitation card which was open. He grabbed it and stared as he read it word by word:

> Respectful Invitation
>
> Master Gao Erchu[5] is hereby invited to teach history in our school for four hours a week, for an honorarium of thirty cents an hour. This serves as a contract.
>
> Deferentially signed by the school principal He Wan Shuzhen[6] on the first of the ninth lunar month, the thirteenth year of the Chinese Republic.

"Erchu Master Gao? Who's he? You? Have you changed your name?" Huang San made haste to ask after reading this.

However, Master Gao simply smiled disdainfully. He had indeed changed his name. But Huang San, good for nothing but mahjong, had not yet paid any attention to the new learning and new art. Since he was ignorant of the existence of the great Russian writer Gorki, how could he grasp the far-reaching significance of this change of name? So he simply smiled disdainfully without answering.

"Hey, Old Gao, don't fool around in this futile way!" Huang San put down the contract. "We have a boys' school here, and the goings-on there are already bad enough. Now they've started this girls' school too — goodness knows what trouble will come of that. Why should you mess about with them? It's beneath you...."

"Not necessarily. Especially as Mrs. He insists on inviting me. I can't get out of it...." Annoyed by Huang San's slander of schools, and by seeing from his watch that it was already 2:30, with just half an hour to go to his class, he let his irritation show.

"All right! Forget it." Huang San tactfully changed the subject. "Let's get down to business. We're having a game this evening. Mao Zifu's eldest son from Mao Family

资甫的大儿子在这里了，来请阳宅先生看坟地去的，手头现带着二百番。我们已经约定，晚上凑一桌，一个我，一个老钵，一个就是你。你一定来罢，万不要误事。我们三个人扫光他！”

老杆——高老夫子——沉吟了，但是不开口。

“你一定来，一定！我还得和老钵去接洽一回。地方还是在我的家里。那傻小子是‘初出茅庐’，我们准可以扫光他！你将那一副竹纹清楚一点的交给我罢！”

高老夫子慢慢地站起来，到床头取了麻将牌盒，交给他；一看手表，两点四十分了。他想：黄三虽然能干，但明知道我已经做了教员，还来当面毁谤学堂，又打搅别人的豫备功课，究竟不应该。他于是冷淡地说道：

“晚上再商量罢。我要上课去了。”

他一面说，一面恨恨地向《了凡纲鉴》看了一眼，拿起教科书，装在新皮包里，又很小心地戴上新帽子，便和黄三出了门。他一出门，就放开脚步，像木匠牵着的钻子似的，肩膀一扇一扇地直走，不多久，黄三便连他的影子也望不见了。

高老夫子一跑到贤良女学校，即将新印的名片交给一个驼背的老门房。不一忽，就听到一声“请”，他于是跟着驼背走，转过两个弯，已到教员豫备室了，也算是客厅。何校长不在校；迎接他的是花白胡子的教务长，大名鼎鼎的万瑶圃，别号“玉皇香案吏”的，新近正将他自己和女仙赠答的诗《仙坛酬唱集》陆续登在《大中日报》上。

“阿呀！础翁！久仰久仰！……”万瑶圃连连拱手，并将膝关节和腿关节接连弯了五六弯，仿佛想要蹲下去似的。

“阿呀！瑶翁！久仰久仰！……”础翁夹着皮包照样地做，并且说。

他们于是坐下；一个似死非死的校役便端上两杯白开水来。高老夫子看看对面的挂钟，还只两点四十分，和他的手表要差半点。

“阿呀！础翁的大作，是的，那个……。是的，

Village is here. He's come to invite a geomancer to look them out a good grave site, and he's brought two hundred silver dollars. We're arranged to make up a foursome this evening, with myself, Old Bo and you. Mind you come, and don't keep us waiting. The three of us can clean him out!"

Master Gao thought this over but said nothing.

"Mind you come for sure! I still have to go to fix it up with Old Bo. We'll play in my place. That young fool's a real country bumpkin, so we can be sure of cleaning him out! Give me that set of yours with the clearly marked tiles."

Master Gao stood up slowly, fetched the mahjong box from his bedside and handed it over, then glanced at his watch — 2:40. He thought: Huang San may be smart, but he knows perfectly well that I'm a teacher now, yet runs down schools to my face and stops me from preparing my lesson — he ought to know better. So he said coldly:

"We'll talk it over this evening. I'm off to class now."

So saying, with a baleful glance at the *Outline*, he picked up his textbook, put it in his new briefcase, and very carefully put on his new hat, then left the house with Huang San. Once outside he quickened his step, striding straight ahead sawing the air with his arms. Before long, Huang San lost sight of him completely.

Master Gao, having hurried to Xianliang Girls' School, presented his newly printed card to the humpbacked old gatekeeper. Invited in presently, he followed the humpback round two corners to the staffroom, which also served as a reception room. In the absence of the head-mistress, he was welcomed by the grey-bearded dean, the celebrated Wan Yaopu, also known as the "Ministrant of the Jade Emperor's Altar." Recently the *Dazhong Daily* had serialized his poems "Interchanged with an Immortal."

"Aha! Brother Chu! This is a long-looked for honour!" Wan Yaopu raised clasped hands in repeated salutes, and bent his knees and leg joints five or six times, as if about to squat down.

"Aha! Brother Yao! This is a long-looked for honour!" Briefcase tucked under one arm, Master Gao went through the same motions as he spoke.

Then they sat down. An orderly, more dead than alive, brought in two cups of boiled water. Master Gao saw that the clock on the opposite wall registered just 2:40 — it was half an hour slower than his watch.

"Ah! That fine article of yours, sir. Yes, indeed...your theory of our 'duty to our

那——‘中国国粹义务论’，真真要言不烦，百读不厌！实在是少年人们的座右铭，座右铭座右铭！兄弟也颇喜欢文学，可是，玩玩而已，怎么比得上础翁。”他重行拱一拱手，低声说，“我们的盛德乩坛天天请仙，兄弟也常常去唱和。础翁也可以光降光降罢。那乩仙，就是蕊珠仙子，从她的语气上看来，似乎是一位谪降红尘的花神。她最爱和名人唱和，也很赞成新党，像础翁这样的学者，她一定大加青眼的。哈哈哈哈！”

但高老夫子却不很能发表什么崇论宏议，因为他的豫备——东晋之兴亡——本没有十分足，此刻又并不足的几分也有些忘却了。他烦躁愁苦着；从繁乱的心绪中，又涌出许多断片的思想来：上堂的姿势应该威严；额角的瘢痕总该遮住；教科书要读得慢；看学生要大方。但同时还模模胡胡听得瑶圃说着话：

“……赐了一个荸荠……。‘醉倚青鸾上碧霄’，多么超脱……那邓孝翁叩求了五回，这才赐了一首五绝……‘红袖拂天河，莫道……’蕊珠仙子说……础翁还是第一回……这就是本校的植物园！”

“哦哦！”尔础忽然看见他举手一指，这才从乱头思想中惊觉，依着指头看去，窗外一小片空地，地上有四五株树，正对面是三间小平房。

“这就是讲堂。”瑶圃并不移动他的手指，但是说。

“哦哦！”

“学生是很驯良的。她们除听讲之外，就专心缝纫……。”

“哦哦！”尔础实在颇有些窘急了，他希望他不再说话，好给自己聚精会神，赶紧想一想东晋之兴亡。

“可惜内中也有几个想学学做诗，那可是不行的。维新固然可以，但做诗究竟不是大家闺秀所宜。蕊珠仙子也不很赞成女学，以为淆乱两仪，非天曹所喜。兄弟还很同她讨论过几回……。”

尔础忽然跳了起来，他听到铃声了。

national quintessence,' one could never tire of discussing it, could read it a hundred times without wearying! It is truly a golden rule for the young, a golden rule! I am devoted to literature too, although a mere dilettante. I cannot compare with you, sir!" He raised clasped hands again, then went on softly, "In our Abounding Virtue Planchette Club, we invoke immortals every day, and I often go to join in. I hope you, sir, will honour us with a visit. Our oracle is the immortal Ruizhu. Judging by her manner of speaking, she is a flower spirit who once descended to this dusty world. She loves to exchange views with men of repute, and is all in favour of the new party. She would certainly look with great favour on a scholar like yourself, sir. Hohohoho!"

"But Master Gao was unable to respond with any exalted disquisition, because he had made an inadequate preparation for his class on the rise and fall of Eastern Jin, and by now he had even forgotten part of that. He was on tenterhooks. In this state of mental confusion, some disjointed ideas crossed his mind: in class he should adopt an imposing attitude; should conceal the scar on his temple; should read the textbook slowly, should look at the students in a dignified way. At the same time, indistinctly, he heard Yaopu saying:

"...bestowed a water-chestnut.... 'Tipsily riding a green phoenix above the azure clouds.' Isn't that superb... Deng Xiao begged five times before he was granted a poem of four lines with five characters to each... 'Red sleeves sweep the Milky Way. Do not say....' The immortal Ruizhu said...Your first time, sir.... This is our school's botanical garden!"

"Oh!" Erchu suddenly saw the other's raised hand pointing, and collected his wandering thoughts. In the direction pointed out, he saw outside the window a small patch of ground with four or five trees and, opposite, a small three-roomed bungalow.

"Those are the classrooms," said Yaopu, still pointing in the same direction.

"Oh."

"Our pupils are very well-behaved. When not attending classes they work hard at their sewing...."

"Oh." Erchu really felt rather desperate, and hoped Yaopu would stop talking, so that he could hurry up and concentrate on the rise and fall of Eastern Jin.

Unfortunately, a few of them want to learn to write poetry. That would never do. Reforms are all very well, but it's not appropriate for girls to write poetry. The immortal Ruizhu is not quite in favour of schools for girls, and considers that blurring distinctions between the sexes would not please the rulers of Heaven. I have had a good many discussions with her on the subject...."

Erchu leapt to his feet at the sound of a bell.

“不，不。请坐！那是退班铃。”

“瑶翁公事很忙罢，可以不必客气……。”

“不，不！不忙，不忙！兄弟以为振兴女学是顺应世界的潮流，但一不得当，即易流于偏，所以天曹不喜，也许不过是防微杜渐的意思。只要办理得人，不偏不倚，合乎中庸，一以国粹为归宿，那是决无流弊的。础翁，你想，可对？这是蕊珠仙子也以为‘不无可采’的话。哈哈哈哈！”

校役又送上两杯白开水来；但是铃声又响了。

瑶圃便请尔础喝了两口白开水，这才慢慢地站起来，引导他穿过植物园，走进讲堂去。

他心头跳着，笔挺地站在讲台旁边，只看见半屋子都是蓬蓬松松的头发。瑶圃从大襟袋里掏出一张信笺，展开之后，一面看，一面对学生们说道：

“这位就是高老师，高尔础高老师，是有名的学者，那一篇有名的《论中华国民皆有整理国史之义务》，是谁都知道的。《大中日报》上还说过，高老师是：骤慕俄国文豪高君尔基之为人，因改字尔础，以示景仰之意，斯人之出，诚吾中华文坛之幸也！现在经何校长再三敦请，竟惠然肯来，到这里来教历史了……”

高老师忽而觉得很寂然，原来瑶翁已经不见，只有自己站在讲台旁边了。他只得跨上讲台去，行了礼，定一定神，又记起了态度应该威严的成算，便慢慢地翻开书本，来开讲“东晋之兴亡”。

“嘻嘻！”似乎有谁在那里窃笑了。

高老夫子脸上登时一热，忙看书本，和他的话并不错，上面印着的的确是：“东晋之偏安”。书脑的对面，也还是半屋子蓬蓬松松的头发，不见有别的动静。他猜想这是自己的疑心，其实谁也没有笑；于是又定一定神，看住书本，慢慢地讲下去。当初，是自己的耳朵也听到自己的嘴说些什么的，可是逐渐胡涂起来，竟至于不再知道说什么，待到发挥“石勒之雄图”的时候，便只听得吃吃地窃笑的声音了。

7. In the third century the Jie people raised troops to subdue Early Zhao and founded Later Zhao. They wiped out the last forces of Western Jin in the morth, and opposed Eastern Jin. Shile (274-333), of Jie nationality, was the founder of Later Zhao.

"No, no. Sit down! That's the bell for the end of class."

"You are very busy, Brother Yao. Don't stand on ceremony...."

"No, no, I'm not busy. I believe that promoting schools for girls conforms to the world trend; but, unless carefully handled, it may easily go off the track, which would not please the rules of Heaven; so we should nip any trouble in the bud. If those in charge don't go to extremes but keeps to the Middle Way, abiding by our national quintessence, then nothing can go wrong. Do you agree, Brother Chu? This is what the immortal Ruizhu means by 'Something can be said for it.' Hohohoho!"

The orderly brought in two more cups of boiled water; but the bell rang again.

Yaopu invited Erchu to sip some water, then slowly rose to his feet and conducted him through the botanical garden towards the classrooms.

His heart thumping, he stood stiffly by the platform. Half the room seemed to be nothing but tousled hair. Yaopu took from his lapel pocket a sheet of stationery, which he unfolded. Looking at it, he told the schoolgirls:

"This is Professor Gao, Gao Erchu, a well-known scholar. Everyone knows his famous work 'On the Duty of All Chinese to Reform the Nation's History.' The *Dazhong Daily* has written that Mr. Gao changed his name to Erchu as a mark of his respect for the brilliant Russian man of letters Gorki. His emergence is a happy event for our Chinese world of letters! Now, at the repeated invitation of Principal He, he has kindly consented to come here to teach history...."

Professor Gao had a sudden sensation of isolation. Yaopu had disappeared, leaving him standing all alone by the platform. He had to step onto it, make a bow, and collect his thoughts. Recalling his decision to adopt an imposing attitude, he slowly opened his book and started his lecture on the rise and fall of Eastern Jin.

"Heehee!" He seemed to hear a stifled gigle.

At once Master Gao's face flushed. He looked hastily at the book, he had made no mistake. On it was certainly printed "The Partial Peace of Eastern Jin."

Confronting the book's spine was still half a roomful of tousled hair, with no movement evident. He suspected that he had been imagining things, and that in fact no one had laughed. So collecting his thoughts once more, his eyes on the book, he slowly continued his lecture. At first he had taken in what he was saying, but gradually he grew so confused he had no idea what it was. By the time he came to "The Great Scheme of the Shile,"[7] all he could hear was giggling.

他不禁向讲台下一看，情形和原先已经很不同：半屋子都是眼睛，还有许多小巧的等边三角形，三角形中都生着两个鼻孔，这些连成一气，宛然是流动而深邃的海，闪烁地汪洋地正冲着他的眼光。但当他瞥见时，却又骤然一闪，变了半屋子蓬蓬松松的头发了。

他也连忙收回眼光，再不敢离开教科书，不得已时，就抬起眼来看看屋顶。屋顶是白而转黄的洋灰，中央还起了一道正圆形的棱线；可是这圆圈又生动了，忽然扩大，忽然收小，使他的眼睛有些昏花。他豫料倘将眼光下移，就不免又要遇见可怕的眼睛和鼻孔联合的海，只好再回到书本上，这时已经是“淝水之战”，苻坚快要骇得“草木皆兵”了。

他总疑心有许多人暗暗地发笑，但还是熬着讲，明明已经讲了大半天，而铃声还没有响，看手表是不行的，怕学生要小觑；可是讲了一会，又到“拓跋氏之勃兴”了，接着就是“六国兴亡表”，他本以为今天未必讲到，没有豫备的。

他自己觉得讲义忽而中止了。

“今天是第一天，就是这样罢……。”他惶惑了一会之后，才断续地说，一面点一点头，跨下讲台去，也便出了教室的门。

“嘻嘻嘻！”

他似乎听到背后有许多人笑，又仿佛看见这笑声就从那深邃的鼻孔的海里出来。他便惘惘然，跨进植物园，向着对面的教员豫备室大踏步走。

他大吃一惊，至于连《中国历史教科书》也失手落在地上了，因为脑壳上突然遭了什么东西的一击。他倒退两步，定睛看时，一枝夭斜的树枝横在他面前，已被他的头撞得树叶都微微发抖。他赶紧弯腰去拾书本，书旁边竖着一块木牌，上面写道：

桑 桑科

8. In 383, at Feishui in Anhui, the Eastern Jin troops defeated a much larger force, whose commander, Fu Jian, mistook all the trees on the hills for enemy soldiers.

9. A branch of the Xianbei people, who in 386 set up the Kingdom of Wei and later extended their rule north of the Yellow River with their capital in Pingcheng, present-day Datong.

Unable to resist looking at the class, he saw that it was much the same as before: half a roomful of eyes, and many dainty little isosceles triangles with two nostrils in the middle of each. These merged to appear a deep, moving sea, and this surging ocean dazzled his eyes. But when he blinked, it turned in a flash into half a roomful of tousled hair.

He hastily lowered his eyes and kept them on his textbook. Then, unable to help it, he raised them to the ceiling, its white plaster turning yellow, with in the centre a projecting circle. But this circle shifted too, now expanding, now contracting, until his eyes grew dim. Foreseeing that if he looked down, he was bound once again to see that fearful ocean of nostrils and eyes, he had to look back at his book. He had now reached the Battle of Feishui.[8] Fu Jian was about to panic, "taking plants and trees for troops."

He kept suspecting the girls of laughing up their sleeves, but he stuck it out. He was sure he had been speaking for a long time, yet still the bell did not go. He couldn't consult his watch, for fear they would despise him; but after a while he came to "The Sudden Rise of the Tobas."[9] After that came the "Chart of the Rise and Fall of the Six Kingdoms," which he had not expected to reach today and had not prepared.

He became aware that the lecture had stopped abruptly halfway.

"As today is the first day, that will do..." he faltered after a panic-stricken pause. Nodding, he stepped down from the platform and walked out of the classroom door.

"Heehee hee!"

Behind him he seemed to hear a number of girls laughing, to see their laughter emerging from that deep ocean of nostrils. In a daze, he stepped into the botanical garden, and strode towards the staff-room opposite.

He gave a start, even dropping *A Textbook of Chinese History*, because something had suddenly knocked him on the head. He fell back a couple of paces. When he looked, a horizontal branch stretched in front of his face, its leaves quivering from the collision with his head. He hastily stooped to retrieve his book. By it stood a board bearing the sign:

MULBERRY
Genus: Morus

他似乎听到背后有许多人笑，又仿佛看见这笑声就从那深邃的鼻孔的海里出来。于是也就不好意思去抚摩头上已经疼痛起来的皮肤，只一心跑进教员豫备室里去。

那里面，两个装着白开水的杯子依然，却不见了似死非死的校役，瑶翁也踪影全无了。一切都黯淡，只有他的新皮包和新帽子在黯淡中发亮。看壁上的挂钟，还只有三点四十分。

高老夫子回到自家的房里许久之后，有时全身还骤然一热；又无端的愤怒；终于觉得学堂确也要闹坏风气，不如停闭的好，尤其是女学堂，——有什么意思呢，喜欢虚荣罢了！

"嘻嘻！"

他还听到隐隐约约的笑声。这使他更加愤怒，也使他辞职的决心更加坚固了。晚上就写信给何校长，只要说自己患了足疾。但是，倘来挽留，又怎么办呢？——也不去。女学堂真不知道要闹到什么样子，自己又何苦去和她们为伍呢？犯不上的。他想。

他于是决绝地将《了凡纲鉴》搬开；镜子推在一旁；聘书也合上了。正要坐下，又觉得那聘书实在红得可恨，便抓过来和《中国历史教科书》一同塞入抽屉里。

一切大概已经打叠停当，桌上只剩下一面镜子，眼界清净得多了。然而还不舒适，仿佛欠缺了半个魂灵，但他当即省悟，戴上红结子的秋帽，径向黄三的家里去了。

"来了，尔础高老夫子！"老钵大声说。

"狗屁！"他眉头一皱，在老钵的头顶上打了一下，说。

"教过了罢？怎么样，可有几个出色的？"黄三热心地问。

"我没有再教下去的意思。女学堂真不知道要闹成什么样子。我辈正经人，确乎犯不上酱在一起……。"

毛家的大儿子进来了，胖到像一个汤圆。

"阿呀！久仰久仰！……"满屋子的手都拱起来，膝关节和腿关节接二连三地屈折，仿佛就要蹲了下去似的。

Behind his back he seemed to hear a number of girls laughing, to see their laughter emerging from that deep ocean of nostrils. So, ashamed to rub the sore place on his head, he hurried straight into the staff-room.

The two cups of boiled water were still there, but there was no sign of the orderly more dead than alive, nor of Wan Yaopu. All was dark and dreary, with nothing but his new briefcase and new hat gleaming in the gloom. The clock on the wall registered only 3:40.

Long after Master Gao returned to his own room, from time to time a burning sensation shot through him from head to foot. He was absolutely furious. He had reached the conclusion that schools would certainly corrupt social customs, and it would be better to close them, especially schools for girls. Love of vainglory — what was the point of it?

"Heehee!"

He could still hear that smothered laughter. This made him even more furious, strengthening his determination to resign. That evening he would write to Principal He, on the pretext that he had foot trouble. But suppose she insisted, what then? — He still wouldn't go. Goodness only knew what trouble would come of schools for girls. Why should he join forces with them? It was beneath his dignity. He thought it over.

So he resolutely set aside the *Outline*, pushed away the mirror and folded up the contract. About to sit down, it struck him that the contract was abominably red, so he snatched it up and stuffed it into a drawer together with *A Textbook of Chinese History*.

When all these dispositions had been made, the desk with nothing left on it but a mirror looked much neater. Still he felt ill at ease, as if short of half his soul; but at once he woke up, put on his autumn hat with the red knot, and set off for Huang San's home.

"Here you are, Master Erchu Gao!" roared Old Bo.

"You dog!" Glaring, he punched the top of Old Bo's head.

"Give your lesson? Well? Were there many pretty ones?" asked Huang San eagerly.

"I've decided to quit. Goodness knows what trouble will come of schools for girls. A respectable man like me certainly can't afford to get mixed up with them...."

In came the Mao family's eldest son, fat as a dumpling.

"Ah! This is a long-looked-for honour!" All the hands in the room were clasped and raised in greeting, while knees and leg joints buckled two or three times as if about to squat down.

“这一位就是先前说过的高干亭兄。”老钵指着高老夫子，向毛家的大儿子说。

“哦哦！久仰久仰！……”毛家的大儿子便特别向他连连拱手，并且点头。

这屋子的左边早放好一顶斜摆的方桌，黄三一面招呼客人，一面和一个小鸦头布置着座位和筹马。不多久，每一个桌角上都点起一枝细瘦的洋烛来，他们四人便入座了。

万籁无声。只有打出来的骨牌拍在紫檀桌面上的声音，在初夜的寂静中清彻地作响。

高老夫子的牌风并不坏，但他总还抱着什么不平。他本来是什么都容易忘记的，惟独这一回，却总以为世风有些可虑；虽然面前的筹马渐渐增加了，也还不很能够使他舒适，使他乐观。但时移俗易，世风也终究觉得好了起来；不过其时很晚，已经在打完第二圈，他快要凑成“清一色”的时候了。

一九二五年五月一日。

"This is Mr. Gao Ganting, of whom I've spoken to you," Old Bo told the Mao family's eldest son, pointing to Master Gao.

"Ah! This is a long-looked-for honour!" The Mao family's eldest son gave Master Gao a special salute and nod.

On the left side of the room, a square table had been set aslant. While greeting his visitors, Huang San and a little serving-girl set ready chairs and chips. Before long, each corner of the table was lit with a thin candle. The four players took their seats.

All was still except for the clunk of ivory tiles on the red sandalwood table, clearly audible in the silence of early night.

Master Gao's luck was not bad, but his sense of injustice still rankled. Normally he could easily banish all cares from his mind but now, for the first time, he was somewhat worried about the state of the world. Although the chips in front of him piled up slowly, this failed to set him at ease or make him optimistic. But customs change with the times, and finally he felt the state of the world was not so bad after all. By then, however, it was very late, they had already finished the second round, and he was on the point of completing a flush.

May 1, 1925

像一匹受伤的狼，当深夜在旷野中嗥叫，
惨伤里夹杂着愤怒和悲哀。

The howl of a wounded wolf crying in the wilderness in the depth of night, anger and sorrow mingled in its agony.

孤独者
The Misanthrope

一

我和魏连殳相识一场，回想起来倒也别致，竟是以送殓始，以送殓终。

那时我在S城，就时时听到人们提起他的名字，都说他很有些古怪：所学的是动物学，却到中学堂去做历史教员；对人总是爱理不理的，却常喜欢管别人的闲事；常说家庭应该破坏，一领薪水却一定立即寄给他的祖母，一日也不拖延。此外还有许多零碎的话柄；总之，在S城里也算是一个给人当做谈助的人。有一年的秋天，我在寒石山的一个亲戚家里闲住；他们就姓魏，是连殳的本家。但他们却更不明白他，仿佛将他当做一个外国人看待，说是“同我们都异样的”。

这也不足为奇，中国的兴学虽说已经二十年了，寒石山却连小学也没有。全山村中，只有连殳是出外游学的学生，所以从村人看来，他确是一个异类；但也很妒羡，说他挣得许多钱。

到秋末，山村中痢疾流行了；我也自危，就想回到城中去。那时听说连殳的祖母就染了病，因为是老年，所以很沉重；山中又没有一个医生。所谓他的家属者，其实就只有一个这祖母，雇一名女工简单地过活；他幼小失了父母，就由这祖母抚养成人的。听说她先前也曾经吃过许多苦，现在可是安乐了。但因为他没有家小，家中究竟非常寂寞，这大概也就是大家所谓异样之一端罢。

寒石山离城是旱道一百里，水道七十里，专使人叫连殳去，往返至少就得四天。山村僻陋，这些事便算大家都要打听的大新闻，第二天便轰传她病势已经极重，专差也出发了；可是到四更天竟咽了气，最后的话，是：“为什么不肯给我会一会连殳的呢？……”

族长，近房，他的祖母的母家的亲丁，闲人，聚集了一屋子，豫计连殳的到来，应该已是入殓的时候了。寿材寿衣早已做成，都无须筹画；他们的第一大问题是在怎样

I

My friendship with Wei Lianshu, now that I come to think of it, was certainly a strange one. It began and ended with a funeral.

When I lived in S— , I often heard him mentioned as an odd fellow: after studying zoology, he had become a history teacher in a middle school; he treated others in cavalier fashion, yet liked to concern himself with their affairs; and while maintaining that the family system should be abolished, he would remit his salary to his grandmother the same day that he drew it. He had many other strange ways, enough to set tongues wagging in the town. One autumn I stayed at Hanshishan with some relatives also named Wei, who were distantly related to him. However, they understood him even less, looking on him as if he were a foreigner. "He's not like us!" they said.

This was not strange, for although China had had modern schools for some twenty years, there was not even a primary school in Hanshishan. He was the only one to have left that mountain village to study; hence in the villagers' eyes he was an undoubted freak. They also envied him, though, saying he had made a lot of money.

Towards the end of autumn, there was an epidemic of dysentery in the village, and in alarm I thought of returning to the town. I heard his grandmother had contracted the disease too, and because of her age her case was serious. Moreover there was not a single doctor in the village. Wei had no other relative but this grandmother, who led a simple life with a maidservant. As he had lost both parents in his childhood, she had brought him up. She was said to have known much hardship earlier, but was now leading a comfortable life. Since he had neither wife nor children, however, his family was very quiet, and this presumably was one of the things considered freakish about him.

The village was a hundred li from the town by land, and seventy li by water; so that it would take four days to fetch Wei back. In this out-of-the-way village such matters were considered momentous news, eagerly canvassed by all. The next day the old woman was reported to be in a critical state, and the messenger on his way. However, before dawn she died, her last words being:

"Why won't you let me see my grandson?"

Elders of the clan, close relatives, members of his grandmother's family and others crowded the room anticipating Wei's return, which would be in time for the funeral. The coffin and shroud had long been ready, but the immediate problem was how to

对付这“承重孙”，因为逆料他关于一切丧葬仪式，是一定要改变新花样的。聚议之后，大概商定了三大条件，要他必行。一是穿白，二是跪拜，三是请和尚道士做法事。总而言之：是全都照旧。

他们既经议妥，便约定在连殳到家的那一天，一同聚在厅前，排成阵势，互相策应，并力作一回极严厉的谈判。村人们都咽着唾沫，新奇地听候消息；他们知道连殳是“吃洋教”的“新党”，向来就不讲什么道理，两面的争斗，大约总要开始的，或者还会酿成一种出人意外的奇观。

传说连殳的到家是下午，一进门，向他祖母的灵前只是弯了一弯腰。族长们便立刻照豫定计画进行，将他叫到大厅上，先说过一大篇冒头，然后引入本题，而且大家此唱彼和，七嘴八舌，使他得不到辩驳的机会。但终于话都说完了，沉默充满了全厅，人们全数悚然地紧看着他的嘴。只见连殳神色也不动，简单地回答道：

“都可以的。”

这又很出于他们的意外，大家的心的重担都放下了，但又似乎反加重，觉得太“异样”，倒很有些可虑似的。打听新闻的村人们也很失望，口口相传道，“奇怪！他说‘都可以’哩！我们看去罢！”都可以就是照旧，本来是无足观了，但他们也还要看，黄昏之后，便欣欣然聚满了一堂前。

我也是去看的一个，先送了一份香烛；待到走到他家，已见连殳在给死者穿衣服了。原来他是一个短小瘦削的人，长方脸，蓬松的头发和浓黑的须眉占了一脸的小半，只见两眼在黑气里发光。那穿衣也穿得真好，井井有条，仿佛是一个大殓的专家，使旁观者不觉叹服。寒石山老例，当这些时候，无论如何，母家的亲丁是总要挑剔的；他却只是默默地，遇见怎么挑剔便怎么改，神色也不动。站在我前面的一个花白头发的老太太，便发出羡慕感叹的声音。

其次是拜；其次是哭，凡女人们都念念有词。其次入棺；其次又是拜；又是哭，直到钉好了棺盖。沉静了一瞬间，大家忽而扰动了，很有惊异和不满的形势。我也不

cope with this grandson, for they expected he would insist on changes in the funeral rites. After a conference they decide on three terms which he must accept. First, he must wear deep mourning; secondly, he must kowtow to the coffin; and, thirdly, he must let Buddhist monks and Taoist priests say mass. In short, all must be done in the traditional manner.

This decision once reached, they decided to gather there in full force when Wei arrived home, to assist each other in this negotiation which could admit of no compromise. Licking their lips, the villagers eagerly awaited developments. Wei, as a "modern," "a follower of foreign creeds," had always proved unreasonable. A struggle would certainly ensue, which might even result in some novel spectacle.

He arrived home, I heard, in the afternoon, and only bowed to his grandmother's shrine as he entered. The elders proceeded at once according to plan. They summoned him to the hall, and after a lengthy preamble led up to the subject. Then, speaking in unison and at length, they gave him no chance to argue. At last, however, they dried up, and a deep silence fell in the hall. All eyes fastened fearfully on his lips. But without changing countenance, he answered simply:

"All right."

This was totally unexpected. A weight had been lifted from their minds, yet their hearts felt heavier than ever, for this was so "freakish" as to give rise to anxiety. The villagers looking for news were also disappointed and said to each other, "Strange. He said, 'All right.' Let's go and watch." Wei's "all right"meant that all would be in accordance with tradition, in which case it was not worth watching; still, they wanted to look on, and after dusk the hall filled with lighthearted spectators.

I was one of those who went, having first sent along my gift of incense and candles. As I arrived he was already putting the shroud on the dead. He was a thin man with an angular face, hidden to a certain extent by his dishevelled hair, dark eyebrows and moustache. His eyes gleamed darkly. He laid out the body very well, as deftly as an expert, so that the spectators were impressed. According to the local custom, at a married woman's funeral members of the dead woman's family found fault even if all was well done; however he remained silent, complying with their wishes with a face devoid of all expression. A grey-haired old woman standing before me gave a sigh of envy and respect.

Then people kowtowed; then they wailed, all the women chanting as they wailed. When the body was put in the coffin, all kowtowed again, then wailed again, until the lid of the coffin was nailed down. Silence reigned for a moment, and then there was stir of surprise and dissatisfaction. I too suddenly realized that Wei had not shed a single

由的突然觉到：连殳就始终没有落过一滴泪，只坐在草荐上，两眼在黑气里闪闪地发光。

大殓便在这惊异和不满的空气里面完毕。大家都怏怏地，似乎想走散，但连殳却还坐在草荐上沉思。忽然，他流下泪来了，接着就失声，立刻又变成长嚎，像一匹受伤的狼，当深夜在旷野中嗥叫，惨伤里夹杂着愤怒和悲哀。这模样，是老例上所没有的，先前也未曾豫防到，大家都手足无措了，迟疑了一会，就有几个人上前去劝止他，愈去愈多，终于挤成一大堆。但他却只是兀坐着号咷，铁塔似的动也不动。

大家又只得无趣地散开；他哭着，哭着，约有半点钟，这才突然停了下来，也不向吊客招呼，径自往家里走。接着就有前去窥探的人来报告：他走进他祖母的房里，躺在床上，而且，似乎就睡熟了。

隔了两日，是我要动身回城的前一天，便听到村人都遭了魔似的发议论，说连殳要将所有的器具大半烧给他祖母，余下的便分赠生时侍奉，死时送终的女工，并且连房屋也要无期地借给她居住了。亲戚本家都说到舌敝唇焦，也终于阻当不住。

恐怕大半也还是因为好奇心，我归途中经过他家的门口，便又顺便去吊慰。他穿了毛边的白衣出见，神色也还是那样，冷冷的。我很劝慰了一番；他却除了唯唯诺诺之外，只回答了一句话，是：

“多谢你的好意。”

二

我们第三次相见就在这年的冬初，S城的一个书铺子里，大家同时点了一点头，总算是认识了。但使我们接近起来的，是在这年底我失了职业之后。从此，我便常常访问连殳去。一则，自然是因为无聊赖；二则，因为听人说，他倒很亲近失意的人的，虽然素性这么冷。但是世事

tear from beginning to end. He was simply sitting on the mourner's mat, his two eyes gleaming darkly.

In this atmosphere of surprise and dissatisfaction, the ceremony ended. The disgruntled mourners seemed about to leave, but Wei was still sitting on the mat, lost in thought. Suddenly, tears fell from his eyes, then he burst into a long wail like a wounded wolf howling in the wilderness at the dead of night, anger and sorrow mingled with his agony. This was not in accordance with tradition and, taken by surprise, we were at a loss. After a little hesitation, some went to try to persuade him to stop, and there were joined by more and more people until finally there was a crowd round him. But he sat there wailing, motionless as an iron statue.

With a sense of anti-climax, the crowd dispersed. Wei continued to cry for about half an hour, then suddenly stopped, and without a word to the mourners went straight inside. Later it was reported by spies that he had gone into his grandmother's room, lain down on the bed and, to all appearances, fallen sound asleep.

Two days later, on the eve of my return to town, I heard the villagers discussing eagerly, as if they were possessed, how Wei intended to burn most of his dead grandmother's furniture and possessions, giving the rest to the maidservant who had served her during her life and attended her on her deathbed. Even the house was to be lent to the maid for an indefinite period. Wei's relatives argued themselves hoarse, but he was adamant.

Largely out of curiosity, perhaps, on my way back I passed his house and went in to express condolence. He received me wearing a hemless white mourning dress, and his expression was as cold as ever. I urged him not to take it so to heart, but apart from grunting non-committally all he said was:

"Thanks for your concern."

II

Early that winter we met for the third time. It was in a bookshop in S— , where we nodded simultaneously, showing at least that we were acquainted. But it was at the end of that year, after I lost my job, that we became friends. Thenceforward I paid Wei many visits. In the first place, of course, I had nothing to do; in the second place he was said to sympathize with lame dogs, despite his habitual reserve.

升沉无定，失意人也不会长是失意人，所以他也就很少长久的朋友。这传说果然不虚，我一投名片，他便接见了。两间连通的客厅，并无什么陈设，不过是桌椅之外，排列些书架，大家虽说他是一个可怕的“新党”，架上却不很有新书。他已经知道我失了职业；但套话一说就完，主客便只好默默地相对，逐渐沉闷起来。我只见他很快地吸完一枝烟，烟蒂要烧着手指了，才抛在地面上。

“吸烟罢。”他伸手取第二枝烟时，忽然说。

我便也取了一枝，吸着，讲些关于教书和书籍的，但也还觉得沉闷。我正想走时，门外一阵喧嚷和脚步声，四个男女孩子闯进来了。大的八九岁，小的四五岁，手脸和衣服都很脏，而且丑得可以。但是连殳的眼里却即刻发出欢喜的光来了，连忙站起，向客厅间壁的房里走，一面说道：

“大良，二良，都来！你们昨天要的口琴，我已经买来了。”

孩子们便跟着一齐拥进去，立刻又各人吹着一个口琴一拥而出，一出客厅门，不知怎的便打将起来。有一个哭了。

“一人一个，都一样的。不要争呵！”他还跟在后面嘱咐。

“这么多的一群孩子都是谁呢？”我问。

“是房主人的。他们都没有母亲，只有一个祖母。”

“房东只一个人么？”

“是的。他的妻子大概死了三四年了罢，没有续娶。——否则，便要不肯将余屋租给我似的单身人。”他说着，冷冷地微笑了。

我很想问他何以至今还是单身，但因为不很熟，终于不好开口。

只要和连殳一熟识，是很可以谈谈的。他议论非常多，而且往往颇奇警。使人不耐的倒是他的有些来客，大抵是读过《沉沦》的罢，时常自命为“不幸的青年”或是“零余者”，螃蟹一般懒散而骄傲地堆在大椅子上，一面唉声叹气，一面皱着眉头吸烟。还有那房主的孩子们，总

1. A contemporary of Lu Xun's, who wrote about repressed young men.

However, fortune being fickle, lame dogs do not remain lame for ever, hence he had few steady friends. Report proved true, for as soon as I sent in my card, he received me. His sitting-room consisted of two rooms thrown into one, quite bare of ornament, with nothing in it apart from table and chairs but some bookcases. Although he was reputed to be terribly "modern," there were few modern books on the shelves. He knew that I had lost my job; but after the usual polite remarks had been exchanged, host and guest sat silent, with nothing to say to each other. I noticed he very quickly finished his cigarette, only dropping it to the ground when it nearly burnt his fingers.

"Have a cigarette," he said suddenly, reaching for another.

"So I took one and, between puffs, spoke of teaching and books, still finding very little to say. I was just thinking of leaving when shouts and footsteps were heard outside the door, and four children rushed in. The eldest was about eight or nine, the smallest four or five. The hands, faces and clothes were very dirty, and they were thoroughly unprepossessing; yet Wei's face lit up with pleasure, and getting up at once he walked to the other room, saying:

"Come, Daliang, Erliang, all of you! I have bought the mouth-organs you wanted yesterday.."

The children rushed in after him, to return immediately with a mouth-organ apiece; but once outside they started fighting, and one of them cried.

"There's one each; they're exactly the same. Don't squabble!" he said as he followed them.

"Whose children are they?" I asked.

"The landlord's. They have no mother, only a grandmother."

"Your landlord is a widower?"

"Yes. His wife died three or four years ago, and he has not remarried. Otherwise, he would not rent his spare rooms to a bachelor like me." He said this with a cold smile.

I wanted very much to ask why he had remained single so long, but I did not know him well enough.

Once you knew him well, he was a good talker. He was full of ideas, many of them quite remarkable. What exasperated me were some of his guest. As a result, probably, of reading Yu Dafu's[1] romantic stories, they constantly referred to themselves as "the young unfortunate" or "the outcast"; and, sprawling on the big chairs like lazy and arrogant crabs, they would sigh, smoke and frown all at the same time.

是互相争吵，打翻碗碟，硬讨点心，乱得人头昏。但连殳一见他们，却再不像平时那样的冷冷的了，看得比自己的性命还宝贵。听说有一回，三良发了红斑痧，竟急得他脸上的黑气愈见其黑了；不料那病是轻的，于是后来便被孩子们的祖母传作笑柄。

“孩子总是好的。他们全是天真……。”他似乎也觉得我有些不耐烦了，有一天特地乘机对我说。

“那也不尽然。”我只是随便回答他。

“不。大人的坏脾气，在孩子们是没有的。后来的坏，如你平日所攻击的坏，那是环境教坏的。原来却并不坏，天真……。我以为中国的可以希望，只在这一点。”

“不。如果孩子中没有坏根苗，大起来怎么会有坏花果？譬如一粒种子，正因为内中本含有枝叶花果的胚，长大时才能够发出这些东西来。何尝是无端……。”我因为闲着无事，便也如大人先生们一下野，就要吃素谈禅一样，正在看佛经。佛理自然是并不懂得的，但竟也不自检点，一味任意地说。

然而连殳气忿了，只看了我一眼，不再开口。我也猜不出他是无话可说呢，还是不屑辩。但见他又显出许久不见的冷冷的态度来，默默地连吸了两枝烟；待到他再取第三枝时，我便只好逃走了。

这仇恨是历了三月之久才消释的。原因大概是一半因为忘却，一半则他自己竟也被“天真”的孩子所仇视了，于是觉得我对于孩子的冒渎的话倒也情有可原。但这不过是我的推测。其时是在我的寓里的酒后，他似乎微露悲哀模样，半仰着头道：

“想起来真觉得有些奇怪。我到你这里来时，街上看见一个很小的小孩，拿了一片芦叶指着我道：杀！他还不很能走路……。”

“这是环境教坏的。”

我即刻很后悔我的话。但他却似乎并不介意，只竭力地喝酒，其间又竭力地吸烟。

“我倒忘了，还没有问你，”我便用别的话来支梧，

Then there were the landlord's children, who were always fighting among themselves, knocking over bowls and plates, begging for cakes, keeping up an ear-splitting din. Yet the sight of them invariably dipelled Wei's customary coldness, and they seemed to be the most precious thing in his life. Once the third child was said to have measles. He was so worried that his dark face took on an even darker hue. The attack proved a light one, however, and thereafter the children's grandmother made a joke of his anxiety.

"Children are always good. They are all so innocent..." he seized an opening to say one day, having, apparently, sensed my impatience.

"Not always," I answered casually.

"Always. Children have none of the faults of grown-ups. If they turn out badly later, as you contend, it is because they have been moulded by their environment. Originally they are not bad, but innocent.... I think China's only hope lies in this."

"I don't agree. Without the root of evil, how could they bear evil fruit in later life? Take a seed, for example. It is because it contains the embryo leaves, flowers and fruits, that it can grow later into these things. There must be a cause...." Since my unemployment, just like those great officials who resigned from office and took up Buddhism, I had been reading the Buddhist sutras. I did not understand Buddhist philosophy though, and was just talking at random.

However, Wei was annoyed. He gave me a look, then said no more. I could not tell whether he had more to say, or whether he felt it not worth arguing with me. But he looked cold again, as he had not done for a long time, and smoked two cigarettes one after the other in silence. By the time he reached for the third cigarette, I had to beat a retreat.

Our estrangement lasted three months. Then, owing in part to forgetfulness, in part to the fact that he fell out with those "innocent" children, he came to consider my slighting remarks about children as excusable. Or so I surmised. This happened in my house after drinking one day, when, with a rather melancholy look, he cocked his head, and said:

"Come to think of it, it's really curious. On my way here I met a small child with a reed in his hand, which he pointed at me, shouting, 'Kill!' He was just a toddler...."

"He must have been moulded by his environment."

As soon as I had said this, I wanted to take it back. However, he did not seem to care, just went on drinking heavily, smoking furiously in between.

"I meant to ask you," I said, trying to change the subject. "You don't usually call on

“你是不大访问人的，怎么今天有这兴致来走走呢？我们相识有一年多了，你到我这里来却还是第一回。”

“我正要告诉你呢：你这几天切莫到我寓里来看我了。我的寓里正有很讨厌的一大一小在那里，都不像人！”

“一大一小？这是谁呢？”我有些诧异。

“是我的堂兄和他的小儿子。哈哈，儿子正如老子一般。”

“是上城来看你。带便玩玩的罢？”

不。说是来和我商量，就要将这孩子过继给我的。”

“呵！过继给你？”我不禁惊叫了，“你不是还没有娶亲么？”

“他们知道我不娶的了。但这都没有什么关系。他们其实是要过继给我那一间寒石山的破屋子。我此外一无所有，你是知道的；钱一到手就完。只有这一间破屋子。他们父子的一生的事业是在逐出那一个借住着的老女工。”

他那词气的冷峭，实在又使我悚然。但我还慰解他说：

“我看你的本家也还不至于此。他们不过思想略旧一点罢了。譬如，你那年大哭的时候，他们就都热心地围着使劲来劝你……。”

“我父亲死去之后，因为夺我屋子，要我在笔据上画花押，我大哭着的时候，他们也是这样热心地围着使劲来劝我……。”他两眼向上凝视，仿佛要在空中寻出那时的情景来。

“总而言之：关键就全在你没有孩子。你究竟为什么老不结婚的呢？”我忽而寻到了转舵的话，也是久已想问的话，觉得这时是最好的机会了。

他诧异地看着我，过了一会，眼光便移到他自己的膝髁上去了，于是就吸烟，没有回答。

三

但是，虽在这一种百无聊赖的境地中，也还不给连殳安住。渐渐地，小报上有匿名人来攻击他，学界上也常

people, what made you come out today? I've known you for more than a year, yet this is the first time you've been here."

"I was just going to tell you: don't call on me for the time being. There are a father and son in my place who are perfect pests. They are scarcely human!"

"Father and son? Who are they?" I was surprised.

"My cousin and his son. Well, the son resembles the father."

"I suppose they came to town to see you and have a good time?"

"No. They came to talk me into adopting the boy."

"What, to adopt the boy?"I exclaimed in amazement. "But you are not married."

"They know I won't marry. But that's nothing to them. Actually they want to inherit that tumble-down house of mine in the village. I have no other property, you know; as soon as I get money I spend it. I've only that house. Their purpose in life is to drive out the old maidservant who is living in the place for the time being."

The cynicism of his remark took me aback. However I tried to soothe him, by saying:

"I don't think your relatives can be so bad. They are only rather old-fashioned. For instance, that year when you cried bitterly, they came forward eagerly to plead with you...."

"When I was a child and my father died, I cried bitterly because they wanted to take the house from me and make me put my mark on the document, and they came forward eagerly then to plead with me...." He looked up, as if searching the air for that bygone scene.

"The crux of the matter is — you have no children. Why don't you get married?" I had found a way to change the subject, and this was something I had been wanting to ask for a long time. It seemed an excellent opportunity.

He looked at me in surprise, then dropped his gaze to his knees, and started smoking. I received no answer to my question.

III

Yet, even this inane existence he was not allowed to enjoy in peace. Gradually there appeared anonymous attacks in the less reputable papers, and in the schools

有关于他的流言，可是这已经并非先前似的单是话柄，大概是于他有损的了。我知道这是他近来喜欢发表文章的结果，倒也并不介意。S城人最不愿意有人发些没有顾忌的议论，一有，一定要暗暗地来叮他，这是向来如此的，连殳自己也知道。但到春天，忽然听说他已被校长辞退了。这却使我觉得有些兀突；其实，这也是向来如此的，不过因为我希望着自己认识的人能够幸免，所以就以为兀突罢了，S城人倒并非这一回特别恶。

其时我正忙着自己的生计，一面又在接洽本年秋天到山阳去当教员的事，竟没有工夫去访问他。待到有些余暇的时候，离他被辞退那时大约快有三个月了，可是还没有发生访问连殳的意思。有一天，我路过大街，偶然在旧书摊前停留，却不禁使我觉到震悚，因为在那里陈列着的一部汲古阁初印本《史记索隐》，正是连殳的书。他喜欢书，但不是藏书家，这种本子，在他是算作贵重的善本，非万不得已，不肯轻易变卖的。难道他失业刚才两三月，就一贫至此么？虽然他向来一有钱即随手散去，没有什么贮蓄。于是我便决意访问连殳去，顺便在街上买了一瓶烧酒，两包花生米，两个熏鱼头。

他的房门关闭着，叫了两声，不见答应。我疑心他睡着了，更加大声地叫，并且伸手拍着房门。

“出去了罢！”大良们的祖母，那三角眼的胖女人，从对面的窗口探出她花白的头来了，也大声说，不耐烦似的。

“那里去了呢？”我问。

“那里去了？谁知道呢？——他能到那里去呢，你等着就是，一会儿总会回来的。”

我便推开门走进他的客厅去。真是“一日不见，如隔三秋”，满眼是凄凉和空空洞洞，不但器具所余无几了，连书籍也只剩了在S城决没有人会要的几本洋装书。屋中间的圆桌还在，先前曾经常常围绕着忧郁慷慨的青年，怀才不遇的奇士和腌臜吵闹的孩子们的，现在却见得很闲静，只在面上蒙着一层薄薄的灰尘。我就在桌上放了酒瓶和纸

2. By Sima Zhen of the Tang Dynasty (618-907).

rumours spread concerning him. This was not the simple gossip of the old days, but deliberately damaging. I knew this was the outcome of articles he had taken to writing for the magazines, so I paid no attention. The citizens of S— disliked nothing more than fearless argument, and anyone guilty of it would indubitably become the object of secret attacks. This was the rule, and Wei knew it too. However, in spring, when I heard he had been asked to resign by the school authorities, I confessed it surprised me. Of course, this was only to be expected, and it surprised me simply because I had hoped my friend could escape. The citizens of S— were not proving more vicious than usual.

I was occupied then with my own problems, negotiating to go to a school in Shanyang that autumn, so I had no time to call on him. Some three months passed before I was at leisure, and even then it had not occurred to me to visit him. One day, passing the main street, I happened to pause before a second-hand bookstall, where I was startled to see displayed an early edition of the *Commentaries on the "Records of the Historian,*[2]" from Wei's collection. He was no connoisseur, but he loved books, and I knew he prized this particular book. He must be very hard pressed to have sold it. It seemed scarcely possible he could have become so poor only two or three months after losing his job; yet he spent money as soon as he had it, and had never saved. So I decided to call on him. On the same street I bought a bottle of liquor, two packages of peanuts and two smoked fish-heads.

His door was closed. I called out twice, but there was no reply. Thinking he was asleep, I called louder, hammering on the door at the same time.

"He's probably out." The children's grandmother, a fat woman with small eyes, thrust her grey head out from the opposite window, and spoke impatiently.

"Where has he gone?" I asked.

"Where? Who knows — where could he go? You can wait, he will be back soon."

So I pushed open the door and went into his sitting-room. It was greatly changed, looking desolate in its emptiness. There was little furniture left, while all that remained of his library were those foreign books which could not be sold. The middle of the room was still occupied by the table round which those woeful and gallant young men, unrecognized geniuses, and dirty, noisy children had formerly gathered. Now it all seemed very quiet, and there was a thin layer of dust on the table. I put the bottle and packages down, pulled over a chair, and sat down by the

包，拖过一把椅子来，靠桌旁对着房门坐下。

的确不过是“一会儿”，房门一开，一个人悄悄地阴影似的进来了，正是连殳。也许是傍晚之故罢，看去仿佛比先前黑，但神情却还是那样。

“阿！你在这里？来得多久了？”他似乎有些喜欢。

“并没有多久。”我说，“你到那里去了？”

“并没有到那里去，不过随便走走。”

他也拖过椅子来，在桌旁坐下；我们便开始喝烧酒，一面谈些关于他的失业的事。但他却不愿意多谈这些；他以为这是意料中的事，也是自己时常遇到的事，无足怪，而且无可谈的。他照例只是一意喝烧酒，并且依然发些关于社会和历史的议论。不知怎地我此时看见空空的书架，也记起汲古阁初印本的《史记索隐》，忽而感到一种淡漠的孤寂和悲哀。

“你的客厅这么荒凉……。近来客人不多了么？”

“没有了。他们以为我心境不佳，来也无意味。心境不佳，实在是可以给人们不舒服的。冬天的公园，就没有人去……。”他连喝两口酒，默默地想着，突然，仰起脸来看着我问道，“你在图谋的职业也还是毫无把握罢？……”

我虽然明知他已经有些酒意，但也不禁愤然，正想发话，只见他侧耳一听，便抓起一把花生米，出去了。门外是大良们笑嚷的声音。

但他一出去，孩子们的声音便寂然，而且似乎都走了。他还追上去，说些话，却不听得有回答。他也就阴影似的悄悄地回来，仍将一把花生米放在纸包里。

“连我的东西也不要吃了。”他低声，嘲笑似的说。

“连殳，”我很觉得悲凉，却强装着微笑，说，“我以为你太自寻苦恼了。你看得人间太坏……。”

他冷冷的笑了一笑。

“我的话还没有完哩。你对于我们，偶而来访问你的我们，也以为因为闲着无事，所以来你这里，将你当做消遣的资料的罢？”

table facing the door.

Very soon, sure enough, the door opened, and someone stepped in as silently as a shadow. It was Wei. It might have been the twilight that made his face look dark; but his expression was unchanged.

"Ah, it's you? How long have you been here?" He seemed pleased.

"Not very long," I said. "Where have you been?"

"Nowhere in particular. Just taking a stroll."

He pulled up a chair too and sat by the table. We started drinking, and spoke of his losing his job. However, he did not care to talk much about it, considering it as only to be expected. He had come across many similar cases. It was not strange at all, and not worth discussing. As usual, he drank heavily, and discoursed on society and the study of history. Something made me glance at the empty bookshelves and, remembering the *Commentaries on the "Records of the Historian,"* I was conscious of a slight loneliness and sadness.

"Your sitting-room has a deserted look.... Have you had fewer visitors recently?"

"None at all. They don't find it much fun when I'm not in a good mood. A bad mood certainly makes people uncomfortable. Just as no one goes to the park in winter...."

He took two sips of liquor in succession, then fell silent. Suddenly, looking up, he asked, "I suppose you have had no luck either in finding work?"

Although I knew we only venting his feelings as a result of drinking, I felt indignant at the way people treated him. Just as I was about to say something, he pricked up his ears, then, scooping up some peanuts, went out. Outside, the laughter and shouts of the children could be heard.

But as soon as he went out, the children became quiet. It sounded as if they had left. He went after them, and said something, but I could hear no reply. Then he came back, as silent as a shadow, and put the handful of peanuts back in the package.

"They don't even want to eat anything I give them," he said sarcastically, in a low voice.

"Old Wei," I said, forcing a smile, although I was sick at heart, "I think you are tormenting yourself unnecessarily. Why think so poorly of your fellow men?"

He only smiled cynically.

"I haven't finished yet. I suppose you consider that people like me, who come here occasionally, do so in order to kill time or amuse themselves at your expense?"

“并不。但有时也这样想。或者寻些谈资。”

“那你可错误了。人们其实并不这样。你实在亲手造了独头茧，将自己裹在里面了。你应该将世间看得光明些。”我叹惜着说。

“也许如此罢。但是，你说：那丝是怎么来的？——自然，世上也尽有这样的人，譬如，我的祖母就是。我虽然没有分得她的血液，却也许会继承她的运命。然而这也没有什么要紧，我早已豫先一起哭过了……。”

我即刻记起他祖母大殓时候的情景来，如在眼前一样。

“我总不解你那时的大哭……。”于是鹘突地问了。

“我的祖母入殓的时候罢？是的，你不解的。”他一面点灯，一面冷静地说，“你的和我交往，我想，还正因为那时的哭哩。你不知道，这祖母，是我父亲的继母；他的生母，他三岁时候就死去了。”他想着，默默地喝酒，吃完了一个熏鱼头。

“那些往事，我原是不知道的。只是我从小时候就觉得不可解。那时我的父亲还在，家景也还好，正月间一定要悬挂祖像，盛大地供养起来。看着这许多盛装的画像，在我那时似乎是不可多得的眼福。但那时，抱着我的一个女工总指了一幅像说：‘这是你自己的祖母。拜拜罢，保佑你生龙活虎似的大得快。’我真不懂得我明明有着一个祖母，怎么又会有什么‘自己的祖母’来。可是我爱这‘自己的祖母’，她不比家里的祖母一般老；她年青，好看，穿着描金的红衣服，戴着珠冠，和我母亲的像差不多。我看她时，她的眼睛也注视我，而且口角上渐渐增多了笑影：我知道她一定也是极其爱我的。

“然而我也爱那家里的，终日坐在窗下慢慢地做针线的祖母。虽然无论我怎样高兴地在她面前玩笑，叫她，也不能引她欢笑，常使我觉得冷冷地，和别人的祖母们有些不同。但我还爱她。可是到后来，我逐渐疏远她了；这也并非因为年纪大了，已经知道她不是我父亲的生母的缘故，倒是看久了终日终年的做针线，机器似的，自然免不

"No, I don't. Well, sometimes I do. Perhaps they come to find something to talk about."

"Then you are wrong. People are not like that. You are really wrapping yourself up in a cocoon. You should take a more cheerful view." I sighed.

"Maybe. But tell me, where does the thread for the cocoon come from? Of course, there are plenty of people like that; take my grandmother, for example. Although I have none of her blood in my veins, I may inherit her fate. But that doesn't matter, I have already bewailed my fate together with hers...."

"I still don't understand why you cried so bitterly," I said bluntly.

"You mean at my grandmother's funeral? No, you wouldn't." He lit the lamp. "I suppose it was because of that that we became friends," he said quietly. "You know, this grandmother was my grandfather's second wife. My father's own mother died when he was three." Growing thoughtful, he drank silently, and finished a smoked fish-head.

"I didn't know it to begin with. Only, from my childhood I was puzzled. At that time my father was still alive, and our family was well off. During the lunar New Year we would hang up the ancestral images and hold a grand sacrifice. It was one of my rare pleasures to look at those splendidly dressed images. At that time a maidservant would always carry me to an image, and point at it, saying, 'This is your own grandmother. Bow to her so that she will protect you and make you grown up strong and healthy.' I could not understand how I came to have another grandmother, in addition to the one beside me. But I liked this grandmother who was 'my own.' She was not as old as the granny at home. Young and beautiful, wearing a red costume with golden embroidery and a headdress decked with pearls, she resembled my mother. When I looked at her, her eyes seemed to gaze down on me, and a faint smile appeared on her lips. I knew she was very fond of me too."

"But I like the granny at home too, who sat all day under the window slowly plying her needle. However, no matter how merrily I laughed and played in front of her, or called to her, I could not make her laugh; and that made me feel she was cold, unlike other children's grandmothers. Still, I liked her. Later on, though, I gradually cooled towards her, not because I had grown older and learned she was not my own grandmother, but rather because I was

了要发烦。但她却还是先前一样，做针线；管理我，也爱护我，虽然少见笑容，却也不加呵斥。直到我父亲去世，还是这样；后来呢，我们几乎全靠她做针线过活了，自然更这样，直到我进学堂……。”

灯火销沉下去了，煤油已经将涸，他便站起，从书架下摸出一个小小的洋铁壶来添煤油。

“只这一月里，煤油已经涨价两次了……。”他旋好了灯头，慢慢地说。“生活要日见其困难起来。——她后来还是这样，直到我毕业，有了事做，生活比先前安定些；恐怕还直到她生病，实在打熬不住了，只得躺下的时候罢……。

“她的晚年，据我想，是总算不很辛苦的，享寿也不小了，正无须我来下泪。况且哭的人不是多着么？连先前竭力欺凌她的人们也哭，至少是脸上很惨然，哈哈！……可是我那时不知怎地，将她的一生缩在眼前了，亲手造成孤独，又放在嘴里去咀嚼的人的一生。而且觉得这样的人还很多哩。这些人们，就使我要痛哭，但大半也还是因为我那时太过于感情用事……。

“你现在对于我的意见，就是我先前对于她的意见。然而我的那时的意见，其实也不对的。便是我自己，从略知世事起，就的确逐渐和她疏远起来了……。”

他沉默了，指间夹着烟卷，低了头，想着。灯火在微微地发抖。

“呵，人要使死后没有一个人为他哭，是不容易的事呵。”他自言自语似的说；略略一停，便仰起脸来向我道，“想来你也无法可想。我也还得赶紧寻点事情做……。”

“你再没有可托的朋友了么？”我这时正是无法可想，连自己。

“那倒大概还有几个的，可是他们的境遇都和我差不多……。”

我辞别连殳出门的时候，圆月已经升在中天了，是极静的夜。

exasperated by the way she kept on sewing mechanically, day in day out. She was unchanged, however. She sewed, looked after me, loved and protected me as before; and though she seldom smiled, she never scolded me. It was the same after my father died. Later on, we lived almost entirely on her sewing, so it was still the same, until I went to school...."

The light flickered as the kerosene gave out, and he stood up to refill the lamp from a small tin kettle under the bookcase.

"The price of kerosene has gone up twice this month," he said slowly, after turning up the wick. "Life will become harder every day. She remained the same until I graduated from school and got a job, when our life became more secure. She didn't change, I suppose, until she was sick and couldn't carry on, but had to take to her bed...."

"Since her later days, I think, were not too unhappy on the whole, and she lived to a great age, I need not have mourned. Besides, weren't there a lot of others there eager to wail? Even those who had tried their hardest to rob her wailed, or appeared bowed down with grief." He laughed. "However, at that moment her whole life rose to my mind — the life of one who created loneliness for herself and tasted its bitterness. And I felt there were many people like that. I wanted to weep for them; but perhaps it was largely because I was too sentimental....

"Your present advice to me is what I felt with regard to her. But actually my ideas at that time were wrong. As for myself, since I grew up my feelings for her cooled...."

He paused, with a cigarette between his fingers and bending his head lost himself in thought. The lamp-light flickered.

"Well, it is hard to live so that no one will mourn for your death," he said, as if to himself. After a pause he looked up at me, and asked, "I suppose you can't help? I shall have to find something to do very soon."

"Have you no other friends you could ask?" I was in no position to help myself then, let alone others.

"I have a few, but they are all in the same boat...."

When I left him, the full moon was high in the sky and the night was very still.

四

山阳的教育事业的状况很不佳。我到校两月，得不到一文薪水，只得连烟卷也节省起来。但是学校里的人们，虽是月薪十五六元的小职员，也没有一个不是乐天知命的，仗着逐渐打熬成功的铜筋铁骨，面黄肌瘦地从早办公一直到夜，其间看见名位较高的人物，还得恭恭敬敬地站起，实在都是不必“衣食足而知礼节”的人民。我每看见这情状，不知怎的总记起连殳临别托付我的话来。他那时生计更其不堪了，窘相时时显露，看去似乎已没有往时的深沉，知道我就要动身，深夜来访，迟疑了许久，才吞吞吐吐地说道：

“不知道那边可有法子想？——便是钞写，一月二三十块钱的也可以的。我……。”

我很诧异了，还不料他竟肯这样的迁就，一时说不出活来。

“我……，我还得活几天……。”

“那边去看一看，一定竭力去设法罢。”

这是我当日一口承当的答话，后来常常自己听见，眼前也同时浮出连殳的相貌，而且吞吞吐吐地说道“我还得活几天”。到这些时，我便设法向各处推荐一番；但有什么效验呢，事少人多，结果是别人给我几句抱歉的话，我就给他几句抱歉的信。到一学期将完的时候，那情形就更加坏了起来。那地方的几个绅士所办的《学理周报》上，竟开始攻击我了，自然是决不指名的，但措辞很巧妙，使人一见就觉得我是在挑剔学潮，连推荐连殳的事，也算是呼朋引类。

我只好一动不动，除上课之外，便关起门来躲着，有时连烟卷的烟钻出窗隙去，也怕犯了挑剔学潮的嫌疑。连殳的事，自然更是无从说起了。这样地一直到深冬。

下了一天雪，到夜还没有止，屋外一切静极，静到要听出静的声音来。我在小小的灯火光中，闭目枯坐，如见

IV

The teaching profession in Shanyang was no bed of roses. I taught for two months without receiving a cent of salary, until I had to cut down on cigarettes. But the school staff, even those earning only fifteen or sixteen dollars a month, were easily contented. They all had iron constitutions steeled by hardship, and, although lean and haggard, would work from morning till night; while if interrupted at work by their superiors, they would stand up respectfully. Thus they all practised plain living and high thinking. This reminded me, somehow, of Wei's parting words. He was then even more hard up, and often looked embarrassed, having apparently lost his former cynicism. When he heard that I was leaving, he had come late at night to see me off, and, after hesitating for some time, had stuttered:

"Would there be anything for me there? Even copying work, at twenty to thirty dollars a month, would do. I...."

I was surprised. I had not thought he would consider anything so low, and did not know how to answer.

"I...I have to live a little longer...."

"I'll look out when I get there. I'll do my best."

This was what I had promised at the time, and the words often rang in my ears later, as if Wei were before me, stuttering, "I have to live a little longer." I tried to interest various people in his case, but to no avail. There were few vacancies, and many unemployed; they always ended by apologizing for being unable to help, and I would write him an apologetic letter. By the end of the term, things had gone from bad to worse. The magazine *Reason*, edited by some of the local gentry, began to attack me. Naturally no names were mentioned, but it cleverly insinuated that I was stirring up trouble in the school, even my recommendation of Wei being interpreted as a manoeuvre to clique about me.

So I had to keep quiet. Apart from attending class, I lay low in my room, sometimes even fearing I might be considered as stirring up trouble when cigarette smoke escaped from my window. For Wei, naturally, I could do nothing. This state of affair prevailed till midwinter.

It had been snowing all day, and the snow had not stopped by evening. Outside was so still, you could almost hear the sound of stillness. I closed my eyes and sat there in

雪花片片飘坠，来增补这一望无际的雪堆；故乡也准备过年了，人们忙得很；我自己还是一个儿童，在后园的平坦处和一伙小朋友塑雪罗汉。雪罗汉的眼睛是用两块小炭嵌出来的，颜色很黑，这一闪动，便变了连殳的眼睛。

“我还得活几天！”仍是这样的声音。

“为什么呢？”我无端地这样问，立刻连自己也觉得可笑了。

这可笑的问题使我清醒，坐直了身子，点起一枝烟卷来；推窗一望，雪果然下得更大了。听得有人叩门；不一会，一个人走进来，但是听熟的客寓杂役的脚步。他推开我的房门，交给我一封六寸多长的信，字迹很潦草，然而一瞥便认出“魏缄”两个字，是连殳寄来的。

这是从我离开S城以后他给我的第一封信。我知道他疏懒，本不以杳无消息为奇，但有时也颇怨他不给一点消息。待到接了这信，可又无端地觉得奇怪了，慌忙拆开来。里面也用了一样潦草的字体；写着这样的话：

“申飞……。

“我称你什么呢？我空着。你自己愿意称什么，你自己添上去罢。我都可以的。

“别后共得三信，没有复。这原因很简单：我连买邮票的钱也没有。

“你或者愿意知道些我的消息，现在简直告诉你罢：我失败了。先前，我自以为是失败者，现在知道那并不，现在才真是失败者了。先前，还有人愿意我活几天，我自己也还想活几天的时候，活不下去；现在，大可以无须了，然而要活下去……。

“然而就活下去么？

“愿意我活几天的，自己就活不下去。这人已被敌人诱杀了。谁杀的呢？谁也不知道。

“人生的变化多么迅速呵！这半年来，我几乎求乞了，实际，也可以算得已经求乞。然而我还有所为，我愿意为此求乞，为此冻馁，为此寂寞，为此辛苦。但灭亡是不愿意的。你看，有一个愿意我活几天的，那力量就这么

the dim lamplight, doing nothing, imagining the snowflakes falling to augment the boundless drifts of snow. It would be nearly New Year at home too, and everybody would be busy. I saw myself a child again, making a snowman with a group of children on the level ground in the back yard. The eyes of the snowman, made of jet-black fragments of coal, suddenly turned into Wei's eyes.

"I have to live a little longer." The same voice again.

"What for?" I asked inadvertently, aware immediately of the ineptitude of my remark.

It was this reply that woke me up. I sat up, lit a cigarette and opened the window, only to find the snow falling even faster. Then I heard a knock at the door, and a moment later it opened to admit the servant, whose step I knew. He handed me a big envelope, more than six inches in length. The address was scrawled, but I saw Wei's name on it.

This is the first letter he had written me since I left S— . Knowing he was a bad correspondent, I had not wondered at his silence, only sometimes I had felt he should have given me some news of himself. So the receipt of this letter was quite a surprise. I tore it open. The letter had been hastily scrawled, and said:

...Shenfei,

How should I address you? I am leaving a blank for you to fill in as you please. It will be all the same to me.

I have altogether received three letters from you. I did not reply for one simple reason: I had no money even to buy stamps.

Perhaps you would like to know what has happened to me. To put it simply: I have failed. I thought I had failed before, but I was wrong then; now, however, I am really a failure. Formerly there was someone who wanted me to live a little longer, and I wished it too, but found it difficult. Now, there is no need, yet I must go in living....

Shall I then live on?

The one who wanted me to live a little longer could not live himself. He was trapped and killed by the enemy. Who killed him? No one knows.

Changes take place so swiftly! During the last half year I have virtually been a beggar; it's true, I could be considered a beggar. However, I had my purpose: I was willing to beg for the cause, to go cold and hungry for it, to be lonely for it, to suffer hardship for it. But I did not want to destroy myself. So you see, the fact that one person wanted me to live on proved extremely potent. But now there is

大。然而现在是没有了，连这一个也没有了。同时，我自己也觉得不配活下去；别人呢？也不配的。同时，我自己又觉得偏要为不愿意我活下去的人们而活下去；好在愿意我好好地活下去的已经没有了，再没有谁痛心。使这样的人痛心，我是不愿意的。然而现在是没有了，连这一个也没有了。快活极了，舒服极了；我已经躬行我先前所憎恶，所反对的一切，拒斥我先前所崇仰，所主张的一切了。我已经真的失败，——然而我胜利了。

“你以为我发了疯么？你以为我成了英雄或伟人了么？不，不的。这事情很简单；我近来已经做了杜师长的顾问，每月的薪水就有现洋八十元了。

“申飞……。

“你将以我为什么东西呢，你自己定就是，我都可以的。

“你大约还记得我旧时的客厅罢，我们在城中初见和将别时候的客厅。现在我还用着这客厅。这里有新的宾客，新的馈赠，新的颂扬，新的钻营，新的磕头和打拱，新的打牌和猜拳，新的冷眼和恶心，新的失眠和吐血……。

“你前信说你教书很不如意。你愿意也做顾问么？可以告诉我，我给你办。其实是做门房也不妨，一样地有新的宾客和新的馈赠，新的颂扬……。

“我这里下大雪了。你那里怎样？现在已是深夜，吐了两口血，使我清醒起来。记得你竟从秋天以来陆续给了我三封信，这是怎样的可以惊异的事呵。我必须寄给你一点消息，你或者不至于倒抽一口冷气罢。

“此后，我大约不再写信的了，我这习惯是你早已知道的。何时回来呢？倘早，当能相见。——但我想，我们大概究竟不是一路的；那么，请你忘记我罢。我从我的真心感谢你先前常替我筹划生计。但是现在忘记我罢；我现在已经‘好’了。

连殳。十二月十四日。”

no one, not one. At the same time I feel I do not deserve to live, nor do some other people either, in my opinion. Yet, I am conscious of wanting to live on to spite those who wish me dead; for at least there is no one left wants me to live decently, and so no one can be hurt. I don't want to hurt such people. But now there is no one, not one. What a joy! Wonderful! I am now doing what I formerly detested and opposed. I am now giving up all I formerly believed in and upheld. I have really failed — but I have won.

Do you think I am mad? Do you think I have won a hero or a great man? No, it is not that, it is very simple; I have become adviser to General Du, hence I have eighty dollars salary a month.

...Shenfei,

What will you think of me? You decide; it is the same to me.

Perhaps you still remember my former sitting-room the one in which we had our first and last talks. I am still using it. There are new guests, new bribes, new flattery, new seeking for promotion, new kowtows and bows, new mahjong and drinking games, new haughtiness and disgust, new sleeplessness and vomiting of blood....

You said in your last letter that your teaching was not going well. Would you like to be an adviser? Say the word, and I will arrange it for you. Actually, work in the gatehouse would be the same. There would be the same guests, bribes and flattery....

It is snowing heavily here. How is it where you are? It is now midnight, and having just vomited some blood has sobered me. I recall that you have actually written three times in succession to me since autumn — amazing! So I must give you some news of myself, hoping you will not be shocked.

I probably shall not write again; you know my ways of old. When will you be back? If you come soon, we may meet again. Still, I suppose we have taken different roads, so you had better forget me. I thank you from the bottom of my heart for trying to find work for me. But now please forget me; I am doing "well."

Wei Lianshu

December 14th

这虽然并不使我“倒抽一口冷气”，但草草一看之后，又细看了一遍，却总有些不舒服，而同时可又夹杂些快意和高兴；又想，他的生计总算已经不成问题，我的担子也可以放下了，虽然在我这一面始终不过是无法可想。忽而又想写一封信回答他，但又觉得没有话说，于是这意思也立即消失了。

我的确渐渐地在忘却他。在我的记忆中，他的面貌也不再时常出现。但得信之后不到十天，S城的学理七日报社忽然接续着邮寄他们的《学理七日报》来了。我是不大看这些东西的，不过既经寄到，也就随手翻翻。这却使我记起连殳来，因为里面常有关于他的诗文，如《雪夜谒连殳先生》，《连殳顾问高斋雅集》等等；有一回，《学理闲谭》里还津津地叙述他先前所被传为笑柄的事，称作“逸闻”，言外大有“且夫非常之人，必能行非常之事”的意思。

不知怎地虽然因此记起，但他的面貌却总是逐渐模胡；然而又似乎和我日加密切起来，往往无端感到一种连自己也莫明其妙的不安和极轻微的震颤。幸而到了秋季，这《学理七日报》就不寄来了；山阳的《学理周刊》上却又按期登起一篇长论文：《流言即事实论》。里面还说，关于某君们的流言，已在公正士绅间盛传了。这是专指几个人的，有我在内；我只好极小心，照例连吸烟卷的烟也谨防飞散。小心是一种忙的苦痛，因此会百事俱废，自然也无暇记得连殳。总之：我其实已经将他忘却了。

但我也终于敷衍不到暑假，五月底，便离开了山阳。

五

从山阳到历城，又到太谷，一总转了大半年，终于寻不出什么事情做，我便又决计回S城去了。到时是春初的下午，天气欲雨不雨，一切都罩在灰色中；旧寓里还有空房，仍然住下。在道上，就想起连殳的了，到后，便决定晚饭后去看他。我提着两包闻喜名产的煮饼，走了许多潮

Though this letter did not "shock" me, when, after a hasty perusal, I read it carefully again, I felt both uneasy and relieved. At least his livelihood was secure, and I need not worry any more. At any rate, I could do nothing here. I thought of writing to him, but felt there was nothing to say.

In fact, I was gradually forgetting him. His face no longer sprang so often to my mind's eye. However, less than ten days after hearing from him the office of the S—*Weekly* started sending me its paper. I did not read such papers as a rule, but since it was sent to me I glance at some of the contents. And this reminded me of Wei, for the paper frequently carried poem and essays about him, such as "Calling on the Scholar Wei at Night During a Snowstorm," "A Poetic Gathering at the Scholarly Abode of Adviser Wei," and so forth. Once, indeed, under the heading "Table Talk," they retailed with gusto certain stories which had previously been considered material for ridicule, but which had now become "Tables of an Eccentric Genius." Only an exceptional man, it was implied, could have done such unusual things.

Although this recalled him to me, my impression of him was growing fainter. Yet all the time he seemed to be gaining a closer hold on me, which often gave me an inexplicable sense of uneasiness and cast a shadow of apprehension. However, by autumn the newspaper stopped coming, while the Shanyang magazine began to publish the first instalment of a long essay called "The Element of Truth in Rumours," which asserted that rumours about certain gentlemen had reached the ears of the mighty. My name was among those attacked. I had then to be very careful. I had to take care that my cigarette smoke did not get in other people's way. All these precautions took so much time I could attend to nothing else, and naturally had no leisure to think of Wei. I had actually forgotten him.

However, I could not hold my job till summer. By the end of May I had left Shanyang.

V

I wandered between Shanyang, Licheng and Taigu for more than half a year, but could find no work, so I decided to go back to S— . I arrived one afternoon in early spring. It was a cloudy day with everything wrapped in mist. Since there were vacant rooms in my old hostel, I stayed there. On the road I had started thinking of Wei, and after my arrival I made up my mind to call on him after dinner. Taking two packages of

湿的路，让道给许多拦路高卧的狗，这才总算到了连殳的门前。里面仿佛特别明亮似的。我想，一做顾问，连寓里也格外光亮起来了，不觉在暗中一笑。但仰面一看，门旁却白白的，分明帖着一张斜角纸。我又想，大良们的祖母死了罢；同时也跨进门，一直向里面走。

微光所照的院子里，放着一具棺材，旁边站一个穿军衣的兵或是马弁，还有一个和他谈话的，看时却是大良的祖母；另外还闲站着几个短衣的粗人。我的心即刻跳起来了。她也转过脸来凝视我。

“阿呀！您回来了？何不早几天……。”她忽而大叫起来。

“谁……谁没有了？”我其实是已经大概知道的了，但还是问。

“魏大人，前天没有的。”

我四顾，客厅里暗沉沉的，大约只有一盏灯；正屋里却挂着白的孝帏，几个孩子聚在屋外，就是大良二良们。

“他停在那里，”大良的祖母走向前，指着说，“魏大人恭喜之后，我把正屋也租给他了；他现在就停在那里。”

孝帏上没有别的，前面是一张条桌，一张方桌；方桌上摆着十来碗饭菜。我刚跨进门，当面忽然现出两个穿白长衫的来拦住了，瞪了死鱼似的眼睛，从中发出惊疑的光来，钉住了我的脸。我慌忙说明我和连殳的关系，大良的祖母也来从旁证实；他们的手和眼光这才逐渐弛缓下去，默许我近前去鞠躬。

我一鞠躬，地下忽然有人呜呜的哭起来了，定神看时，一个十多岁的孩子伏在草荐上，也是白衣服，头发剪得很光的头上还络着一大绺苎麻丝。

我和他们寒暄后，知道一个是连殳的从堂兄弟，要算最亲的了；一个是远房侄子。我请求看一看故人，他们却竭力拦阻，说是“不敢当”的。然而终于被我说服了，将孝帏揭起。

这回我会见了死的连殳。但是奇怪！虽然穿一套皱的

3. White is the mourning colour in China. White paper on the door indicated that there had been a death in the house.

the well-known Wenxi cakes, I threaded my way through several damp streets, stepping cautiously past many sleeping dogs, until I reached his door. It seemed very bright inside. I thought even his rooms were better lit since he had become an adviser, and smiled to myself. However, when I looked up, I saw a strip of white paper[3] stuck on the door. It occurred to me, as I stepped inside, that the children's grandmother might be dead; but I went straight in.

In the dimly lit courtyard there was a coffin, by which some soldier or orderly in uniform was standing, talking to the children's grandmother. A few workers in short coats were loitering there too. My heart began to beat faster. Just then she turned to look at me.

"Ah, you're back? Why didn't you come earlier?" she suddenly exclaimed.

"Who...who has passed away?" Actually by now I knew, but yet I asked.

"Adviser Wei died the day before yesterday."

I looked around. The sitting-room was dimly lit, probably by one lamp only; the front room, however, was decked with white funeral curtains, and the woman's grandchildren had gathered outside that room.

"His body is there," she said, coming forward and pointing to the front room. "After Mr. Wei was promoted, I let him my front room too; that is where he is now."

There was no writing on the funeral curtain. In front stood a long table, then a square table, spread with some dozen dishes. As I went in, two men in long white gowns suddenly appeared to bar the way, their eyes, like those of a dead fish, fixed in surprise and mistrust on my face. I hastily explained my relation with Wei, and the landlady came up to confirm my statement. Then their hands and eyes dropped, and they allowed me to go forward to bow to the dead.

As I bowed, a wail sounded beside me from the floor. Looking down I saw a child of about ten, kneeling on a mat, also dressed in white. His hair had been cut short, and had some hemp attached to it.

Later I found out that one of these men was Wei's cousin, his nearest in kin, while the other was a distant nephew. I asked to be allowed to see Wei, but they tried their best to dissuade me, saying I was too "polite." Finally they gave in, and lifted the curtain.

This time I saw Wei in death. But, strangely enough, though he was wearing

短衫裤，大襟上还有血迹，脸上也瘦削得不堪，然而面目却还是先前那样的面目，宁静地闭着嘴，合着眼，睡着似的，几乎要使我伸手到他鼻子前面，去试探他可是其实还在呼吸着。

一切是死一般静，死的人和活的人。我退开了，他的从堂兄弟却又来周旋，说“舍弟”正在年富力强，前程无限的时候，竟遽尔“作古”了，这不但是“衰宗”不幸，也太使朋友伤心。言外颇有替连殳道歉之意；这样地能说，在山乡中人是少有的。但此后也就沉默了，一切是死一般静，死的人和活的人。

我觉得很无聊，怎样的悲哀倒没有，便退到院子里，和大良们的祖母闲谈起来。知道入殓的时候是临近了，只待寿衣送到；钉棺材钉时，“子午卯酉”四生肖是必须躲避的。她谈得高兴了，说话滔滔地泉流似的涌出，说到他的病状，说到他生时的情景，也带些关于他的批评。

“你可知道魏大人自从交运之后，人就和先前两样了，脸也抬高起来，气昂昂的。对人也不再先前那么迂。你知道，他先前不是像一个哑子，见我是叫老太太的么？后来就叫‘老家伙’。唉唉，真是有趣。人送他仙居术，他自己是不吃的，就摔在院子里，——就是这地方，——叫道，‘老家伙，你吃去罢。’他交运之后，人来人往，我把正屋也让给他住了，自己便搬在这厢房里。他也真是一走红运，就与众不同，我们就常常这样说笑。要是你早来一个月，还赶得上看这里的热闹，三日两头的猜拳行令，说的说，笑的笑，唱的唱，做诗的做诗，打牌的打牌……。

“他先前怕孩子们比孩子们见老子还怕，总是低声下气的。近来可也两样了，能说能闹，我们的大良们也很喜欢和他玩，一有空，便都到他的屋里去。他也用种种方法逗着玩；要他买东西，他就要孩子装一声狗叫，或者磕一个响头。哈哈，真是过得热闹。前两月二良要他买鞋，还磕了三个响头哩，哪，现在还穿着，没有破呢。”

一个穿白长衫的人出来了，她就住了口。我打听连

a crumpled shirt, stained in front with blood, and his face was very lean, his expression was unchanged. He was sleeping so placidly, with closed mouth and eyes, that I was tempted to put my finger before his nostrils to see if he were still breathing.

Everything was deathly still, both the living and the dead. As I withdrew, his cousin accosted me to state that Wei's untimely death, just when he was in the prime of life and had a great future before him, was not only a calamity for his humble family but a cause of sorrow for his friends. He seemed to be apologizing for Wei for dying. Such eloquence is rare among villagers. However, after that he fell silent again, and everything was deathly still, both the living and the dead.

Feeling cheerless, but by no means sad, I withdrew to the courtyard to chat with the old woman. She told me the funeral would soon take place; they were waiting for the shroud. And when the coffin was nailed down, people born under certain stars should not be near. She rattled on, her words pouring out like a flood. She spoke of Wei's illness, incidents during his life, and even voiced certain criticisms.

"You know, after Mr. Wei came into luck, he was a different man. He held his head high and looked very haughty. He stopped treating people in his old pedantic way. Did you know, he used to act like an idiot, and call me madam? Later on," she chuckled, "he called me 'old bitch'; it was too funny for words. When people sent him rare herbs like atractylis, instead of eating them himself, he would throw them into the courtyard, just here, and call out, 'You take this, old bitch!' After he came into luck, he had scores of visitors; so I vacated my front room for him, and moved into a side one. As we have always said jokingly, he became a different man after his good luck. If you had come one month earlier, you could have seen all the fun here: drinking games practically every day, talking, laughing, singing, poetry writing and mahjong games....

"He used to be more afraid of children than they are of their own father, practically grovelling to them. But recently that changed too, and he was a good one for jokes. My grandchildren liked to play with him, and would go to his rooms whenever they could. He would think up all sorts of practical jokes. For instance, when they wanted him to buy things for them, he would make them bark like dogs or make a thumping kowtow. Ah, that was fun. Two months ago, my second grandchild asked him to buy him a pair of shoes, and had to make three thumping kowtows. He's still wearing them; they aren't worn out yet."

When one of the men in white came out, she stopped talking. I asked about Wei's

殳的病症，她却不大清楚，只说大约是早已瘦了下去的罢，可是谁也没理会，因为他总是高高兴兴的。到一个多月前，这才听到他吐过几回血，但似乎也没有看医生；后来躺倒了；死去的前三天，就哑了喉咙，说不出一句话。十三大人从寒石山路远迢迢地上城来，问他可有存款，他一声也不响。十三大人疑心他装出来的，也有人说有些生痨病死的人是要说不出话来的，谁知道呢……。

“可是魏大人的脾气也太古怪，”她忽然低声说，“他就不肯积蓄一点，水似的钱。十三大人还疑心我们得了什么好处。有什么屁好处呢？他就冤里冤枉胡里胡涂地化掉了。譬如买东西，今天买进，明天又卖出，弄破，真不知道是怎么一回事。待到死了下来，什么也没有，都糟掉了。要不然，今天也不至于这样地冷静……。

“他就是胡闹，不想办一点正经事。我是想到过的，也劝过他。这么年纪了，应该成家；照现在的样子，结一门亲很容易；如果没有门当户对的，先买几个姨太太也可以：人是总应该像个样子的。可是他一听到就笑起来，说道，‘老家伙，你还是总替别人惦记着这等事么？’你看，他近来就浮而不实，不把人的好话当好话听。要是早听了我的话，现在何至于独自冷清清地在阴间摸索，至少，也可以听到几声亲人的哭声……。”

一个店伙背了衣服来了。三个亲人便检出里衣，走进帏后去。不多久，孝帏揭起了，里衣已经换好，接着是加外衣。这很出我意外。一条土黄的军裤穿上了，嵌着很宽的红条，其次穿上去的是军衣，金闪闪的肩章，也不知道是什么品级，那里来的品级。到入棺，是连殳很不妥帖地躺着，脚边放一双黄皮鞋，腰边放一柄纸糊的指挥刀，骨瘦如柴的灰黑的脸旁，是一顶金边的军帽。

三个亲人扶着棺沿哭了一场，止哭拭泪；头上络麻线的孩子退出去了，三良也避去，大约都是属“子午卯酉”之一的。

粗人扛起棺盖来，我走近去最后看一看永别的连殳。

illness, but there was little she could tell me. She knew only that he had been losing weight for a long time, but they had though nothing of it because he always looked so cheerful. About a month before, they heard he had been coughing blood, but it seemed he had not seen a doctor. Then he had to stay in bed, and three days before he died he seemed to have lost the power of speech. His cousin had come all the way from the village to ask him if he had any savings, but he said not a word. His cousin thought he was shamming, but some people had said those dying of consumption did lose the power of speech....

"But Mr. Wei was a queer man," she suddenly whispered. "He never saved money, always spent it like water. His cousin still suspects we got something out of him. Heaven knows, we got nothing. He just spent it in his haphazard way. Buying something today, selling it tomorrow, or breaking it up — God knows what happened. When he died there was nothing left, all spent! Otherwise it would not be so dismal today...."

"He just fooled about, not wanting to do the proper thing. I had thought of that, and spoken to him. At his age, he should have got married; it would have been easy for him then. And if no suitable family could be found, at least he could keep up appearances. But he would laugh whenever I brought it up. 'Old bitch, you are always worrying about such things for other people,' he would say. He was never serious, you see; he wouldn't listen to good advice. If he had listened to me, he wouldn't be wandering lonely in the nether world now; at least there would be wailing from his dear ones...."

A shop assistant arrived, bringing some clothes with him. The three relatives of the dead picked out the underwear, then disappeared behind the curtain. Soon, the curtain was lifted; the new underwear had been put on the corpse, and they proceeded to put on his outer garments. I was surprised to see them dress him in a pair of khaki military trousers with broad red stripes, and a tunic with glittering epaulettes. I could not say what rank these indicated, or how he acquired it. Then the body was placed in the coffin. Wei lay there awkwardly, a pair of brown leather shoes beside his feet, a paper sword at his waist, and beside his lean and ashen face a military cap with a gilt band.

The three relatives wailed beside the coffin, then stopped and wiped their tears. The boy with hemp attached to his hair withdrew, as did the old woman's third grandchild — no doubt they had been born under the wrong stars.

As the labourers lifted the coffin lid, I stepped forward to see Wei for the last time.

他在不妥帖的衣冠中，安静地躺着，合了眼，闭着嘴，口角间仿佛含着冰冷的微笑，冷笑着这可笑的死尸。

敲钉的声音一响，哭声也同时迸出来。这哭声使我不能听完，只好退到院子里；顺脚一走，不觉出了大门了。潮湿的路极其分明，仰看太空，浓云已经散去，挂着一轮圆月，散出冷静的光辉。

我快步走着，仿佛要从一种沉重的东西中冲出，但是不能够。耳朵中有什么挣扎着，久之，久之，终于挣扎出来了，隐约像是长嗥，像一匹受伤的狼，当深夜在旷野中嗥叫，惨伤里夹杂着愤怒和悲哀。

我的心地就轻松起来，坦然地在潮湿的石路上走，月光底下。

一九二五年十月十七日毕。

In his awkward costume he lay placidly, with closed mouth and eyes. There seemed to be an ironical smile on his lips, mocking the ridiculous corpse.

When the nails began to be hammered in, the wailing started afresh. I could not stand it very long, so withdrew to the courtyard; then, somehow, I was out of the gate. The damp road glistened, and I looked up at the sky where the cloud banks had scattered and a full moon hung, shedding a cool light.

I walked with quickened steps, as if eager to break through some heavy barrier, but finding it impossible. Something struggled in my ears, and, after a long, long time, burst out. It was like a long howl, the howl of a wounded wolf crying in the wilderness in the depth of night, anger and sorrow mingled in its agony.

Then my heart felt lighter, and I paced calmly on along the damp cobbled road under the moon.

October 17, 1925

我也将寻觅子君，当面说出我的悔恨和悲哀，
祈求她的饶恕；

I would seek out Zijun to tell her of my remorse and grief,
to beg for her forgiveness.

伤逝

——涓生的手记

Regret for the Past

— Juansheng's Notes

如果我能够，我要写下我的悔恨和悲哀，为子君，为自己。

会馆里的被遗忘在偏僻里的破屋是这样地寂静和空虚。时光过得真快，我爱子君，仗着她逃出这寂静和空虚，已经满一年了。事情又这么不凑巧，我重来时，偏偏空着的又只有这一间屋。依然是这样的破窗，这样的窗外的半枯的槐树和老紫藤，这样的窗前的方桌，这样的败壁，这样的靠壁的板床。深夜中独自躺在床上，就如我未曾和子君同居以前一般，过去一年中的时光全被消灭，全未有过，我并没有曾经从这破屋子搬出，在吉兆胡同创立了满怀希望的小小的家庭。

不但如此。在一年之前，这寂静和空虚是并不这样的，常常含着期待；期待子君的到来。在久待的焦躁中，一听到皮鞋的高底尖触着砖路的清响，是怎样地使我骤然生动起来呵！于是就看见带着笑涡的苍白的圆脸，苍白的瘦的臂膊，布的有条纹的衫子，玄色的裙。她又带了窗外的半枯的槐树的新叶来，使我看见，还有挂在铁似的老干上的一房一房的紫白的藤花。

然而现在呢，只有寂静和空虚依旧，子君却决不再来了，而且永远，永远地！……

子君不在我这破屋里时，我什么也看不见。在百无聊赖中，随手抓过一本书来，科学也好，文学也好，横竖什么都一样；看下去，看下去，忽而自己觉得，已经翻了十多页了，但是毫不记得书上所说的事。只是耳朵却分外地灵，仿佛听到大门外一切往来的履声，从中便有子君的，而且橐橐地逐渐临近，——但是，往往又逐渐渺茫，终于消失在别的步声的杂沓中了。我憎恶那不像子君鞋声的穿布底鞋的长班的儿子，我憎恶那太像子君鞋声的常常穿着新皮鞋的邻院的搽雪花膏的小东西！

莫非她翻了车么？莫非她被电车撞伤了么？……

我便要取了帽子去看她，然而她的胞叔就曾经当面骂过我。

I want, if I can, to record my remorse and grief, for Zijun's sake as well as for my own.

How silent and empty it is, this shabby room in a forgotten corner of the hostel. Time certainly flies. A whole year has passed since I fell in love with Zijun and, thanks to her, escaped from this silence and emptiness. On my return here, as ill luck would have it, this was the only room vacant. The broken window with the half-withered locust tree and old wistaria outside it and the square table in front of it are unchanged. Unchanged too are the mouldering wall and wooden bed beside it. At night I lie alone, just as I did before living with Zijun. The past year has been blotted out as if it had never been, as if I had never moved out of this shabby room to set up house, in a small way but with high hopes, in Lucky Lane.

Nor is that all. A year ago there was a difference in this silence and emptiness for it held expectancy, the expectancy of Zijun's arrival. The tapping of high heels on the brick pavement, cutting into my long, restless waiting, would galvanize me into life. Then I would see her pale round face dimpling in a smile, her thin white arms, striped cotton blouse and black skirt. And she would bring in to show me a new leaf from the half-withered locust tree outside the window, or clusters of the mauve wistaria flowers that hung from a vine which looked as if made of iron.

But now there is only silence and emptiness. Zijun will never come back — never, never again.

When Zijun was not here, I could see nothing in this shabby room. Out of sheer boredom I would pick up a book — science or literature, it was all the same to me — and read on and on till it suddenly dawned on me that I had turned a dozen pages without taking in a word. My sense of hearing, however, was so acute that I seemed able to hear all the footsteps outside the gate, including those of Zijun, gradually approaching — but all too often they faded away again to be lost at last in the medley of other footfalls. I hated the steward's son who wore cloth-soled shoes which sounded quite different from those of Zijun. I hated the little wretch next door who used face-cream, often wore new leather shoes, and whose steps sounded all too like those of Zijun.

Could her rickshaw have been upset? Could she have been run over by a tram?...

I would want to put on my hat to go and find her, but her uncle had cursed me to my face.

蓦然，她的鞋声近来了，一步响于一步，迎出去时，却已经走过紫藤棚下，脸上带着微笑的酒窝。她在她叔子的家里大约并未受气；我的心宁帖了，默默地相视片时之后，破屋里便渐渐充满了我的语声，谈家庭专制，谈打破旧习惯，谈男女平等，谈伊孛生，谈泰戈尔，谈雪莱……。她总是微笑点头，两眼里弥漫着稚气的好奇的光泽。壁上就钉着一张铜板的雪莱半身像，是从杂志上裁下来的，是他的最美的一张像。当我指给她看时，她却只草草一看，便低了头，似乎不好意思了。这些地方，子君就大概还未脱尽旧思想的束缚，——我后来也想，倒不如换一张雪莱淹死在海里的记念像或是伊孛生的罢；但也终于没有换，现在是连这一张也不知那里去了。

"我是我自己的，他们谁也没有干涉我的权利！"

这是我们交际了半年，又谈起她在这里的胞叔和在家的父亲时，她默想了一会之后，分明地，坚决地，沉静地说了出来的话。其时是我已经说尽了我的意见，我的身世，我的缺点，很少隐瞒；她也完全了解的了。这几句话很震动了我的灵魂，此后许多天还在耳中发响，而且说不出的狂喜，知道中国女性，并不如厌世家所说那样的无法可施，在不远的将来，便要看见辉煌的曙色的。

送她出门，照例是相离十多步远；照例是那鲇鱼须的老东西的脸又紧帖在脏的窗玻璃上了，连鼻尖都挤成一个小平面；到外院，照例又是明晃晃的玻璃窗里的那小东西的脸，加厚的雪花膏。她目不邪视地骄傲地走了，没有看见；我骄傲地回来。

"我是我自己的，他们谁也没有干涉我的权利！"这彻底的思想就在她的脑里，比我还透澈，坚强得多。半瓶雪花膏和鼻尖的小平面，于她能算什么东西呢？

我已经记不清那时怎样地将我的纯真热烈的爱表示给她。岂但现在，那时的事后便已模胡，夜间回想，早只剩

Then, abruptly, I would hear her draw nearer, step by step, so that by the time I went out to meet her would already have passed the wistaria trellis, her face dimpling in a smile. Probably she wasn't badly treated after all in her uncle's home. I would calm down and, after we had gazed at each other in silence for a moment, the shabby room would gradually be filled with the sound of my pronouncements on the tyranny of the family, the need to break with tradition, the equality of men and women, Ibsen, Tagore and Shelley.... She would nod her head, smiling, her eyes filled with a childlike look of wonder. On the wall was pinned a copper-plate reproduction of a bust of Shelley, cut out from a magazine. It was one of the best-looking likenesses of him, but when I pointed it out to her she only gave it a hasty glance, then hung her head as if in embarrassment. In matters like this, Zijun had probably not freed herself completely from the trammels of old ideas. It occurred to me later that it might be better to substitute a picture of Shelley drowning at sea, or a portrait of Ibsen. But I never got round to it. And now even this print has vanished.

"I'm my own mistress. None of them has any right to imterfere with me."

She came out with this statement clearly, firmly and gravely after a thoughtful silence, following a conversation about her uncle who was here and her father in the country. We had known each other then for half a year. By that time I had told her all my views, all about myself, and what my failings were. I had hidden very little, and she understood me completely. These few words of hers stirred me to the bottom of my heart and rang in my ears for many days afterwards. I was unspeakably happy to know that Chinese women were not as hopeless as the pessimists made out, and that we should see in the not too distant future the splendour of the dawn.

Each time I saw her out, I kept several paces behind her. And each time the old wretch's face, bewhiskered as if with fish tentacles, would be pressed so hard against the dirty window-pane that the tip of his nose was flattened. And each time we reached the outer courtyard, against the bright glass window there was the little wretch's face, plastered with facecream. But looking neither right nor left as she walked proudly out, she did not see them. And I walked proudly back.

"I'm my own mistress. None of them has any right to interfere with me." Her mind was completely made up on this point. She was by far the more thoroughgoing and resolute of the two of us. What did she care about the half pot of facecream or the flattened nose tip?

I cannot remember clearly how I expressed my true, passionate love for her. Not

了一些断片了；同居以后一两月，便连这些断片也化作无可追踪的梦影。我只记得那时以前的十几天，曾经很仔细地研究过表示的态度，排列过措辞的先后，以及倘或遭了拒绝以后的情形。可是临时似乎都无用，在慌张中，身不由己地竟用了在电影上见过的方法了。后来一想到，就使我很愧恧，但在记忆上却偏只有这一点永远留遗，至今还如暗室的孤灯一般，照见我含泪握着她的手，一条腿跪了下去……。

不但我自己的，便是子君的言语举动，我那时就没有看得分明；仅知道她已经允许我了。但也还仿佛记得她脸色变成青白，后来又渐渐转作绯红，——没有见过，也没有再见的绯红；孩子似的眼里射出悲喜，但是夹着惊疑的光，虽然力避我的视线，张皇地似乎要破窗飞去。然而我知道她已经允许我了，没有知道她怎样说或是没有说。

她却是什么都记得：我的言辞，竟至于读熟了的一般，能够滔滔背诵；我的举动，就如有一张我所看不见的影片挂在眼下，叙述得如生，很细微，自然连那使我不愿再想的浅薄的电影的一闪。夜阑人静，是相对温习的时候了，我常是被质问，被考验，并且被命复述当时的言语，然而常须由她补足，由她纠正，像一个丁等的学生。

这温习后来也渐渐稀疏起来。但我只要看见她两眼注视空中，出神似的凝想着，于是神色越加柔和，笑窝也深下去，便知道她又在自修旧课了，只是我很怕她看到我那可笑的电影的一闪。但我又知道，她一定要看见，而且也非看不可的。

然而她并不觉得可笑。即使我自己以为可笑，甚而至于可鄙的，她也毫不以为可笑。这事我知道得很清楚，因为她爱我，是这样地热烈，这样地纯真。

去年的暮春是最为幸福，也是最为忙碌的时光。我的心平静下去了，但又有别一部分和身体一同忙碌起来。我们这时才在路上同行，也到过几回公园，最多的是寻住

only now: my impression just after the event itself was hazy. Thinking back that night, I recollected only a few disjointed scraps; while a month or two after we started living together, even these vanished like dreams without a trace. All I can remember is that for about a fortnight beforehand I had considered very carefully what attitude to take, how to make my declaration, and how to behave if turned down. But when the time came it was all in vain. In my nervousness, something constrained me to use a method seen in films. The thought of this makes me thoroughly ashamed, yet it is the only thing I remember clearly. Even today it is like a solitary lamp in a dark room, showing me clasping her hand with tears in my eyes and going down on one knee....

At the time I did not even notice Zijun's reaction clearly. All I knew was that she accepted my proposal. However, I seem to remember that her face first turned pale then gradually flushed red, redder than I ever saw it before or after. Sadness and joy mingled with apprehension flashed from her childlike eyes, although she tried to avoid my gaze, looking ready in her confusion to fly out of the window. Then I knew she accepted my proposal, although not knowing what she said or whether she said anything at all.

She, however, remembered everything. She could reel off the speech I made as if she had learned it by heart. She described my conduct in detail, to the life, like a film unfolding itself before her eyes, including of course that trashy scene from the movies which I was only too anxious to forget. The night, when all was still, was our time for review. I was often interrogated and examined, or ordered to repeat everything said on that occasion; yet she often had to fill in gaps and correct my mistakes as if I were a Grade D student.

Gradually these reviews became few and far between. But whenever I saw her gazing raptly into space, a tender look dawning on her dimpling face, I knew she was going over that old lesson again and feared she was visualizing my ridiculous act from the movies. I knew, though, that she must be visualizing it, that she insisted on visualizing it.

But she didn't find it ridiculous. Though I thought it laughable, even contemptible, to her it was no joke. And I knew this beyond a doubt because of her true, passionate love for me.

Late spring last year was our happiest and also our busiest time. I had calmed down by then, although bestirring my mental faculties in step with my physical activity. This was when we started walking side by side in the street. We went several times to the park, but most of our outings were in search of lodgings. On the road I was conscious of searching looks, sarcastic smiles or lewd and contemptuous glances which

所。我觉得在路上时时遇到探索，讥笑，猥亵和轻蔑的眼光，一不小心，便使我的全身有些瑟缩，只得即刻提起我的骄傲和反抗来支持。她却是大无畏的，对于这些全不关心，只是镇静地缓缓前行，坦然如入无人之境。

寻住所实在不是容易事，大半是被托辞拒绝，小半是我们以为不相宜。起先我们选择得很苛酷，——也非苛酷，因为看去大抵不像是我们的安身之所；后来，便只要他们能相容了。看了二十多处，这才得到可以暂且敷衍的处所，是吉兆胡同一所小屋里的两间南屋；主人是一个小官，然而倒是明白人，自住着正屋和厢房。他只有夫人和一个不到周岁的女孩子，雇一个乡下的女工，只要孩子不啼哭，是极其安闲幽静的。

我们的家具很简单，但已经用去了我的筹来的款子的大半；子君还卖掉了她唯一的金戒指和耳环。我拦阻她，还是定要卖，我也就不再坚持下去了；我知道不给她加入一点股分去，她是住不舒服的。

和她的叔子，她早经闹开，至于使他气愤到不再认她做侄女；我也陆续和几个自以为忠告，其实是替我胆怯，或者竟是嫉妒的朋友绝了交。然而这倒很清静。每日办公散后，虽然已近黄昏，车夫又一定走得这样慢，但究竟还有二人相对的时候。我们先是沉默的相视，接着是放怀而亲密的交谈，后来又是沉默。大家低头沉思着，却并未想着什么事。我也渐渐清醒地读遍了她的身体，她的灵魂，不过三星期，我似乎于她已经更加了解，揭去许多先前以为了解而现在看来却是隔膜，即所谓真的隔膜了。

子君也逐日活泼起来。但她并不爱花，我在庙会时买来的两盆小草花，四天不浇，枯死在壁角了，我又没有照顾一切的闲暇。然而她爱动物，也许是从官太太那里传染的罢，不一月，我们的眷属便骤然加得很多，四只小油鸡，在小院子里和房主人的十多只在一同走。但她们却认识鸡的相貌，各知道那一只是自家的。还有一只花白的叭儿狗，从庙会买来，记得似乎原有名字，子君却给它另起

unless I was on my guard set me shivering, so that at every instant I had to summon all my pride and defiance to my support. She, however, was completely fearless and impervious to all this. She continued slowly and calmly on her way, as if there were no one in sight.

It was no easy matter finding lodgings. In most cases we were refused on some pretext or other, while we ourselves turned down a few places as unsuitable. To start with we were very particular — and yet not too particular either, because we saw that most of these lodgings did not look the sort of place where we could live. Later on, all we asked was to be tolerated. We had looked at over twenty places before we found one we could make do: two rooms with a northern exposure in a small house in Lucky Lane. The owner was a petty official but an intelligent man, who occupied only the central and the side rooms. His household consisted simply of a wife, a baby girl not yet one year old, and a maidservant from the country. As long as the child didn't cry, it would be very quiet.

Our furniture, simple as it was, had already taken the greater part of the money I had raised; and Zijun had sold her only gold ring and earrings too. I tried to stop her, but when she insisted I didn't press the point. I knew that unless allowed to make a small investment in our home she would feel uncomfortable.

She had already quarrelled with her uncle, so enraging him in fact that he had disowned her. And I had broken with several friends who thought they were giving me good advice but were actually either afraid for me, or jealous. Still, this meant we were very quiet. Although it was getting on for dusk when I left the office and the rickshaw man always went slowly, at last the time came when we were together again. First we would look at each other in silence, then relax and talk intimately, and finally fall silent again. We both bowed our heads pensively then, without anything particular in mind. Little by little, body and soul alike, she became an open book to me. In the short space of three weeks I learned more about her, overcoming many impediments which I had fancied I understood but now discovered to have been real barriers.

As the days passed, Zijun became more lively. She had no liking for flowers though, and when I bought two pots of flowers at the market she left them unwatered for four days so that they died neglected in corner. I hadn't the time to see to everything. She had a liking for animals, however, which she may have picked up from the official's wife; and in less than a month our household was greatly increased as four chicks of ours started picking their way across the courtyard with the landlady's dozen. But the two mistresses could tell them apart, each able to identify her own. Then there was a spotted peke, bought at the market. I believe he had a name of his own to begin with, but Zijun gave him another one — Asui. And I called him Asui too, though I didn't

了一个，叫作阿随。我就叫它阿随，但我不喜欢这名字。

这是真的，爱情必须时时更新，生长，创造。我和子君说起这，她也领会地点点头。

唉唉，那是怎样的宁静而幸福的夜呵！

安宁和幸福是要凝固的，永久是这样的安宁和幸福。我们在会馆里时，还偶有议论的冲突和意思的误会，自从到吉兆胡同以来，连这一点也没有了；我们只在灯下对坐的怀旧谭中，回味那时冲突以后的和解的重生一般的乐趣。

子君竟胖了起来，脸色也红活了；可惜的是忙。管了家务便连谈天的工夫也没有，何况读书和散步。我们常说，我们总还得雇一个女工。

这就使我也一样地不快活，傍晚回来，常见她包藏着不快活的颜色，尤其使我不乐的是她要装作勉强的笑容。幸而探听出来了，也还是和那小官太太的暗斗，导火线便是两家的小油鸡。但又何必硬不告诉我呢？人总该有一个独立的家庭。这样的处所，是不能居住的。

我的路也铸定了，每星期中的六天，是由家到局，又由局到家。在局里便坐在办公桌前钞，钞，钞些公文和信件；在家里是和她相对或帮她生白炉子，煮饭，蒸馒头。我的学会了煮饭，就在这时候。

但我的食品却比在会馆里时好得多了。做菜虽不是子君的特长，然而她于此却倾注着全力；对于她的日夜的操心，使我也不能不一同操心，来算作分甘共苦。况且她又这样地终日汗流满面，短发都粘在脑额上；两只手又只是这样地粗糙起来。

况且还要饲阿随，饲油鸡，……都是非她不可的工作。

我曾经忠告她：我不吃，倒也罢了；却万不可这样地操劳。她只看了我一眼，不开口，神色却似乎有点凄然；我也只好不开口。然而她还是这样地操劳。

我所豫期的打击果然到来。双十节的前一晚，我呆

like the name.

It is true that love must be constantly renewed, must grow and create. When I spoke of this to Zijun, she nodded understandingly.

Ah, what peaceful, happy evenings those were!

Tranquillity and happiness will grow stale if unchanged, unrenewed. While in the hostel, we had occasional differences of opinion or misunderstandings; but even these vanished after we moved to Lucky Lane. We just sat facing each other in the lamplight, reminiscing, savouring again the joy of the new harmony which had followed our disputes.

Zijun grew plumper, her cheeks became rosier; the only pity was that she was too busy. Housekeeping left her no time even to chat, much less to read or go for walks. We often said we would have to get a maid.

Another thing that upset me on my return in the evening was her covert look of unhappiness, or the forced smile which depressed me even more. Luckily I discovered that this was owing to her secret feud with the petty official's wife, the bone of contention being the two families' chicks. But why wouldn't she tell me outright? People ought to have a home of their own. A lodging of this kind was no place to live in.

I had my routine too. Six days of the week I went from home to the bureau and from the bureau home. In the office I sat at my desk copying, copying endless official documents and letters. At home I kept her company or helped her light the stove, boil rice or steam rolls. This was when I learned to cook.

Still, I ate much better here than in the hostel. Although cooking was not Zijun's forte, she threw herself into it heart and soul. Her ceaseless anxieties on this score made me anxious too, and in this way we shared the sweet and the bitter together. She kept at it so hard all day, perspiration made her short hair cling to her brows, and her hands began to grow rough.

And then she had to feed Asui and the chicks....No one else could do this chore.

I told her I would rather go without food than see her work herself to the bone like this. She just glanced at me without a word, looking rather wistful, so that I couldn't very well say any more. But she went on working as hard as ever.

Finally the blow I had been expecting fell. The evening before the Double Tenth Festival, I was sitting idle while she washed the dishes when we heard a knock on the

坐着，她在洗碗。听到打门声，我去开门时，是局里的信差，交给我一张油印的纸条。我就有些料到了，到灯下去一看，果然，印着的就是：

奉
局长谕史涓生着毋庸到局办事
秘书处启　十月九号

这在会馆里时，我就早已料到了；那雪花膏便是局长的儿子的赌友，一定要去添些谣言，设法报告的。到现在才发生效验，已经要算是很晚的了。其实这在我不能算是一个打击，因为我早就决定，可以给别人去钞写，或者教读，或者虽然费力，也还可以译点书，况且《自由之友》的总编辑便是见过几次的熟人，两月前还通过信。但我的心却跳跃着。那么一个无畏的子君也变了色，尤其使我痛心；她近来似乎也较为怯弱了。

"那算什么。哼，我们干新的。我们……。"她说。

她的话没有说完；不知怎地，那声音在我听去却只是浮浮的；灯光也觉得格外黯淡。人们真是可笑的动物，一点极微末的小事情，便会受着很深的影响。我们先是默默地相视，逐渐商量起来，终于决定将现有的钱竭力节省，一面登"小广告"去寻求钞写和教读，一面写信给《自由之友》的总编辑，说明我目下的遭遇，请他收用我的译本，给我帮一点艰辛时候的忙。

"说做，就做罢！来开一条新的路！"

我立刻转身向了书案，推开盛香油的瓶子和醋碟，子君便送过那黯淡的灯来。我先拟广告；其次是选定可译的书，迁移以来未曾翻阅过，每本的头上都满漫着灰尘了；最后才写信。

我很费踌蹰，不知道怎样措辞好，当停笔凝思的时候，转眼去一瞥她的脸，在昏暗的灯光下，又很见得凄然。我真不料这样微细的小事情，竟会给坚决的，无畏的

door. When I opened it, the messenger from our bureau handed me a mimeographed slip of paper. I had a good idea what it was and, when I took it to the lamp, sure enough it read:

> By order of the commissioner, Shi Juansheng is discharged.
> The secretariat, October 9th

I had foreseen this while we were still in the hostel. Face-Cream, being one of the gambling friends of the commissioner's son, was bound to have spread rumours and tried to make trouble. I was only surprised that this hadn't happened sooner. In face this was really no blow, because I had already decided that I could work as a clerk somewhere else or teach, or even, though it was more difficult, do some translation work. I knew the editor of *Freedom's Friend*, and had corresponded with him a couple of months previously. But all the same, my heart was thumping. What distressed me most was that even Zijun, fearless as she was, had turned pale. Recently she seemed to be weaker, more faint-hearted.

"What does it matter?" she said. "We can make a fresh start. We...."

Her voice trailed off and to my ears, it failed to carry conviction. The lamplight, too, seemed unusually dim. Men are really ludicrous creatures, so easily upset by trifles. First we gazed at each other in silence, then started discussing what to do. Finally we decided to live as economically as possible on the money we had, to advertise in the paper for a post as clerk or teacher, and to write at the same time to the editor of *Freedom's Friend* explaining my present situation and asking him to accept a translation from me to help tide me over this difficult period.

"Suit the action to the word! Let's make a fresh start."

I went straight to the table and pushed aside the bottle of sesame oil and saucer of vinegar, while Zijun brought over the dim lamp. First I drew up the advertisement; then I made a selection of books to translate. I hadn't looked at my books since we moved house, and each volume was thick with dust. Last of all I wrote the letter.

I hesitate for a long time over the wording of the letter. When I stopped writing to think, and glanced at her in the dusky lamplight, she was looking very wistful again. I had never imagined a trifle like this could cause such a striking change in someone so firm and fearless as Zijun. She really had grown much weaker lately; this wasn't

子君以这么显著的变化。她近来实在变得很怯弱了，但也并不是今夜才开始的。我的心因此更缭乱，忽然有安宁的生活的影像——会馆里的破屋的寂静，在眼前一闪，刚刚想定睛凝视，却又看见了昏暗的灯光。

许久之后，信也写成了，是一封颇长的信；很觉得疲劳，仿佛近来自己也较为怯弱了。于是我们决定，广告和发信，就在明日一同实行。大家不约而同地伸直了腰肢，在无言中，似乎又都感到彼此的坚忍倔强的精神，还看见从新萌芽起来的将来的希望。

外来的打击其实倒是振作了我们的新精神。局里的生活，原如鸟贩子手里的禽鸟一般，仅有一点小米维系残生，决不会肥胖；日子一久，只落得麻痹了翅子，即使放出笼外，早已不能奋飞。现在总算脱出这牢笼了，我从此要在新的开阔的天空中翱翔，趁我还未忘却了我的翅子的扇动。

小广告是一时自然不会发生效力的；但译书也不是容易事，先前看过，以为已经懂得的，一动手，却疑难百出了，进行得很慢。然而我决计努力地做，一本半新的字典，不到半月，边上便有了一大片乌黑的指痕，这就证明着我的工作的切实。《自由之友》的总编辑曾经说过，他的刊物是决不会埋没好稿子的。

可惜的是我没有一间静室，子君又没有先前那么幽静，善于体帖了，屋子里总是散乱着碗碟，弥漫着煤烟，使人不能安心做事；但是这自然还只能怨我自己无力置一间书斋。然而又加以阿随，加以油鸡们。加以油鸡们又大起来了，更容易成为两家争吵的引线。

加以每日的"川流不息"的吃饭；子君的功业，仿佛就完全建立在这吃饭中。吃了筹钱，筹来吃饭，还要喂阿随，饲油鸡；她似乎将先前所知道的全都忘掉了，也不想到我的构思就常常为了这催促吃饭而打断。即使在坐中给看一

something that had just started that evening. More put out than ever, I had a sudden vision of a peaceful life — the quiet of my shabby room in the hostel flashed before my eyes, and I was just about to take a good look at when I found myself back in the dusky lamplight again.

It took me a long time to finish the letter, a very lengthy letter. And I was so tired after writing it that I realized I must have grown weaker myself lately too. We decided to send in the advertisement and post the letter the next day. Then with one accord we straightened up silently, as if conscious of each other's fortitude and strength, able to see new hope growing from this fresh beginning.

Indeed, this blow from outside infused new spirit into us. While in the bureau I had been like a wild bird in a cage, given just enough bird-seed by its captor to keep alive but not to thrive; doomed as time passed to lose the use of its wings, so that if ever released it would be unable to fly. Now, at any rate, I had got out of the cage. I must soar anew through the boundless sky before it was too late, before I had forgotten how to flap my wings.

Of course we could not expect results from a small advertisement right away. However, translating is not so simple either. You read something and think you understand it, but when you come to translate it difficulties crop up everywhere, and progress is very slow. Still, I was determined to do my best. In less than a fortnight, the edge of a fairly new dictionary was black with my fingerprints, which shows how seriously I took my work. The editor of *Freedom's Friend* had said that his magazine would never ignore a good manuscript.

Unfortunately, there was no room where I could be undisturbed, and Zijun was not as quiet or considerate as she had been. Our place was so cluttered up with dishes and bowls, so filled with smoke, that it was impossible to work steadily there. But of course I had only myself to blame for not being able to afford a study. On top of this there were Asui and the chicks. The chicks, moreover, had now grown into hens and were more of a bone of contention than ever between the two families.

Then there was the never-ending business of eating every day. All Zijun's energies seemed to go to this. One ate to earn and earned to eat, while Asui and the hens had to be fed too. Apparently she had forgotten all she had ever learned, and did not realize that she was interrupting my train of thought when she called me to meals. And although I sometimes showed a little displeasure as I sat down, she paid no attention at all, just went on munching away quite unconcerned.

点怒色，她总是不改变，仍然毫无感触似的大嚼起来。

使她明白了我的作工不能受规定的吃饭的束缚，就费去五星期。她明白之后，大约很不高兴罢，可是没有说。我的工作果然从此较为迅速地进行，不久就共译了五万言，只要润色一回，便可以和做好的两篇小品，一同寄给《自由之友》去。只是吃饭却依然给我苦恼。菜冷，是无妨的，然而竟不够；有时连饭也不够，虽然我因为终日坐在家里用脑，饭量已经比先前要减少得多。这是先去喂了阿随了，有时还并那近来连自己也轻易不吃的羊肉。她说，阿随实在瘦得太可怜，房东太太还因此嗤笑我们了，她受不住这样的奚落。

于是吃我残饭的便只有油鸡们。这是我积久才看出来的，但同时也如赫胥黎的论定“人类在宇宙间的位置”一般，自觉了我在这里的位置：不过是叭儿狗和油鸡之间。

后来，经多次的抗争和催逼，油鸡们也逐渐成为肴馔，我们和阿随都享用了十多日的鲜肥；可是其实都很瘦，因为它们早已每日只能得到几粒高粱了。从此便清静得多。只有子君很颓唐，似乎常觉得凄苦和无聊，至于不大愿意开口。我想，人是多么容易改变呵！

但是阿随也将留不住了。我们已经不能再希望从什么地方会有来信，子君也早没有一点食物可以引它打拱或直立起来。冬季又逼近得这么快，火炉就要成为很大的问题；它的食量，在我们其实早是一个极易觉得的很重的负担。于是连它也留不住了。

倘使插了草标到庙市去出卖，也许能得几文钱罢，然而我们都不能，也不愿这样做。终于是用包袱蒙着头，由我带到西郊去放掉了，还要追上来，便推在一个并不很深的土坑里。

我一回寓，觉得又清静得多多了；但子君的凄惨的神色，却使我很吃惊。那是没有见过的神色，自然是为阿随。但又何至于此呢？我还没有说起推在土坑里的事。

1. *Man's Place in Nature*, published in 1863, is one of T. H. Huxley's well-known works.

It took her five weeks to realize that my work would not be restricted by regular meal-time. When the realization came she was probably annoyed, but she said nothing. After that my work did go forward faster, and soon I had translated 50,000 words. I had only to polish the manuscript, and it could be sent in with two already completed shorter pieces to *Freedom's Friend*. Those meals were still a headache though. I didn't mind the dishes being cold, but there wasn't enough to go round. Although my appetite was much smaller than before now that I was sitting at home all day using my brain, even so there wasn't always even enough rice. It had been given to Asui, sometimes along with the mutton which I myself rarely had a chance of eating recently. Asui was so thin, she said, it was really pathetic; besides it made the landlady sneer at us. She couldn't stand being laughed at.

So there were only the hens to eat my left-overs. It was a long time before I realized this. I was very conscious however that my "place in nature,"[1] as Huxley describes it, was only somewhere between the peke and the hens.

Later on, after much argument and insistence, the hens started appearing on our table and we and Asui were able to enjoy them for over the days. They were very thin though, because for a long time they had been fed only a few grains of sorghum a day. After that, life became much more peaceful. Only Zijun was very dispirited and often seemed sad and bored, or even sulky. How easily people change!

But we couldn't keep Asui either. We had stopped hoping for a letter from anywhere, and Zijun had long had not even a scrap of food with which to get him to beg or stand on his hindlegs. Besides, winter was fast approaching, and we didn't know what to do about stove. His appetite had long been a heavy liability, of which we were all too conscious. So even the dog had to go.

If we had tied a tag to him and put him on sale in the market, we might have made a few coppers. But neither of us could bring ourselves to do this. Finally I muffled his head in a cloth and took him outside the West Gate, where I let him loose. When he ran after me, I pushed him into a pit — not a very deep one.

When I got home, I found the place much more peaceful; but Zijun's tragic expression quite staggered me. I had never seen such a look on her face before. Of course it was because of Asui, but why take it so to heart? And I hadn't told her about pushing him into the pit.

到夜间，在她的凄惨的神色中，加上冰冷的分子了。

“奇怪。——子君，你怎么今天这样儿了？”我忍不住问。

“什么？”她连看也不看我。

“你的脸色……。”

“没什么，——什么也没有。”

我终于从她言动上看出，她大概已经认定我是一个忍心的人。其实，我一个人，是容易生活的，虽然因为骄傲，向来不与世交来往，迁居以后，也疏远了所有旧识的人，然而只要能远走高飞，生路还宽广得很。现在忍受着这生活压迫的苦痛，大半倒是为她，便是放掉阿随，也何尝不如此。但子君的识见却似乎只是浅薄起来，竟至于连这一点也想不到了。

我拣了一个机会，将这些道理暗示她；她领会似的点头。然而看她后来的情形，她是没有懂，或者是并不相信的。

天气的冷和神情的冷，逼迫我不能在家庭中安身。但是，往那里去呢？大道上，公园里，虽然没有冰冷的神情，冷风究竟也刺得人皮肤欲裂。我终于在通俗图书馆里觅得了我的天堂。

那里无须买票；阅书室里又装着两个铁火炉。纵使不过是烧着不死不活的煤的火炉，但单是看见装着它，精神上也就总觉得有些温暖。书却无可看：旧的陈腐，新的是几乎没有的。

好在我到那里去也并非为看书。另外时常还有几个人，多则十余人，都是单薄衣裳，正如我，各人看各人的书，作为取暖的口实。这于我尤为合式。道路上容易遇见熟人，得到轻蔑的一瞥，但此地却决无那样的横祸，因为他们是永远围在别的铁炉旁，或者靠在自家的白炉边的。

那里虽然没有书给我看，却还有安闲容得我想。待到孤身枯坐，回忆从前，这才觉得大半年来，只为了爱，——盲目的爱，——而将别的人生的要义全盘疏忽了。第一，便是生活。人必生活着，爱才有所附丽。世界

That night, something icy crept into her tragic expression.

"Really!" I couldn't help blurting out. "What's got into you today, Zijun?"

"What?" She didn't even glance at me.

"The way you look...."

"It's nothing — nothing at all."

Eventually I guessed from her behaviour that she considered me callous. Actually, when on my own I had managed all right, although too proud to mix much with family connections. Since my move I had become estranged from my former friends. But if I could only take wing and fly away, I still had plenty of ways to make a living. The wretchedness of my present life was largely due to her — getting rid of Asui was a case in point. But Zijun seemed too obtuse now even to understand that.

When I took an opportunity to hint this to her, she nodded as if she understood. But judging by her later behaviour, she either didn't take it in or else she didn't believe me.

The cold weather and her cold looks made it impossible for me to be comfortable at home. But where could I go? I could get away from her icy looks in the street and parks, but the cold wind there cut like a knife. Finally I found a heaven in the public library.

Admission was free, and there were two stoves in the reading room. Although the fires were very low, the mere sight of the stoves made one warmer. There were no books worth reading: the old ones were out of date, and there were no new ones to speak of.

But I didn't go there to read. There were usually a few other people there, sometimes as many as a dozen, all thinly clad like me. We kept up a pretence of reading in order to keep out of the cold. This suited me down to the ground. In the streets you were liable to meet people you knew who would glance at you contemptuously, but here there was no uncalled-for trouble of that kind, because my acquaintances were all gathered round other stoves or warming themselves at the stoves in their own homes.

Although there were no books for me to read there, I found quiet in which to think. As I sat there alone thinking over the past, I realized that during the last half year, for love — blind love — I had neglected all the other important things in life. First and foremost, livelihood. A man must make a living before

上并非没有为了奋斗者而开的活路；我也还未忘却翅子的扇动，虽然比先前已经颓唐得多……。

屋子和读者渐渐消失了，我看见怒涛中的渔夫，战壕中的兵士，摩托车中的贵人，洋场上的投机家，深山密林中的豪杰，讲台上的教授，昏夜的运动者和深夜的偷儿……。子君，——不在近旁。她的勇气都失掉了，只为着阿随悲愤，为着做饭出神；然而奇怪的是倒也并不怎样瘦损……。

冷了起来，火炉里的不死不活的几片硬煤，也终于烧尽了，已是闭馆的时候。又须回到吉兆胡同，领略冰冷的颜色去了。近来也间或遇到温暖的神情，但这却反而增加我的苦痛。记得有一夜，子君的眼里忽而又发出久已不见的稚气的光来，笑着和我谈到还在会馆时候的情形，时时又很带些恐怖的神色。我知道我近来的超过她的冷漠，已经引起她的忧疑来，只得也勉力谈笑，想给她一点慰藉。然而我的笑貌一上脸，我的话一出口，却即刻变为空虚，这空虚又即刻发生反响，回向我的耳目里，给我一个难堪的恶毒的冷嘲。

子君似乎也觉得的，从此便失掉了她往常的麻木似的镇静，虽然竭力掩饰，总还是时时露出忧疑的神色来，但对我却温和得多了。

我要明告她，但我还没有敢，当决心要说的时候，看见她孩子一般的眼色，就使我只得暂且改作勉强的欢容。但是这又即刻来冷嘲我，并使我失却那冷漠的镇静。

她从此又开始了往事的温习和新的考验，逼我做出许多虚伪的温存的答案来，将温存示给她，虚伪的草稿便写在自己的心上。我的心渐被这些草稿填满了，常觉得难于呼吸。我在苦恼中常常想，说真实自然须有极大的勇气的；假如没有这勇气，而苟安于虚伪，那也便是不能开辟新的生路的人。不独不是这个，连这人也未尝有！

子君有怨色，在早晨，极冷的早晨，这是从未见过

there can be any place for love. There must be a way out for those who struggle, and I hadn't yet forgotten how to flap my wings, although I was much weaker than before....

The reading room and the readers gradually faded. I saw fishermen on the angry sea, soldiers in the trenches, dignitaries in their cars, speculators at the stock exchange, heroes in mountain forests, teachers on their platforms, night prowlers, thieves in the dark.... Zijun was nowhere near me. She had lost all her courage in her resentment over Asui and absorption in her cooking. The strange thing was that she didn't look particularly thin....

It grew colder. The few lumps of slow-burning hard coal in the stove had at last burnt out, and it was closing time. I had to go back to Lucky Lane to expose myself to that icy look. Of late I had sometimes been met with warmth, but this only upset me more. One evening, I remember, from Zijun's eyes flashed the childlike look I had not seen for so long, as she reminded me with a smile of something that happened at the hostel. But there was a constant look of fear in her eyes as well. I knew she was worried by the fact that my behaviour recently had been colder than her own; so sometimes, to comfort her, I forced myself to talk and laugh. But each forced laugh and remark at once rang hollow. And the way this hollowness immediately re-echoed in my ears, like a hateful sneer, was more than I could bear.

Zijun may have felt this too, for after this she lost her wooden calm and, though she tried her best to hide it, often showed anxiety. She treated me, however, much more tenderly.

I wanted to speak to her plainly, but lacked the courage. Whenever I made up my mind to speak, the sight of those childlike eyes compelled me, for the time being, to force a smile. But my smile turned straightway into a sneer at myself and made me lose my cold composure.

After that shc revived the old questions and started new tests, forcing me to give all sorts of hypocritical answers to show my affection for her. Hypocrisy became branded on my heart, so filling it with falseness that it was hard to breathe. I often felt, in my depression, that really great courage was needed to tell the truth; for a man who lacked courage and reconciled himself to hypocrisy could never open up a new path in life. What's more, he just could not exist.

Then Zijun started looking resentful. This happened for the first time one morning,

的，但也许是从我看来的怨色。我那时冷冷地气愤和暗笑了；她所磨练的思想和豁达无畏的言论，到底也还是一个空虚，而对于这空虚却并未自觉。她早已什么书也不看，已不知道人的生活的第一着是求生，向着这求生的道路，是必须携手同行，或奋身孤往的了，倘使只知道捶着一个人的衣角，那便是虽战士也难于战斗，只得一同灭亡。

我觉得新的希望就只在我们的分离；她应该决然舍去，——我也突然想到她的死，然而立刻自责，忏悔了。幸而是早晨，时间正多，我可以说我的真实。我们的新的道路的开辟，便在这一遭。

我和她闲谈，故意地引起我们的往事，提到文艺，于是涉及外国的文人，文人的作品：《诺拉》，《海的女人》。称扬诺拉的果决……。也还是去年在会馆的破屋里讲过的那些话，但现在已经变成空虚，从我的嘴传入自己的耳中，时时疑心有一个隐形的坏孩子，在背后恶意地刻毒地学舌。

她还是点头答应着倾听，后来沉默了。我也就断续地说完了我的话，连余音都消失在虚空中了。

“是的。”她又沉默了一会，说，“但是，……涓生，我觉得你近来很两样了。可是的？你，——你老实告诉我。”

我觉得这似乎给了我当头一击，但也立即定了神，说出我的意见和主张来：新的路的开辟，新的生活的再造，为的是免得一同灭亡。

临末，我用了十分的决心，加上这几句话：

“……况且你已经可以无须顾虑，勇往直前了。你要我老实说；是的，人是不该虚伪的。我老实说罢：因为，因为我已经不爱你了！但这于你倒好得多，因为你更可以毫无挂念地做事……。”

我同时豫期着大的变故的到来，然而只有沉默。她脸色陡然变成灰黄，死了似的；瞬间便又苏生，眼里也发了稚气的闪闪的光泽。这眼光射向四处，正如孩子在饥渴中寻求着慈爱的母亲，但只在空中寻求，恐怖地回避着我的眼。

one bitterly cold morning, or so I imagined. I laughed up my sleeve with freezing indignation. All the ideas and intelligent, fearless phrases she had learned were empty after all; yet she had no inkling of their emptiness. She had given up reading long ago, so did not understand that the first thing in life is to make a living and that to do this people must advance hand in hand, or else soldier on alone. All she could do was cling to someone else's clothing, making it hard for even a fighter to struggle, and bringing ruin on both.

I felt that our only hope lay in parting. She ought to make a clean break. The thought of her death occurred to me abruptly, but at once I reproached myself and felt remorse. Happily it was morning, and there was plenty of time for me to tell her the truth. Whether or not we could make a fresh start depended on this.

I deliberately brought up the past. I spoke of literature, then of foreign authors and their works, of Ibsen's *A Doll's House* and *The Lady from the Sea*. I praised Nora for being strong-minded.... All this had been said the previous year in the shabby room in the hostel, but now it rang hollow. As the words left my mouth I could not free myself from the suspicion that an unseen urchin behind me was maliciously parroting everything I said.

She listened, nodding agreement, then was silent. And I wound up abruptly, the last echo of my voice vanishing in the emptiness.

"Yes," she said presently, after another silence. "But.... Juansheng, I feel you're a different person these days. Is that true? Tell me honestly."

This was a head-on blow. But taking a grip of myself, I explained my views and proposals: only by making a fresh start and building a new life could we both avoid ruin.

To clinch the matter I said firmly:

"...Besides, you can go boldly ahead now without any scruples. You asked me for the truth. You're right: we shouldn't be hypocritical. Well, the truth is it's because I don't love you any more. Actually, this makes it much better for you, because it'll be easier for you to go ahead without any regret...."

I was expecting a scene, but all that followed was silence. Her face turned ashen pale, as pale as death; but in a moment her colour came back and that childlike look darted from her eyes. She gazed around like a hungry or thirsty child searching for its kindly mother. But she only stared into space, fearfully avoiding my eyes.

我不能看下去了，幸而是早晨，我冒着寒风径奔通俗图书馆。

在那里看见《自由之友》，我的小品文都登出了。这使我一惊，仿佛得了一点生气。我想，生活的路还很多，——但是，现在这样也还是不行的。

我开始去访问久已不相闻问的熟人，但这也不过一两次；他们的屋子自然是暖和的，我在骨髓中却觉得寒冽。夜间，便蜷伏在比冰还冷的冷屋中。

冰的针刺着我的灵魂，使我永远苦于麻木的疼痛。生活的路还很多，我也还没有忘却翅子的扇动，我想。——我突然想到她的死，然而立刻自责，忏悔了。

在通俗图书馆里往往瞥见一闪的光明，新的生路横在前面。她勇猛地觉悟了，毅然走出这冰冷的家，而且，——毫无怨恨的神色。我便轻如行云，漂浮空际，上有蔚蓝的天，下是深山大海，广厦高楼，战场，摩托车，洋场，公馆，晴明的闹市，黑暗的夜……。

而且，真的，我豫感得这新生面便要来到了。

我们总算度过了极难忍受的冬天，这北京的冬天就如蜻蜓落在恶作剧的坏孩子的手里一般，被系着细线，尽情玩弄，虐待，虽然幸而没有送掉性命，结果也还是躺在地上，只争着一个迟早之间。

写给《自由之友》的总编辑已经有三封信，这才得到回信，信封里只有两张书券：两角的和三角的。我却单是催，就用了九分的邮票，一天的饥饿，又都白挨给于己一无所得的空虚了。

然而觉得要来的事，却终于来到了。

这是冬春之交的事，风已没有这么冷，我也更久地在外面徘徊；待到回家，大概已经昏黑。就在这样一个昏黑的晚上，我照常没精打采地回来，一看见寓所的门，也照常更加丧气，使脚步放得更缓。但终于走进自己的屋子里

The sight was more than I could stand. Fortunately it was still early. Braving the cold wind, I hurried to the public library.

There I saw *Freedom's Friend*, with my short articles in it. This took me by surprise and breathed a little fresh life into me. "There are plenty of ways open to me," I reflected. "But things can't go on like this."

I started calling on old friends with whom I had long been out of touch, but didn't go more than once or twice. Naturally their rooms were warm, yet I felt chilled to the marrow. And in the evenings I huddled in a room colder than ice.

An icy needle was piercing my heart so that it kept aching numbly. "There are plenty of ways open to me," I reflected. "I haven't forgotten how to flap my wings." The thought of her death occurred to me abruptly, but at once I reproached myself and felt remorse.

In the library the new path ahead of me often flashed before my eyes. She had faced up bravely to the facts and boldly left this icy home. Left it, what's more, without any sense of grievance. Then light as a cloud I floated through the void, the blue sky above me and, below, mountain ranges, mighty oceans, sky-scrapers, battlefields, motor-cars, thoroughfares, rich men's mansions, bright busy shopping centers, and the dark night....

What's more, indeed, I foresaw that this new life was just around the corner.

Somehow we managed to live through the fearful winter, a bitter Beijing winter. But like dragonflies caught by mischievous boys who tie them up to play with and torment at will, although we had come through alive we were prostrate — the end was only a matter of time.

I wrote three letters to the editor of *Freedom's Friend* before receiving a reply. The envelope contained nothing but two book tokens, one for twenty cents, the other for thirty cents. So my nine cents spent on postage to press for payment and my whole day without food had all gone for nothing.

Then what I had been expecting finally happened.

As winter gave place to spring and the wind became less icy, I spent more time roaming the streets, not getting home generally before dark. On one such dark evening I came home listlessly as usual and as usual, grew so depressed at the sight of our gate that my feet began to drag. Eventually, however, I reached my room. It was dark inside.

了，没有灯火；摸火柴点起来时，是异样的寂寞和空虚！

正在错愕中，官太太便到窗外来叫我出去。

“今天子君的父亲来到这里，将她接回去了。”她很简单地说。

这似乎又不是意料中的事，我便如脑后受了一击，无言地站着。

“她去了么？”过了些时，我只问出这样一句话。

“她去了。”

“她，——她可说什么？”

“没说什么。单是托我见你回来时告诉你，说她去了。”

我不信；但是屋子里是异样的寂寞和空虚。我遍看各处，寻觅子君；只见几件破旧而黯淡的家具，都显得极其清疏，在证明着它们毫无隐匿一人一物的能力。我转念寻信或她留下的字迹，也没有；只是盐和干辣椒，面粉，半株白菜，却聚集在一处了，旁边还有几十枚铜元。这是我们两人生活材料的全副，现在她就郑重地将这留给我一个人，在不言中，教我借此去维持较久的生活。

我似乎被周围所排挤，奔到院子中间，有昏黑在我的周围；正屋的纸窗上映出明亮的灯光，他们正在逗着孩子玩笑。我的心也沉静下来，觉得在沉重的迫压中，渐渐隐约地现出脱走的路径：深山大泽，洋场，电灯下的盛筵，壕沟，最黑最黑的深夜，利刃的一击，毫无声响的脚步……。

心地有些轻松，舒展了，想到旅费，并且嘘一口气。

躺着，在合着的眼前经过的豫想的前途，不到半夜已经现尽；暗中忽然仿佛看见一堆食物，这之后，便浮出一个子君的灰黄的脸来，睁了孩子气的眼睛，恳托似的看着我。我一定神，什么也没有了。

但我的心却又觉得沉重。我为什么偏不忍耐几天，要这样急急地告诉她真话的呢？现在她知道，她以后所有的只是她父亲——儿女的债主——的烈日一般的严威和旁人的赛过冰霜的冷眼。此外便是虚空。负着虚空的重担，在

As I groped for the matches and struck a light, the place seemed extraordinarily quiet and empty.

I was standing there in bewilderment, when the official's wife called me outside.

"Zijun's father came today and took her away," she said simply.

This was not what I had expected. I felt as if hit on the back of the head, and stood speechless.

"She went?" I finally managed to ask.

"Yes."

"Did — did she say anything?"

"No. Just asked me to tell you when you came back that she'd gone."

I couldn't believe it; yet the room was extraordinarily quiet and empty. I gazed around in search of Zijun, but all I could see were some shabby sticks of furniture scattered sparsely about the room, as if to prove their inability to conceal anyone or anything. It occurred to me that she might have left a letter or at least jotted down a few words, but no. Only salt, dried chilli, flour and half a cabbage had been placed together, with a few dozen coppers at the side. These were all our worldly goods, and now she had solemnly left these all to me, mutely bidding me to use them to eke out my existence a little longer.

As if repelled by my surroundings, I hurried out to the middle of the courtyard where all around me was dark. Bright lamplight showed on the window-paper of the central room, where they were teasing the baby to make her laugh. My heart grew calmer as by degrees I glimpsed a way out of this heavy oppression: high mountains and marshlands, thoroughfares, brightly lit banquets, trenches, pitch-black night, the thrust of a sharp knife, utterly noiseless footsteps....

Relaxing, I thought about travelling expenses and sighed.

As I lay with closed eyes I conjured up a picture of the future, but before the night was half over it had vanished. In the gloom I suddenly seemed to see a pile of groceries, then Zijun's ashen face appeared to gaze at me beseechingly with childlike eyes. But as soon as I pulled myself together, there was nothing there.

However, my heart was still heavy. Why couldn't I have waited a few days instead of blurting out the truth to her like that? Now she knew all that was left to her was the blazing fury of her father — to his children he was heartless creditor — and the cold looks of bystanders, colder than frost or ice. Apart from this there was only emptiness. What a fearful thing it is to bear the heavy burden of emptiness, walking what is

严威和冷眼中走着所谓人生的路，这是怎么可怕的事呵！而况这路的尽头，又不过是——连墓碑也没有的坟墓。

我不应该将真实说给子君，我们相爱过，我应该永久奉献她我的说谎。如果真实可以宝贵，这在子君就不该是一个沉重的空虚。谎语当然也是一个空虚，然而临末，至多也不过这样地沉重。

我以为将真实说给子君，她便可以毫无顾虑，坚决地毅然前行，一如我们将要同居时那样。但这恐怕是我错误了。她当时的勇敢和无畏是因为爱。

我没有负着虚伪的重担的勇气，却将真实的重担卸给她了。她爱我之后，就要负了这重担，在严威和冷眼中走着所谓人生的路。

我想到她的死……。我看见我是一个卑怯者，应该被摈于强有力的人们，无论是真实者，虚伪者。然而她却自始至终，还希望我维持较久的生活……。

我要离开吉兆胡同，在这里是异样的空虚和寂寞。我想，只要离开这里，子君便如还在我的身边；至少，也如还在城中，有一天，将要出乎意表地访我，像住在会馆时候似的。

然而一切请托和书信，都是一无反响；我不得已，只好访问一个久不问候的世交去了。他是我伯父的幼年的同窗，以正经出名的拔贡，寓京很久，交游也广阔的。

大概因为衣服的破旧罢，一登门便很遭门房的白眼。好容易才相见，也还相识，但是很冷落。我们的往事，他全都知道了。

“自然，你也不能在这里了，”他听了我托他在别处觅事之后，冷冷地说，“但那里去呢？很难。——你那，什么呢，你的朋友罢，子君，你可知道，她死了。”

我惊得没有话。

“真的？”我终于不自觉地问。

“哈哈。自然真的。我家的王升的家，就和她家同村。”

2. A successful candidate of a certain grade in the official examination system of the Qing Dynasty.

called one's path in life amid cold looks and blazing fury! This path ends, moreover, in nothing but a grave without so much as a tombstone.

I ought not to have told Zijun the truth. Since we had loved each other, I should have indulged her to the last with lies, if truth is precious, it should not have proved such a heavy burden of emptiness to Zijun. Of course lies are empty too, but at least they would not have proved so crushing a burden in the end.

I had imagined that if I told Zijun the truth she could go forward boldly without scruples, just as when we started living together. But I must have been wrong. Her courage and fearlessness then were owing to love.

Lacking the courage to shoulder the heavy burden of hypocrisy, I thrust the burden of the truth on to her. Because she had loved me she would have to bear this heavy burden amid cold looks and blazing fury to the end of her days.

I had thought of her death.... I saw that I was a weakling who deserved to be cast out by the strong, honest men and hypocrites both. Yet she, from first to last, had hoped that I could eke out my existence....

I must leave Lucky Lane, which was so extraordinarily empty and lonely. To my mind, if only I could get away, it would be as if Zijun were still at my side; or at least as if she were still in town and might drop in on me at any time, as she had when I lived in the hostel.

However, all my letters went unanswered, as did applications to friends to find me a post. There was nothing for it but to seek out a family connection whom I had not visited for a long time. This was an old classmate of my uncle's, a highly respected senior licentiate[2] who had lived in Beijing for many years and had a wide circle of acquaintances.

The gatekeeper eyed me scornfully, no doubt on account of my shabby clothes. When finally I was admitted, my uncle's friend still acknowledged our acquaintance but treated me very coldly. He knew all about us.

"Obviously you can't stay here," he told me coldly, after being asked to recommend me to a job elsewhere. "But where will you go? It's extremely difficult....That, h'm, that friend of yours, Zijun, I suppose you know, is dead."

I was dumbfounded.

"Are you sure?" I blurted out at last.

He laughed drily. "Of course I am. My servant Wang Sheng comes from the same village as her family."

"但是，——不知道是怎么死的？"

"谁知道呢。总之是死了就是了。"

我已经忘却了怎样辞别他，回到自己的寓所。我知道他是不说谎话的；子君总不会再来的了，像去年那样。她虽是想在严威和冷眼中负着虚空的重担来走所谓人生的路，也已经不能。她的命运，已经决定她在我所给与的真实——无爱的人间死灭了！

自然，我不能在这里了；但是，"那里去呢？"

四围是广大的空虚，还有死的寂静。死于无爱的人们的眼前的黑暗，我仿佛一一看见，还听得一切苦闷和绝望的挣扎的声音。

我还期待着新的东西到来，无名的，意外的。但一天一天，无非是死的寂静。

我比先前已经不大出门，只坐卧在广大的空虚里，一任这死的寂静侵蚀着我的灵魂。死的寂静有时也自己战栗，自己退藏，于是在这绝续之交，便闪出无名的，意外的，新的期待。

一天是阴沉的上午，太阳还不能从云里面挣扎出来，连空气都疲乏着。耳中听到细碎的步声和咻咻的鼻息，使我睁开眼。大致一看，屋子里还是空虚；但偶然看到地面，却盘旋着一匹小小的动物，瘦弱的，半死的，满身灰土的……。

我一细看，我的心就一停，接着便直跳起来。

那是阿随。它回来了。

我的离开吉兆胡同，也不单是为了房主人们和他家女工的冷眼，大半就为着这阿随。但是，"那里去呢？"新的生路自然还很多，我约略知道，也间或依稀看见，觉得就在我面前，然而我还没有知道跨进那里去的第一步的方法。

经过许多回的思量和比较，也还只有会馆是还能相容的地方。依然是这样的破屋，这样的板床，这样的半枯的槐树和紫藤，但那时使我希望，欢欣，爱，生活的，却全

"But — how did she die?"

"Who knows? At any rate, she's dead."

I have forgotten how I took my leave and went home. I knew he wouldn't tell a lie. Zijun would never come back as she had last year. Although she had thought to bear the burden of emptiness amid cold looks and blazing fury till the end of her days, it had been too much for her. Fate had decreed that she should die believing the truth I had told her — die in a world without love.

Obviously I could not stay there. But where could I go?

Around me was a great void and deathlike silence. I seemed to see the darkness before the eyes of those, each one in turn, who died unloved; to hear all their bitter, despairing cries as they struggled.

I was waiting for something new, something nameless and unexpected. But day after day passed in the same deathlike silence.

I went out much less than before, sitting or lying in the great void, allowing this deathlike silence to eat away my soul. Sometimes the silence itself seemed afraid, seemed to recoil. At such times there flashed into my mind nameless, unexpected new hope.

One overcast morning when the sun had failed to struggle out from behind the clouds and the very air was tired, sounds of pattering paws and snuffling made me open my eyes. A glance around the room revealed nothing, but looking down I saw a tiny creature perambulating the floor. It was thin, covered with dust, more dead than alive....

When I took a closer look, my heart missed a beat. I jumped up.

It was Asui. He had come back.

I left Lucky Lane not just because of the cold glances of my landlord, his wife and their maid, but largely on account of Asui. But where could I go? There were many ways open to me of course, this I knew, and sometimes I glimpsed them stretching out before me. What I didn't know was how to take the first step.

After much cogitation and weighing of pros and cons, I decided that the hostel was the only possible lodging place for me. Here is the same shabby room as before, the same wooden bed, half-withered locust tree and wistaria vine. But all that formerly gave

都逝去了，只有一个虚空，我用真实去换来的虚空存在。

新的生路还很多，我必须跨进去，因为我还活着。但我还不知道怎样跨出那第一步。有时，仿佛看见那生路就像一条灰白的长蛇，自己蜿蜒地向我奔来，我等着，等着，看看临近，但忽然便消失在黑暗里了。

初春的夜，还是那么长。长久的枯坐中记起上午在街头所见的葬式，前面是纸人纸马，后面是唱歌一般的哭声。我现在已经知道他们的聪明了，这是多么轻松简截的事。

然而子君的葬式却又在我的眼前，是独自负着虚空的重担，在灰白的长路上前行，而又即刻消失在周围的严威和冷眼里了。

我愿意真有所谓鬼魂，真有所谓地狱，那么，即使在孽风怒吼之中，我也将寻觅子君，当面说出我的悔恨和悲哀，祈求她的饶恕；否则，地狱的毒焰将围绕我，猛烈地烧尽我的悔恨和悲哀。

我将在孽风和毒焰中拥抱子君，乞她宽容，或者使她快意……。

但是，这却更虚空于新的生路；现在所有的只是初春的夜，竟还是那么长。我活着，我总得向着新的生路跨出去，那第一步，——却不过是写下我的悔恨和悲哀，为子君，为自己。

我仍然只有唱歌一般的哭声，给子君送葬，葬在遗忘中。

我要遗忘；我为自己，并且要不再想到这用了遗忘给子君送葬。

我要向着新的生路跨进第一步去，我要将真实深深地藏在心的创伤中，默默地前行，用遗忘和说谎做我的前导……。

一九二五年十月二十一日毕。

me love and life, hope and happiness, has vanished. Nothing remains but emptiness, the empty existence I exchanged for the truth.

There are many ways open to me and I must take one of them, because I am still living. I still don't know, though, how to take the first step. Sometimes the road seems like a great grey serpent, writhing and darting at me. I wait and wait, watching it approach, but it always vanishes suddenly in the darkness.

The early spring nights are as long as ever. Sitting idle as the time drags, I recall a funeral procession I saw in the street this morning. There were paper figures and paper horses in front and, behind, weeping like singing. Now I see how clever they are — this is so simple.

Then Zijun's funeral springs to my mind. She bore the heavy burden of emptiness alone, advancing down the long grey road only to be swallowed up amid cold looks and blazing fury.

If only there really were ghosts, really were a hell! Then, no matter how the infernal whirlwind roared, I would seek out Zijun to tell her of my remorse and grief, to beg for her forgiveness. Failing this, the poisonous flames of hell would engulf me and fiercely consume all my remorse and grief.

In the whirlwind and flames I would put my arms round Zijun and ask her pardon, or let her take her revenge....

However, this is emptier than my new life. I have nothing now but the early spring night which is still as long as ever. Since I am living, I must make a fresh start. And the first step is just to record my remorse and grief, for Zijun's sake as well as for my own.

All I have is weeping like singing as I mourn for Zijun, burying her in oblivion.

I want to forget. For my own sake, I do not want to remember the oblivion I gave Zijun for her burial.

I must make a fresh start in life. Hiding the truth deep in my wounded heart, I must advance silently, taking oblivion and falsehood as my guide....

October 21, 1925

而且看见床前站着一个满脸流血的孩子，

自己正要去打她。

Her face streaming with blood, whom he was about to beat.

兄則友弟則
長幼序友
則敬臣

弟兄
Brothers

公益局一向无公可办，几个办事员在办公室里照例的谈家务。秦益堂捧着水烟筒咳得喘不过气来，大家也只得住口。久之，他抬起紫涨着的脸来了，还是气喘吁吁的，说：

“到昨天，他们又打起架来了，从堂屋一直打到门口。我怎么喝也喝不住。”他生着几根花白胡子的嘴唇还抖着。“老三说，老五折在公债票上的钱是不能开公账的，应该自己赔出来……。”

“你看，还是为钱，”张沛君就慷慨地从破的躺椅上站起来，两眼在深眼眶里慈爱地闪烁。“我真不解自家的弟兄何必这样斤斤计较，岂不是横竖都一样？……”

“像你们的弟兄，那里有呢。”益堂说。

“我们就是不计较，彼此都一样。我们就将钱财两字不放在心上。这么一来，什么事也没有了。有谁家闹着要分的，我总是将我们的情形告诉他，劝他们不要计较。益翁也只要对令郎开导开导……。”

“那～～里……。”益堂摇头说。

“这大概也怕不成。”汪月生说，于是恭敬地看着沛君的眼，“像你们的弟兄，实在是少有的；我没有遇见过。你们简直是谁也没有一点自私自利的心思，这就不容易……。”

“他们一直从堂屋打到大门口……。”益堂说。

“令弟仍然是忙？……”月生问。

“还是一礼拜十八点钟功课，外加九十三本作文，简直忙不过来。这几天可是请假了，身热，大概是受了一点寒……。”

“我看这倒该小心些，”月生郑重地说。“今天的报上就说，现在时症流行……。”

“什么时症呢？”沛君吃惊了，赶忙地问。

“那我可说不清了。记得是什么热罢。”

沛君迈开步就奔向阅报室去。

“真是少有的，”月生目送他飞奔出去之后，向着秦益堂赞叹着。“他们两个人就像一个人。要是所有的弟兄都这样，家里那里还会闹乱子。我就学不来……。”

There was never any business to transact in the Public Welfare Bureau, where several civil servants were as usual discussing family affairs in the office. Qin Yitang, hookah in hand, started coughing so convulsively that the conversation broke off. After some time he raised his swollen purple face and gasped:

"And yesterday they started fighting, fighting all the way from the main hall to the gate. I couldn't stop them, no matter how I shouted." His lips and sparse white beard quivered. "Number Three said the money Number Five had spent on government bonds couldn't be charged to the family account, he should repay it...."

"See, money again." Zhang Peijun bounded up from the chaise-longue, his eyes in their deep sockets flashing compassionately. "I really can't understand why brothers squabble like this over trifles. What difference do these things make anyway?"

"Other people aren't like you and your brother," replied Yitang.

"We don't squabble, but share and share alike. Money and property aren't things we worry about. That's why we never have any trouble. Whenever any family wants to divide the property, I always tell them how it is with us, and urge them not to squabble. If you just explain things to your honourable sons, Brother Yi...."

"Impossible." Yitang shook his head.

"I'm afraid that wouldn't work," said Wang Yuesheng, looking Peijun admiringly in the eyes. "You and your brother are really exceptional; I've met no others like you. Neither of you has the least thought of self — that's not easy...."

"They fought all the way from the hall to the gate..." reiterated Yitang.

"Is your honourable younger brother still as busy as ever?"

"He still had eighteen hours of classes a week, and on top of that ninety-three essays to correct, simply more than he can cope with. But the last few days he's asked for leave. He's feverish, most likely caught a chill."

"I think he'd better be careful," said Yuesheng gravely. "According to today's paper, there's an epidemic now...."

"What epidemic?" asked Peijun hastily, taken aback.

"I can't say for sure. Some kind of fever, as far as I remember."

Peijun hurried to the reading-room.

"They're really exceptional," said Yuesheng admiringly to Qin Yitang, as he watched Peijun hurry away. "The two of them seem just like one. If all brothers were the same, there would never be any family rows. I wish I could emulate them, but I can't."

“说是折在公债票上的钱不能开公账……。”益堂将纸煤子插在纸煤管子里，恨恨地说。

办公室中暂时的寂静，不久就被沛君的步声和叫听差的声音震破了。他仿佛已经有什么大难临头似的，说话有些口吃了，声音也发着抖。他叫听差打电话给普悌思普大夫，请他即刻到同兴公寓张沛君那里去看病。

月生便知道他很着急，因为向来知道他虽然相信西医，而进款不多，平时也节省，现在却请的是这里第一个有名而价贵的医生。于是迎了出去，只见他脸色青青的站在外面听听差打电话。

“怎么了？”

“报上说……说流行的是猩……猩红热。我我午后来局的时，靖甫就是满脸通红……。已经出门了么？请……请他们打电话找，请他即刻来，同兴公寓，同兴公寓……。”

他听听差打完电话，便奔进办公室，取了帽子。汪月生也代为着急，跟了进去。

“局长来时，请给我请假，说家里有病人，看医生……。”他胡乱点着头，说。

“你去就是。局长也未必来。”月生说。

但是他似乎没有听到，已经奔出去了。

他到路上，已不再较量车价如平时一般，一看见一个稍微壮大，似乎能走的车夫，问过价钱，便一脚跨上车去，道，“好。只要给我快走！”

公寓却如平时一般，很平安，寂静；一个小伙计仍旧坐在门外拉胡琴。他走进他兄弟的卧室，觉得心跳得更利害，因为他脸上似乎见得更通红了，而且发喘。他伸手去一摸他的头，又热得炙手。

“不知道是什么病？不要紧罢？”靖甫问，眼里发出忧疑的光，显系他自己也觉得不寻常了。

“不要紧的，……伤风罢了。”他支梧着回答说。

他平时是专爱破除迷信的，但此时却觉得靖甫的样子

"Says the money spent on government bonds can't be charged to the family account..." fumed Yitang, as he stuck a spill in the spill-holder.

There was quiet in the office for a while, till it was broken by the sound of Peijun's steps and his call to the orderly. He sounded as if confronted by disaster, stuttering, his voice quavering. He told the orderly to ring up Putisi, Dr. Pu, and ask him to go at once to Zhang Peijun's flat in the Tongxing Mansions to see a patient.

Yuesheng realized how worried he must be, because although he had faith in Western doctors his salary was low and normally he economized, yet now he was calling in his most celebrated doctor whose fees were high. Going out to meet him he saw that his face was pale as he stood outside listening while the orderly telephoned.

"Well?"

"The papers say... there's an epidemic of scarlet... scarlet fever. I... when I came to the office after lunch, Jingfu's face was a hectic red.... He's gone out? Ask them... to ring him up and ask him to go at once to the Tongxing Mansions, the Tongxing Mansions...."

Having heard the orderly pass on this message, he dashed into the office to pick up his hat. Wang Yuesheng, sharing his anxiety, followed him in.

"When the commissioner comes, please ask leave for me. Tell him one of my family's ill and I'm getting a doctor..." he said, nodding at random.

"Just go along. The commissioner may not be coming," said Yuesheng.

But he had already dashed off, as if without having heard.

In the street, he did not bargain in his usual way for a rickshaw. As soon as he saw a sturdy rickshaw man who looked like a good runner, he asked the price and got in, saying, "All right. As long as you hurry!"

His block of flats, as usual, was peaceful and quiet. A young attendant was still sitting outside the gate fiddling. When he entered his brother's bedroom, his heart beat even faster, for his face seemed a more hectic red and he was panting for breath. Peijun felt his forehead — it burned to his touch.

"What illness can this be? Not serious is it?" asked Jingfu, his eyes bright with anxiety.

"No, it's not serious...a cold," Peijun stammered.

Normally he loved to debunk superstition, but now he sensed something ill-

和说话都有些不祥，仿佛病人自己就有了什么豫感。这思想更使他不安，立即走出，轻轻地叫了伙计，使他打电话去问医院：可曾找到了普大夫？

"就是啦，就是啦。还没有找到。"伙计在电话口边说。

沛君不但坐不稳，这时连立也不稳了；但他在焦急中，却忽而碰着了一条生路：也许并不是猩红热。然而普大夫没有找到，……同寓的白问山虽然是中医，或者于病名倒还能断定的，但是他曾经对他说过好几回攻击中医的话：况且追请普大夫的电话，他也许已经听到了……。

然而他终于去请白问山。

白问山却毫不介意，立刻戴起玳瑁边墨晶眼镜，同到靖甫的房里来。他诊过脉，在脸上端详一回，又翻开衣服看了胸部，便从从容容地告辞。沛君跟在后面，一直到他的房里。

他请沛君坐下，却是不开口。

"问山兄，舍弟究竟是……？"他忍不住发问了。

"红斑痧。你看他已经'见点'了。"

"那么，不是猩红热？"沛君有些高兴起来。

"他们西医叫猩红热，我们中医叫红斑痧。"

这立刻使他手脚觉得发冷。

"可以医么？"他愁苦地问。

"可以。不过这也要看你们府上的家运。"

他已经胡涂得连自己也不知道怎样竟请白问山开了药方，从他房里走出；但当经过电话机旁的时候，却又记起普大夫来了。他仍然去问医院，答说已经找到了，可是很忙，怕去得晚，须待明天早晨也说不定的。然而他还叮嘱他要今天一定到。

他走进房去点起灯来看，靖甫的脸更觉得通红了，的确还现出更红的点子，眼睑也浮肿起来。他坐着，却似乎所坐的是针毡；在夜的渐就寂静中，在他的翘望中，每一辆汽车的汽笛的呼啸声更使他听得分明，有时竟无端疑为

omened in Jingfu's appearance and question, as if the patient himself had some premonition. This notion upset him still more. At once he left the room, softly called the attendant, and told him to telephone to the hospital: Had Dr. Pu been found?

"I see, I see. They haven't traced him yet," said the attendant by the telephone.

Peijun could not sit quietly, by now he could not even stand steadily; but in his anxiety he hit on a gleam of hope: this might not be scarlet fever. However, they had not found Dr. Pu.... Bai Wenshan in that block of flats was a Chinese doctor, but he might be able to diagnose the illness. However, several times when talking to him Beijun had attacked traditional Chinese medicine; besides, he'd already asked several times for the Western doctor, who might have had a telephone call by this time....

But in the end he went to call in Bai Wenshan.

Evidently Bai Wenshan bore him no grudge. He promptly put on his dark glasses with tortoise-shell rims, and went with him to Jingfu's room. Having felt his pulse and examined his face, he undid his clothes to look at his chest, then slowly took his leave. Peijun followed him back to his room.

He invited Peijun to sit down, but then said nothing.

"Brother Wenshan, what's wrong with my brother?" Peijun blurted out.

"Red rash. You saw how the spots had come out."

"Then it's not scarlet fever?" Peijun took heart.

"Western doctors call it scarlet fever. We Chinese doctors call it red rash."

At once his hands and feet turned cold.

"Is there a cure?" he asked frantically.

"Yes. But it also depends on your family's luck."

He was too stupefied to grasp how he asked Bai Wenshan to make out a prescription or how he left his room; but when he passed the telephone he remembered Dr. Pu. Once more he rang up the hospital, only to learn that the doctor had been found but was too busy to call until late — maybe not until the next morning. He urged them to ask him to come that day without fail.

When he went in and lit the lamp, he found Jingfu's face a still more hectic red, and more red spots had certainly appeared. His face and eyes were puffy too. He sat down, but felt as if sitting on needles. In the growing silence of the night, in his desperation he distinctly heard the honking of each car; and once, thinking

普大夫的汽车，跳起来去迎接。但是他还未走到门口，那汽车却早经驶过去了；惘然地回身，经过院落时，见皓月已经西升，邻家的一株古槐，便投影地上，森森然更来加浓了他阴郁的心地。

突然一声乌鸦叫。这是他平日常常听到的；那古槐上就有三四个乌鸦窠。但他现在却吓得几乎站住了，心惊肉跳地轻轻地走进靖甫的房里时，见他闭了眼躺着，满脸仿佛都见得浮肿；但没有睡，大概是听到脚步声了，忽然张开眼来，那两道眼光在灯光中异样地凄怆地发闪。

“信么？”靖甫问。

“不，不。是我。”他吃惊，有些失措，吃吃地说，“是我。我想还是去请一个西医来，好得快一点。他还没有来……。”

靖甫不答话，合了眼。他坐在窗前的书桌旁边，一切都静寂，只听得病人的急促的呼吸声，和闹钟的札札地作响。忽而远远地有汽车的汽笛发响了，使他的心立刻紧张起来，听它渐近，渐近，大概正到门口，要停下了罢，可是立刻听出，驶过去了。这样的许多回，他知道了汽笛声的各样：有如吹哨子的，有如击鼓的，有如放屁的，有如狗叫的，有如鸭叫的，有如牛吼的，有如母鸡惊啼的，有如呜咽的……。他忽而怨愤自己：为什么早不留心，知道，那普大夫的汽笛是怎样的声音的呢？

对面的寓客还没有回来，照例是看戏，或是打茶围去了。但夜却已经很深了，连汽车也逐渐地减少。强烈的银白色的月光，照得纸窗发白。

他在等待的厌倦里，身心的紧张慢慢地弛缓下来了，至于不再去留心那些汽笛。但凌乱的思绪，却又乘机而起；他仿佛知道靖甫生的一定是猩红热，而且是不可救的。那么，家计怎么支持呢，靠自己一个？虽然住在小城里，可是百物也昂贵起来了……。自己的三个孩子，他的两个，养活尚且难，还能进学校去读书么？只给一两个读书呢，那自然是自己的康儿最聪明，——然而大家一定要批评，说是薄待了兄弟的孩子……。

this must be Dr. Pu's car, he leapt up to go and meet him. But before he reached the gate, the car had already driven past. Turning back, disappointed, as he crossed the yard he saw that the bright moon had risen in the west, and his neighbour's old locust tree was casting a shadow on the ground, so murky that it added to his gloom.

Suddenly a crow cawed. A familiar sound, as there were three or four crows' nests in the old locust tree. But now he was no appalled that he nearly stopped dead, Tiptoeing fearfully into Jingfu's room, he found him lying with closed eyes, his whole face apparently swollen. But he was not asleep, for he suddenly opened his eyes, no doubt on hearing footsteps. In the lamplight his eyes glittered strangely, disconsolately.

"A letter?" Jingfu asked.

"No, no. It's me," he stuttered, started and rather at a loss. "It's me." I'm still going to fetch a Western doctor, to speed up your cure. He hasn't come yet...."

Jingfu closed his eyes without answering. His brother sat by the desk in front of the window. All that could be heard in the silence was the patient's gasping breath and the ticking of the alarm-clock. Suddenly a car honked in the distance. At once he tensed. He heard it come nearer and nearer. It must surely be reaching the gate now and going to stop. But the next second he heard it drive past. When this had happened a number of times, he could tell the difference between various horns: some sounded like whistling, others like drumming, farting, dogs barking, ducks quacking, cows mooing, hens squawking, sobbing.... He felt a sudden self-reproach: why hadn't he paid attention earlier, so that he could recognize Dr. Pu's horn?

The tenant who lived opposite was, as usual, still out at an opera or bawdy-house. But it was already very late, and cars were few and far between now. Brilliant silver moonlight whitened the window-paper.

Tired out with waiting, his tension relaxed by degrees, until he stopped paying attention to the horns. But wild fancies seized this chance to cross his mind. It seemed to him certain that Jingfu had scarlet fever, and it was incurable. In that case how was he, on his own, to support the family? Although the town where they lived was small, prices were going up.... It would be hard enough feeding his own three children and Jingfu's two, and how could they go to school? If one or two only had chance to study, then of course his Kang'er was the most intelligent — but people were bound to protest that he was ill-treating his brother's children....

后事怎么办呢，连买棺木的款子也不够，怎么能够运回家，只好暂时寄顿在义庄里……。

忽然远远地有一阵脚步声进来，立刻使他跳起来了，走出房去，却知道是对面的寓客。

“先帝爷，在白帝城……。”

他一听到这低微高兴的吟声，便失望，愤怒，几乎要奔上去叱骂他。但他接着又看见伙计提着风雨灯，灯光中照出后面跟着的皮鞋，上面的微明里是一个高大的人，白脸孔，黑的络腮胡子。这正是普悌思。

他像是得了宝贝一般，飞跑上去，将他领入病人的房中。两人都站在床面前，他擎了洋灯，照着。

“先生，他发烧……。”沛君喘着说。

“什么时候，起的？”普悌思两手插在裤侧的袋子里，凝视着病人的脸，慢慢地问。

“前天。不，大……大大前天。”

普大夫不作声，略略按一按脉，又叫沛君擎高了洋灯，照着他在病人的脸上端详一回；又叫揭去被卧，解开衣服来给他看。看过之后，就伸出手指在肚子上去一摩。

“Measles……”普悌思低声自言自语似的说。

“疹子么？”他惊喜得声音也似乎发抖了。

“疹子。”

“就是疹子？……”

“疹子。”

“你原来没有出过疹子？……”

他高兴地刚在问靖甫时，普大夫已经走向书桌那边去了，于是也只得跟过去。只见他将一只脚踏在椅子上，拉过桌上的一张信笺，从衣袋里掏出一段很短的铅笔，就桌上飕飕地写了几个难以看清的字，这就是药方。

“怕药房已经关了罢？”沛君接了方，问。

“明天不要紧。明天吃。”

明天再看？……”

“不要再看了。酸的，辣的，太咸的，不要吃。热

1. A phrase from an opera about Liu Bei, the first emperor of Han, who died in Baidi City in Sichuan.

How to manage the funeral? He couldn't even afford to buy a coffin, so how could he have it sent to their old home? He'd have to deposit it for the time being in the public mortuary.

Abruptly, he heard distant footsteps approaching. At once he jumped up and went out, knowing that this was the tenant who lived opposite.

"The First Emperor in Baidi City...."[1]

The sound of this soft, cheerful singing disappointed and exasperated him. He nearly charged over to curse him. But then he saw the attendant holding a lantern which lit up a pair of leather shoes behind, and in the faint light above was a tall man with a white face and black beard and whiskers. It was Putisi.

As if he had found a treasure, he flew forward to lead him to the patient's room. They stood in front of the bed, which he lit up by bringing over the lamp.

"He's feverish, sir..." Peijun gasped.

"Since when ? How long?" Putisi demanded slowly, his hands in his trouser pockets.

"The day before yesterday. No...three days ago."

Dr. Pu said nothing, but cursorily felt his pulse. Then he told Peijun to hold the lamp higher so that he could look at the patient's face. He also told him to draw back the quilt and unbutton his jacket. After looking at his chest, he reached over to feel his stomach.

"Measles," he said softly, as if to himself.

"Measles?" quavered Peijun in astonished relief.

"Measles."

"Just measles?"

"Yes."

"Haven't you had measles before?"

Elatedly, he was just asking Jingfu this when Dr. Pu walked over to the desk, and he had to follow him. He saw him put one foot on the chair, pull over a sheet of stationery, and take from his pocket a pencil stub. With this he scrawled a few almost illegible characters — the prescription.

"Won't the pharmacies have closed by now?" asked Peijun as he took this.

"Tomorrow will do. He can take that medicine tomorrow."

"Will you come again tomorrow?..."

"There's no need. He mustn't eat anything acid, peppery or salty. When his fever has

退了之后，拿小便，送到我的，医院里来，查一查，就是了。装在，干净的，玻璃瓶里；外面，写上名字。”

普大夫且说且走，一面接了一张五元的钞票塞入衣袋里，一径出去了。他送出去，看他上了车，开动了，然后转身，刚进店门，只听背后 gö gö 的两声，他才知道普悌思的汽车的叫声原来是牛吼似的。但现在是知道也没有什么用了，他想。

房子里连灯光也显得愉悦；沛君仿佛万事都已做讫，周围都很平安，心里倒是空空洞洞的模样。他将钱和药方交给跟着进来的伙计，叫他明天一早到美亚药房去买药，因为这药房是普大夫指定的，说惟独这一家的药品最可靠。

“东城的美亚药房！一定得到那里去。记住：美亚药房！”他跟在出去的伙计后面，说。

院子里满是月色，白得如银；“在白帝城”的邻人已经睡觉了，一切都很幽静。只有桌上的闹钟愉快而平匀地札札地作响；虽然听到病人的呼吸，却是很调和。他坐下不多久，忽又高兴起来。

“你原来这么大了，竟还没有出过疹子？”他遇到了什么奇迹似的，惊奇地问。

“………”

“你自己是不会记得的。须得问母亲才知道。”

“………”

“母亲又不在这里。竟没有出过疹子。哈哈哈！”

沛君在床上醒来时，朝阳已从纸窗上射入，刺着他朦胧的眼睛。但他却不能即刻动弹，只觉得四肢无力，而且背上冷冰冰的还有许多汗，而且看见床前站着一个满脸流血的孩子，自己正要去打她。

但这景象一刹那间便消失了，他还是独自睡在自己的房里，没有一个别的人。他解下枕衣来拭去胸前和背上的冷汗，穿好衣服，走向靖甫的房里去时，只见“在白帝城”的邻人正在院子里漱口，可见时候已经很不早了。

gone, bring me a specimen of his urine. Take it to the hospital for a test, that's all. Put it in a clean glass bottle with his name on it."

While speaking Dr. Pu started out, stuffing into his pocket the five-yuan note handed to him. He went straight to the gate. Having seen him out, Peijun watched him get into his car and start it up. He then turned and was re-entering the gate when he heard two honks behind him and discovered that Putisi's horn sounded like a bull bellowing. But the knowledge was of no use to him now, he reflected.

In the bedroom even the lamplight looked cheerful now. Peijun felt he had done all that could be done. All around was very peaceful, yet his heart seemed strangely empty. He gave the prescription and the money for it to the attendant who had followed him in, telling him to go first thing in the morning to the Meiya Pharmacy to buy the medicine. Because this was the pharmacy recommended by Dr. Pu as the only one with reliable drugs.

"Meiya Pharmacy in the east city! Mind you go there. Remember: Meiya Pharmacy!" he said following the attendant out again.

The courtyard was flooded with moonlight, silver-white. His neighbour was asleep in "Baidi City," and all was very still. Only the alarm-clock on the desk was ticking cheerfully and steadily. The patient's breathing, although audible, was very regular too. Before he had sat there long, his spirits rose again.

"You've never had measles in all those years?" he asked incredulously, as if this were miraculous.

"...."

"You wouldn't remember. We should have had to ask mother."

"...."

"But she isn't here. So you never had measles!" He laughed heartily.

When Peijun woke in his bed, the morning sun shining through the window-paper stung his sleepy eyes. But he could not move, he felt too limp, and his back was still clammy with cold sweat. Besides, standing by the bed he saw child, her face streaming with blood, whom he was about to beat.

But in a flash this apparition vanished, and he was sleeping alone with no one else in his room. He pulled off his pillowcase to wipe the sweat from his chest and back, then dressed. By the time he headed for Jingfu's room, he saw his "Baidi City" neighbour rinsing his mouth in the courtyard, and knew that it was already fairly late.

靖甫也醒着了，眼睁睁地躺在床上。

“今天怎样？”他立刻问。

“好些……。”

“药还没有来么？”

“没有。”

他便在书桌旁坐下，正对着眠床；看靖甫的脸，已没有昨天那样通红了。但自己的头却还觉得昏昏的，梦的断片，也同时闪闪烁烁地浮出：

——靖甫也正是这样地躺着，但却是一个死尸。他忙着收殓，独自背了一口棺材，从大门外一径背到堂屋里去。地方仿佛是在家里，看见许多熟识的人们在旁边交口赞颂……。

——他命令康儿和两个弟妹进学校去了；却还有两个孩子哭嚷着要跟去。他已经被哭嚷的声音缠得发烦，但同时也觉得自己有了最高的威权和极大的力。他看见自己的手掌比平常大了三四倍，铁铸似的，向荷生的脸上一掌批过去……。

他因为这些梦迹的袭击，怕得想站起来，走出房外去，但终于没有动。也想将这些梦迹压下，忘却，但这些却像搅在水里的鹅毛一般，转了几个圈，终于非浮上来不可：

——荷生满脸是血，哭着进来了。他跳在神堂上……。

那孩子后面还跟着一群相识和不相识的人。他知道他们是都来攻击他的……。

——“我快不至于昧了良心。你们不要受孩子的诳话的骗……。”他听得自己这样说。

——荷生就在他身边，他又举起了手掌……。

他忽而清醒了，觉得很疲劳，背上似乎还有些冷。靖甫静静地躺在对面，呼吸虽然急促，却是很调匀。桌上的闹钟似乎更用了大声札札地作响。

他旋转身子去，对了书桌，只见蒙着一层尘，再转脸去看纸窗，挂着的日历上，写着两个漆黑的隶书：廿七。

伙计送药进来了，还拿着一包书。

“什么？”靖甫睁开了眼睛，问。

Jingfu had woken too, and was lying in bed open-eyed.

"How do you feel today?" he promptly asked.

"Better...."

"Hasn't the medicine come yet?"

"No."

He sat down by the desk, facing the bed, and saw that Jingfu's face was less red than the previous day. But his own head still felt muddled, and fragments of his dream kept flashing before him:

— Jingfu was lying like this, but he was a corpse. He hastily laid him out and carried the coffin on his back all the way from outside the gate to the main hall. The place seemed to be their old home. He fancied he saw many acquaintances standing on either side praising him....

— He ordered Kang'er and his younger brother and sister to go to school; but two other sobbing children clamoured to go with them. Their sobbing got on his nerves, but at the same time he felt that he had absolute power and great strength. He saw the palm of his hand, three or four times bigger than normal and hard as iron, slap Hesheng on the face....

Afraid of these vestiges of his dream which assailed him, he wanted to stand up and leave the room, but could not move. He also wanted to suppress and forget these dream fragments; but they seemed like goose-feathers plunged into the water, which after floating round several times finally surfaced again.

— Hesheng came in sobbing, his face streaming with blood. He jumped onto the shrine.... Behind the child trooped a crowd of people, some known to him, some strangers. All come to attack him, he knew.

— "I would never be so heartless. Don't be taken in by the children's lies," he heard himself saying.

— Hesheng was beside him. He raised his palm again....

He suddenly came to his senses. He felt worn out and his back still seemed clammy. Jingfu was lying quietly opposite. His breathing, although rapid, was regular. The clock on the desk seemed to be ticking more loudly.

He wheeled round to face the desk which was covered with dust. When he turned to look at the window, the calendar hanging on the wall had printed on it in clerical script: Twenty-seven.

The attendant brought in the medicine, as well as a parcel — a book.

"What's that?" asked Jingfu, opening his eyes.

“药。”他也从倘恍中觉醒，回答说。

“不，那一包。”

“先不管它。吃药罢。”他给靖甫服了药，这才拿起那包书来看，道，“索士寄来的。一定是你向他去借的那一本：《Sesame and Lilies》。”

靖甫伸手要过书去，但只将书面一看，书脊上的金字一摩，便放在枕边，默默地合上眼睛了。过了一会，高兴地低声说：

“等我好起来，译一点寄到文化书馆去卖几个钱，不知道他们可要……。”

这一天，沛君到公益局比平日迟得多，将要下午了；办公室里已经充满了秦益堂的水烟的烟雾。汪月生远远地望见，便迎出来。

“嚄！来了。令弟全愈了罢？我想，这是不要紧的；时症年年有，没有什么要紧。我和益翁正惦记着呢；都说：怎么还不见来？现在来了，好了！但是，你看，你脸上的气色，多少……。是的，和昨天多少两样。”

沛君也仿佛觉得这办公室和同事都和昨天有些两样，生疏了。虽然一切也还是他曾经看惯的东西：断了的衣钩，缺口的唾壶，杂乱而尘封的案卷，折足的破躺椅，坐在躺椅上捧着水烟筒咳嗽而且摇头叹气的秦益堂……。

“他们也还是一直从堂屋打到大门口……。”

“所以呀，”月生一面回答他，“我说你该将沛兄的事讲给他们，教他们学学他。要不然，真要把你老头儿气死了……。”

“老三说，老五折在公债票上的钱是不能算公用的，应该……应该……。”益堂咳得弯下腰去了。

“真是‘人心不同’……。”月生说着，便转脸向了沛君，“那么，令弟没有什么？”

“没有什么。医生说是疹子。”

“疹子？是呵，现在外面孩子们正闹着疹子。我的同院住着的三个孩子也都出了疹子了。那是毫不要紧的。但

2. A collection of essays by John Ruskin (1819-1900).

"Your medicine," he answered, roused from his stupefaction.

"No, that parcel."

"Never mind that now. Take your medicine first." Only after giving Jingfu his medicine did he pick up the parcel. "Suoshi sent this," he said. "It must be the volume of *Sesame and Lilies*[2] that you asked him to lend you."

Jingfu reached out for the book, but simply glanced at the cover and ran his fingers over the gold letters on the spine, then put it down by his pillow and closed his eyes in silence. Presently he murmured happily:

"When I'm better, I shall translate a little and send it to the Culture Library to earn a bit of money. That is, if they'll accept it...."

Today, Peijun arrived at the Public Welfare Bureau much later than usual, after noon. The office was already wreathed with smoke from Qin Yitang's hookah. Wang Yuesheng, seeing him in the distance, came out to meet him.

"Ah! You've come. Is your honourable younger brother better? I didn't think it could be serious. Every year there are these epidemics, which don't amount to much. Yitang and I were talking about you, wondering why you hadn't come. Now here you are, good! But you look a little off colour...you weren't like this yesterday."

To Peijun, this office and his colleagues had also changed since the previous day and seemed strange. Although everything there was familiar: the broken clothes-hanger, the spittoon cracked at the edge, the clutter of dusty files, the rickety chaise-longue with its broken leg, and Qin Yitang lying back on it with his hookah, coughing, shaking his head and sighing....

"They kept it up all the way from the hall to the gate...."

"That's why," rejoined Yuesheng, "you should tell them about Brother Pei, get them to learn from him. Otherwise, they'll really make you die of rage, old fellow...."

"Number Three says the money Number Five spent on government bonds can't be charged to the family, he should...should..." Yitang doubled up, coughing.

"How true it is that 'the hearts of men differ'..." Yuesheng turned towards Peijun. "So your honourable brother is all right?"

"He's all right. According to the doctor, it's measles."

"Measles? Yes, all the children outside are getting measles. The three in the compound where I live have all come down with it. It's nothing serious. But to think

你看，你昨天竟急得那么样，叫旁人看了也不能不感动，这真所谓‘兄弟怡怡’。”

“昨天局长到局了没有？”

“还是‘杳如黄鹤’。你去簿子上补画上一个‘到’就是了。”

“说是应该自己赔。”益堂自言自语地说。“这公债票也真害人，我是一点也莫名其妙。你一沾手就上当。到昨天，到晚上，也还是从堂屋一直打到大门口。老三多两个孩子上学，老五也说他多用了公众的钱，气不过……。”

“这真是愈加闹不清了！”月生失望似的说。“所以看见你们弟兄，沛君，我真是‘五体投地’。是的，我敢说，这决不是当面恭维的话。”

沛君不开口，望见听差的送进一件公文来，便迎上去接在手里。月生也跟过去，就在他手里看着，念道：

“‘公民郝上善等呈：东郊倒毙无名男尸一具请饬分局速行拨棺抬埋以资卫生而重公益由’。我来办。你还是早点回去罢，你一定惦记着令弟的病。你们真是鹡鸰在原’……。

“不！”他不放手，“我来办。”

月生也就不再去抢着办了。沛君便十分安心似的沉静地走到自己的桌前，看着呈文，一面伸手去揭开了绿锈斑斓的墨盒盖。

一九二五年十一月三日。

3. A phrase from *The Analects of Confucius*.

4. An allusion to a poem by Cui Hao of the Tang Dynasty.

5. A poem in the *Book of Songs* has the lines : Pied wagtails in the wasteland ; brothers are concerned for each other's difficulties.

how worried you were yesterday! People seeing you couldn't help being moved. Yours is truly a case of 'brotherly harmony.'"[3]

"Did the commissioner show up yesterday?"

"No, still not a sign — 'gone like the yellow stork.'[4] Go and sign the register and that will be that."

"Says he should repay it," muttered Yitang to himself. "These government bonds are a menace, you don't know where you are with them. Touch them and you land in trouble. Up to yesterday evening, they were still fighting from the hall to the gate. Number Three has two more children in school, and Number Five is furious, claiming he's used more of the family money...."

"That complicates matters still more!" Yuesheng sounded disappointed. "So when I look at you and your brother, Peijun, I 'fall prostrate in admiration.' Believe me, that's the truth, I'm not flattering you to your face — no, indeed."

Peijun said nothing as he saw the orderly bring in a dispatch, which he stepped forward to take. Yuesheng followed and read it out as he held it:

"Hao Shangshan and other citizens petition: 'In the eastern suburb an unknown male has died. Your bureau is requested to issue a coffin at once and have him buried, in the interest of hygiene and the public welfare.' I'll see to that. You'd better go home early, you must be worried about your brother's illness. You two are really 'pied wagtails in the wasteland.'..."[5]

"No!" He kept hold of the dispatch. "I'll see to it."

Yuesheng did not insist. Peijun, looking very much at ease, walked quietly to his desk, read the petition, and reached out to remove the cover from his black ink-box blotched with patina.

November 3, 1925

爱姑觉得自己是完全孤立了；

Aigu felt completely isolated.

离婚
The Divorce

“阿阿，木叔！新年恭喜，发财发财！”

“你好，八三！恭喜恭喜！……”

“唉唉，恭喜！爱姑也在这里……”

“阿阿，木公公！……”

庄木三和他的女儿——爱姑——刚从木莲桥头跨下航船去，船里面就有许多声音一齐嗡的叫了起来，其中还有几个人捏着拳头打拱；同时，船旁的坐板也空出四人的坐位来了。庄木三一面招呼，一面就坐，将长烟管倚在船边；爱姑便坐在他左边，将两只钩刀样的脚正对着八三摆成一个“八”字。

“木公公上城去？”一个蟹壳脸的问。

“不上城，”木公公有些颓唐似的，但因为紫糖色脸上原有许多皱纹，所以倒也看不出什么大变化，“就是到庞庄去走一遭。”

合船都沉默了，只是看他们。

“也还是为了爱姑的事么？”好一会，八三质问了。

“还是为她。……这真是烦死我了，已经闹了整三年，打过多少回架，说过多少回和，总是不落局……。”

“这回还是到慰老爷家里去？……”

“还是到他家。他给他们说和也不止一两回了，我都不依。这倒没有什么。这回是他家新年会亲，连城里的七大人也在……。”

“七大人？”八三的眼睛睁大了。“他老人家也出来说话了么？……那是……。其实呢，去年我们将他们的灶都拆掉了，总算已经出了一口恶气。况且爱姑回到那边去，其实呢，也没有什么味儿……。”他于是顺下眼睛去。

我倒并不贪图回到那边去，八三哥！”爱姑愤愤地昂起头，说，“我是赌气。你想，‘小畜生’姘上了小寡妇，就不要我，事情有这么容易的？‘老畜生’只知道帮儿子，也不要我，好容易呀！七大人怎样？难道和知县大老爷换帖，就不说人话了么？他不能像慰老爷似的不通，只说是‘走散好走散好’。我倒要对他说说我这几年的艰难，且看七大人说谁不错！”

"Ah, Uncle Mu! A happy New Year and good luck to you!"

"How are you, Basan? Happy New Year!"

"Happy New Year! So Aigu's as well."

"Well met, Grandad Mu!"

As Zhuang Musan and his daughter Aigu stepped down into the boat from Magnolia Bridge Wharf a hum of voices broke out on board. Some of the passengers clasped their hands and bowed, and four places were vacated on the benches of the cabin. Calling out greetings, Zhuang Musan sat down, leaning his long pipe against the side of the boat. Aigu sat on his left opposite Basan, her scythe-shaped feet fanning out to form a V.

"Going into town, Grandad Mu?" asked a man with a ruddy face like the shell of a crab.

"Not to town." Grandad Mu sounded rather dispirited. But his dark red face was so wrinkled in any case that he looked much the same as usual. "We're making a trip to Pang Village."

All on board stopped talking to stare at them.

"Is it Aigu's business again?" asked Basan at last.

"It is.... This affair will be the death of me. It's dragged on now for three years. We've quarrelled and patched it up time after time; yet still the thing isn't settled...."

"Will you be going to Mr. Wei's house again?"

"That's right. This won't be the first time he's acted as peace-maker; but I've never agreed to his terms. Not that it matters. Their family's having their New Year reunion now. even Seventh Master form the city will be there."

"Seventh Master?" Basan opened his eyes very wide. "So he'll be there to put his word in too, eh?....Well.... As a matter of fact, since we pulled down their kitchen range last year we've had our revenge more or less. Besides, there's really no point in Aigu going back there." He lowered his eyes again.

"I'm not set on going back there, Brother Basan!"Aigu looked up indignantly. "I'm doing this to spite them. Just think! Young Beast carried on with that little widow and decided he didn't want me. But is it as simple as that? Old Beast just egged on his son and tried to get rid of me too — as if it were all that easy! What about Seventh Master? Just because he exchanges cards with the magistrate, does that mean he can't talk our language? He can't be such a blockhead as Mr. Wei, who says nothing but: 'Separate, better separate.' I'll tell him what I've had to put up with all these years, and we'll see who he says is right!"

八三被说服了，再开不得口。

只有潺潺的船头激水声；船里很静寂。庄木三伸手去摸烟管，装上烟。

斜对面，挨八三坐着的一个胖子便从肚兜里掏出一柄打火刀，打着火绒，给他按在烟斗上。

“对对。”木三点头说。

“我们虽然是初会，木叔的名字却是早已知道的。”胖子恭敬地说。“是的，这里沿海三六十八村，谁不知道？施家的儿子姘上了寡妇，我们也早知道。去年木叔带了六位儿子去拆平了他家的灶，谁不说应该？……你老人家是高门大户都走得进的，脚步开阔，怕他们甚的！……”

“你这位阿叔真通气，”爱姑高兴地说，“我虽然不认识你这位阿叔是谁。”

“我叫汪得贵。”胖子连忙说。

“要撇掉我，是不行的。七大人也好，八大人也好。我总要闹得他们家败人亡！慰老爷不是劝过我四回么？连爹也看得赔贴的钱有点头昏眼热了……。”

“你这妈的！”木三低声说。

“可是我听说去年年底施家送给慰老爷一桌酒席哩，八公公。”蟹壳脸道。

“那不碍事。”汪得贵说，“酒席能塞得人发昏么？酒席如果能塞得人发昏，送大菜又怎样？他们知书识理的人是专替人家讲公道话的，譬如，一个人受众人欺侮，他们就出来讲公道话，倒不在乎有没有酒喝。去年年底我们敝村的荣大爷从北京回来，他见过大场面的，不像我们乡下人一样。他就说，那边的第一个人物要算光太太，又硬……。”

“汪家汇头的客人上岸哩！”船家大声叫着，船已经要停下来。

“有我有我！”胖子立刻一把取了烟管，从中舱一跳，随着前进的船走在岸上了。

“对对！”他还向船里面的人点头，说。

船便在新的静寂中继续前进；水声又很听得出了，潺

Basan was convinced, and kept his mouth shut. The boat was very quiet, with no sound but the plash of water against the bow. Zhuang Musan reached for his pipe and filled it.

A fat man sitting opposite, next to Basan, rummaged in his girdle for a flint and struck a light, which he held to Zhuang Musan's pipe.

"Thank you, thank you," said Zhuang Musan, nodding to him.

"Though this is the first time we've met," said the fat man respectfully, "I heard of you long age. Yes, who is there in all the eighteen villages by the coast who doesn't know of Uncle Mu? We've known too for some time that Young Shi was carrying on with a little widow. When you took your six sons to tear down their kitchen range last year, who didn't say you were right?... All the big gates open for you, you have plenty of face. Why be afraid of *them*?"

"This uncle is a truly discerning man," said Aigu approvingly. "I don't know who he is, though."

"My name is Wang Degui," replied the fat man promptly.

"They can't just push me out! I don't care whether it's Seventh Master or Eighth Master. I'll go on making trouble till their family's ruined and all of them are dead! Mr. Wei has been at me four times, hasn't he? Even Dad's been thrown off his balance by the sight of that settlement money...."

Zhuang Musan swore softly to himself.

"But, Grandad Mu, didn't the Shi family send Mr. Wei a whole feast at the end of last year?" asked Crab-face.

"Makes no difference," said Wang Degui. "Can a feast blind a man completely? If so, what happens when you send him a foreign banquet? Those scholars who know the truth will always stick up for justice. If anyone's bullied by everyone else, for instance, they will up and speak for him no matter whether there's wine to be had or not. At the end of last year, Mr. Rong of our humble village came back from Beijing. He's one who has seen the great world, not like us villagers. He said that a Madame Guang there, who's the best..."

"Wang Jetty!" shouted the boatmen, preparing to moor. "Any passengers for Wang Jetty?"

"Here, me!" Fatty grabbed his pipe, and darted out of the cabin, jumping ashore just as the boat drew in.

"Excuse me!" he called back with a nod to the passengers.

The boat rowed on in fresh silence, broken only by the plash of water. Basan began to doze off, facing Aigu's scythe-shaped shoes, and his mouth fell open by degrees. The

潺的。八三开始打磕睡了，渐渐地向对面的钩刀式的脚张开了嘴。前舱中的两个老女人也低声哼起佛号来，她们撷着念珠，又都看爱姑，而且互视，努嘴，点头。

爱姑瞪着眼看定篷顶，大半正在悬想将来怎样闹得他们家败人亡；“老畜生”，“小畜生”，全都走投无路。慰老爷她是不放在眼里的，见过两回，不过一个团头团脑的矮子：这种人本村里就很多，无非脸色比他紫黑些。

庄木三的烟早已吸到底，火逼得斗底里的烟油吱吱地叫了，还吸着。他知道一过汪家汇头，就到庞庄；而且那村口的魁星阁也确乎已经望得见。庞庄，他到过许多回，不足道的，以及慰老爷。他还记得女儿的哭回来，他的亲家和女婿的可恶，后来给他们怎样地吃亏。想到这里，过去的情景便在眼前展开，一到惩治他亲家这一局，他向来是要冷冷地微笑的，但这回却不，不知怎的忽而横梗着一个胖胖的七大人，将他脑里的局面挤得摆不整齐了。

船在继续的寂静中继续前进；独有念佛声却宏大起来；此外一切，都似乎陪着木叔和爱姑一同浸在沉思里。

“木叔，你老上岸罢，庞庄到了。”

木三他们被船家的声音警觉时，面前已是魁星阁了。

他跳上岸，爱姑跟着，经过魁星阁下，向着慰老爷家走。朝南走过三十家门面，再转一个弯，就到了，早望见门口一列地泊着四只乌篷船。

他们跨进黑油大门时，便被邀进门房去；大门后已经坐满着两桌船夫和长年。爱姑不敢看他们，只是溜了一眼，倒也并不见有“老畜生”和“小畜生”的踪迹。

当工人搬出年糕汤来时，爱姑不由得越加局促不安起来了，连自己也不明白为什么。“难道和知县大老爷换帖，就不说人话么？”她想。“知书识理的人是讲公道话的。我要细细地对七大人说一说，从十五岁嫁过去做媳妇的时候起……。”

她喝完年糕汤；知道时机将到。果然，不一会，她已经跟着一个长年，和她父亲经过大厅，又一弯，跨进客厅

two old women in the front cabin began softly chanting Buddhist prayers and telling their beads. They looked at Aigu and exchanged significant glances, pursing their lips and nodding.

Aigu was staring at the awning above her, probably considering how best to raise such trouble that Old Beast's family would be ruined and he and Young Beast would have no way to turn. She was not afraid of Mr. Wei. She had seen him twice and he was nothing but a squat, round-headed fellow — there were plenty like him in her own village, only a little darker.

Zhuang Musan had come to the end of his tobacco, and the oil in the pipe was sputtering, but still he went on puffing. He knew the stop after Wang Jetty was Pang Village. Already, in fact, you could see Literary Star Pavilion at the entrance to the village. He had been here so often it was not worth talking about, any more than Mr. Wei. He remembered how his daughter had come crying home, how badly her husband and father-in-law had behaved, and how they had worsted him. The past unfolded again before his eyes. Usually when he recalled how he had punished the evil-doers, he would give a bleak smile — but not this time. The fat form of Seventh Master had somehow intervened, and was squeezing his thoughts out of any semblance of order.

The boat went on in continued silence. Only the Buddhist prayers swelled in volume. Everyone else seemed sunk in thoughts like Aigu and her father.

"Here you are, Uncle Mu, Pang Village."

Roused by the boatman's voice, they looked up to see Literary Star Pavilion before them.

Zhuang jumped ashore, and Aigu followed him. They passed the pavilion and headed for Mr. Wei's house. After passing thirty houses on their way south, they turned a corner and reached their destination. Four boats with black awnings were moored in a row at the gate.

As they stepped through the great, black-lacquered gate, they were asked into the gatehouse. It was full of boatmen and farmhands, who were seated at two tables. Aigu dared not stare at them, but she took one hasty look round, and saw there was not a sign of Old Beast and Young Beast.

When a servant brought in soup containing sweet New Year cakes, without knowing why, she felt even more uncomfortable and uneasy. "Just because he exchanges cards with the magistrate doesn't mean he can't talk our language, does it?" she thought. "These scholars who know the truth will always stick up for justice. I must tell Seventh Master the whole story, beginning from the time I married at the age of fifteen...."

When she finished the soup, she knew the time was at hand. Sure enough, before long she found herself following one of the farmhands, who ushered her and her father

的门槛去了。

客厅里有许多东西，她不及细看；还有许多客，只见红青缎子马挂发闪。在这些中间第一眼就看见一个人，这一定是七大人了。虽然也是团头团脑，却比慰老爷们魁梧得多；大的圆脸上长着两条细眼和漆黑的细胡须；头顶是秃的，可是那脑壳和脸都很红润，油光光地发亮。爱姑很觉得稀奇，但也立刻自己解释明白了：那一定是擦着猪油的。

"这就是'屁塞'，就是古人大殓的时候塞在屁股眼里的。"七大人正拿着一条烂石似的东西，说着，又在自己的鼻子旁擦了两擦，接着道，"可惜是'新坑'。倒也可以买得，至迟是汉。你看，这一点是'水银浸'……。"

"水银浸"周围即刻聚集了几个头，一个自然是慰老爷；还有几位少爷们，因为被威光压得像瘪臭虫了，爱姑先前竟没有见。

她不懂后一段话；无意，而且也不敢去研究什么"水银浸"，便偷空向四处一看望，只见她后面，紧挨着门旁的墙壁，正站着"老畜生"和"小畜生。"虽然只一瞥，但较之半年前偶然看见的时候，分明都见得苍老了。

接着大家就都从"水银浸"周围散开；慰老爷接过"屁塞"，坐下，用指头摩挲着，转脸向庄木三说话。

"就是你们两个么？"

"是的。"

"你的儿子一个也没有来？"

"他们没有工夫。"

"本来新年正月又何必来劳动你们。但是，还是只为那件事，……我想，你们也闹得够了。不是已经有两年多了么？我想，冤仇是宜解不宜结的。爱姑既然丈夫不对，公婆不喜欢……。也还是照先前说过那样：走散的好。我没有这么大面子，说不通。七大人是最爱讲公道话的，你们也知道。现在七大人的意思也这样：和我一样。

1. It was the custom for small pieces of jade to be inserted in a dead man's orifices, for people believed this prevented the corpse from decaying.

2. The Han Dynasty (206 B.C.-220 A.D.)

3. The jade and metal objects found in tombs are often stained with mercury, which was placed in corpses to prevent them from decaying too rapidly.

across the great hall, and round a corner into the reception room.

The room was so crammed with things she could not take in all it contained. There were many guests as well, whose short jackets of red and blue satin were shimmering all around her. And in the midst of them was a man who she knew at once must be Seventh Master. Though he had a round head and a round face too, he was a great deal bigger than Mr. Wei and the others. He had narrow slits of eyes in his great round face, and a wispy black moustache; and though he was bald his head and face were ruddy and glistening. Aigu was quite puzzled for a moment, then concluded he must have rubbed his skin with lard.

"This is an anus-stop,[1] which the ancients used in burials."

Seventh Master was holding something which looked like a corroded stone, and he rubbed his nose twice with this object as he spoke. "Unfortunately, it comes from a recent digging. Still, it's worth having: it can't be later than Han.[2] Look at this 'mercury stain.'..."[3]

The "mercury stain" was at once surrounded by several heads, one of which, of course, was Mr. Wei's. There were several sons of the house as well, whom Aigu had not yet noticed, for so awed were they by Seventh Master that they looked like flattened bedbugs.

She did not understand all he had just said; she was not interested in this "mercury stain," nor did she dare investigate it; so she took this chance instead to look round. Standing behind her by the wall, close to the door, were both Old Beast and Young Beast. She saw at a glance that they looked older than when she had met them by chance half a years ago.

Then everybody drifted away from the "mercury stain." Mr. Wei took the anus-stop and sat down to stroke it, turning to ask Zhuang Musan:

"Did just the two of you come?"

"Just the two of us."

"Why have none of your sons come?"

"They hadn't time."

"We wouldn't have troubled you to come at New Year, if not for this business.... I'm sure you've had enough of it yourself. It's over two years now, isn't it? Better to remove enmity than keep it, I say. Since Aigu's husband didn't get on with her, and his parents didn't like her...better take the advice I gave you before and let them separate. I haven't enough face to convince you. But Seventh Master, you know, is a champion of justice. And Seventh Master, you know, is a champion of justice. And Seventh Master's view is the same as mine. However, he says both sides must make some concessions, and

可是七大人说，两面都认点晦气罢，叫施家再添十块钱：九十元！”

“……”

“九十元！你就是打官司打到皇帝伯伯跟前，也没有这么便宜。这话只有我们的七大人肯说。”

七大人睁起细眼，看着庄木三，点点头。

爱姑觉得事情有些危急了，她很怪平时沿海的居民对他都有几分惧怕的自己的父亲，为什么在这里竟说不出话。她以为这是大可不必的；她自从听到七大人的一段议论之后，虽不很懂，但不知怎的总觉得他其实是和蔼近人，并不如先前自己所揣想那样的可怕。

“七大人是知书识理，顶明白的；”她勇敢起来了。“不像我们乡下人。我是有冤无处诉；倒正要找七大人讲讲。自从我嫁过去，真是低头进，低头出，一礼不缺。他们就是专和我作对，一个个都像个‘气杀钟馗’。那年的黄鼠狼咬死了那匹大公鸡，那里是我没有关好吗？那是那只杀头癞皮狗偷吃糠拌饭，拱开了鸡橱门。那‘小畜生’不分青红皂白，就夹脸一嘴巴……。”

七大人对她看了一眼。

“我知道那是有缘故的。这也逃不出七大人的明鉴；知书识理的人什么都知道。他就是着了那滥婊子的迷，要赶我出去。我是三茶六礼定来的，花轿抬来的呵！那么容易吗？……我一定要给他们一个颜色看，就是打官司也不要紧。县里不行，还有府里呢……。”

“那些事是七大人都知道的。”慰老爷仰起脸来说。“爱姑，你要是不转头，没有什么便宜的。你就总是这模样。你看你的爹多少明白；你和你的弟兄都不像他。打官司打到府里，难道官府就不会问问七大人么？那时候是，‘公事公办’，那是，……你简直……。”

“那我就拼出一条命，大家家败人亡。”

“那倒并不是拼命的事，“七大人这才慢慢地说了。“年纪青青。一个人总要和气些：‘和气生财’。对不对？我一添就是十块，那简直已经是‘天外道理’了。要

he's told the Shi family to add another ten dollars to the settlement, making it ninety dollars!"

"...."

"Ninety dollars! If you took the case right up to the emperor, you couldn't get such favourable terms. Nobody but Seventh Master would make such a handsome offer!"

Seventh Master widened his slits of eyes to nod at Zhuang Musan.

Aigu saw that the situation was critical and marvelled that her father, of whom all the coastal families stood in awe, should have not a word to say for himself here. This was quite uncalled for, she thought. Although she could not follow all Seventh Master said, he somehow struck her as a kindly old soul, not nearly as frightening as she had imagined.

"Seventh Master's a scholar who knows the truth," she said boldly. "He's not like us country folk. I had no one to complain to of all the wrong that's been done me; but now I'll tell Seventh Master. All the time I was married I tried to be a good wife — I bowed my head as I went in and out, and I didn't fail in a single wifely duty. But they kept finding fault with me — each one was a regular bully. That year the weasel killed that bit cock, how could they blame me for not closing the coop? It was that mangy cur — curse it! — who pushed open the door of the coop to steal some rice mixed with husks. But that Young Beast wouldn't distinguish black from white. He gave me a slap on the cheek..."

Seventh Master looked at her.

"I knew there must be a reason. This is something Seventh Master will not fail to notice, for scholars who know the truth know everything. He was bewitched by that bitch, and wanted to drive me away! I married him with the proper ceremonies — three lots of tea and six presents — and was carried to his house in a bridal sedan! Is it so easy for him to toss me aside?...I mean to show them, I don't mind going to court. If it can't be settled at the district court, we'll go to the prefecture...."

"Seventh Master knows all this," said Mr. Wei, looking up. "If you persist in this attitude, Aigu, it won't be to your advantage. You haven't changed in the least. Look, how sensible your father is! It's a pity you and your brothers aren't like him. Suppose you do take this matter to the prefect, won't he consult Seventh Master? But then the case will be dealt with publicly, and nobody's feelings will be spared....That being so...."

"I'll stake my life if need be, even if it ruins both families!"

"There's no need for such desperate measures," put in Seventh Master slowly. "You're still young. We should all keep the peace. 'Peace breeds wealth.' Isn't

不然，公婆说‘走！’就得走。莫说府里，就是上海北京，就是外洋，都这样。你要不信，他就是刚从北京洋学堂里回来的，自己问他去。”于是转脸向着一个尖下巴的少爷道，“对不对？”

“的的确确。”尖下巴少爷赶忙挺直了身子，必恭必敬地低声说。

爱姑觉得自己是完全孤立了；爹不说话，弟兄不敢来，慰老爷是原本帮他们的，七大人又不可靠，连尖下巴少爷也低声下气地像一个瘪臭虫，还打“顺风锣”。但她在胡里胡涂的脑中，还仿佛决定要作一回最后的奋斗。

“怎么连七大人……。”她满眼发了惊疑和失望的光。“是的……。我知道，我们粗人，什么也不知道。就怨我爹连人情世故都不知道，老发昏了。就专凭他们‘老畜生’‘小畜生’摆布；他们会报丧似的急急忙忙钻狗洞，巴结人……。”

“七大人看看，”默默地站在她后面的“小畜生”忽然说话了。“她在大人面前还是这样，那在家里是，简直闹得六畜不安。叫我爹是‘老畜生’，叫我是口口声声‘小畜生’，‘逃生子’。”

“那个‘娘滥十十万人生’的叫你‘逃生子’？爱姑回转脸去大声说，便又向着七大人道，“我还有话要当大众面前说说哩。他那里有好声好气呵，开口‘贱胎’，闭口‘娘杀’。自从结识了那婊子，连我的祖宗都入起来了。七大人，你给我批评批评，这……。”

她打了一个寒噤，连忙住口，因为她看见七大人忽然两眼向上一翻，圆脸一仰，细长胡子围着的嘴里同时发出一种高大摇曳的声音来了。

“来……兮！”七大人说。

她觉得心脏一停，接着便突突地乱跳，似乎大势已去，局面都变了；仿佛失足掉在水里一般，但又知道这实在是自己错。

立刻进来一个蓝袍子黑背心的男人，对七大人站定，垂手挺腰，像一根木棍。

that true? I've added a whole ten dollars: that's more than generous. For if your father-in-law and mother-in-law say 'Go!' then go you must. Don't talk about the prefecture, this would be the same in Shanghai, Beijing or even abroad. If you don't believe me, ask *him*! He's just come back from the foreign school in Beijing." He turned towards a sharp-chinned son of the house. "Isn't that so?" he asked.

"Ab-so-lutely," Sharp-chin hastily straightened up to answer in low, respectful tones.

Aigu felt completely isolated. Her father refused to speak, her brother had not dared come, Mr. Wei had always been on the other side, and now Seventh Master had failed her, while even this young sharp-chin, with his soft talk and air of a flattened bug, was simply saying what was expected of him. But confused as she was, she resolved to make a last stand.

"What, does even Seventh Master..." Her eyes showed surprise and disappointment. "Yes...I know, we rough folk are ignorant. My father's to blame for not even understanding how to deal with people — he's lost his old wits completely. He let Old Beast and Young Beast have their way in everything. They stoop to every means, however foul, to fawn on those above them...."

"Look at her, Seventh Master!" Young Beast, who had been standing silently behind her, suddenly spoke up now. "She dares act like this even in Seventh Masters presence. At home she gave us simply to peace at all. She calls my father Old Beast and me Young Beast or Bastard."

"Who the devil is calling you a bastard?" Aigu rounded on him fiercely, then turned back to Seventh Master. "I've something else I'd like to say in public. He was always mean to me. It was 'slut' and 'bitch' all the time. After he started carrying on with that whore, he even cursed my ancestors. Judge between us, Seventh Master...."

She gave a start, and the words died on her lips, for suddenly Seventh Master rolled his eyes and lifted his round face. From the mouth framed by that wispy moustache issued a shrill, trailing cry:

"Come here!..."

Her heart, which had missed a beat, suddenly started pounding. The battle was lost, the tables were turned it seemed. She had taken a false step and fallen into the water, and she knew it was all her own fault.

A man in a blue gown and black jacket promptly came in, and stood like a stick with his arms at his side in front of Seventh Master.

全客厅里是“鸦雀无声”。七大人将嘴一动，但谁也听不清说什么。然而那男人，却已经听到了，而且这命令的力量仿佛又已钻进了他的骨髓里，将身子牵了两牵，“毛骨耸然”似的；一面答应道：

“是。”他倒退了几步，才翻身走出去。

爱姑知道意外的事情就要到来，那事情是万料不到，也防不了的。她这时才又知道七大人实在威严，先前都是自己的误解，所以太放肆，太粗卤了。她非常后悔，不由的自己说：

“我本来是专听七大人吩咐……。”

全客厅里是“鸦雀无声。”她的话虽然微细得如丝，慰老爷却像听到霹雳似的了；他跳了起来。

“对呀！七大人也真公平；爱姑也真明白！”他夸赞着，便向庄木三，“老木，那你自然是没有什么说的了，她自己已经答应。我想你红绿帖是一定已经带来了的，我通知过你。那么，大家都拿出来……。”

爱姑见她爹便伸手到肚兜里去掏东西；木棍似的那男人也进来了，将小乌龟模样的一个漆黑的扁的小东西递给七大人。爱姑怕事情有变故，连忙去看庄木三，见他已经在茶几上打开一个蓝布包裹，取出洋钱来。

七大人也将小乌龟头拔下，从那身子里面倒一点东西在掌心上；木棍似的男人便接了那扁东西去。七大人随即用那一只手的一个指头蘸着掌心，向自己的鼻孔里塞了两塞，鼻孔和人中立刻黄焦焦了。他皱着鼻子，似乎要打喷嚏。

庄木三正在数洋钱。慰老爷从那没有数过的一叠里取出一点来，交还了“老畜生”；又将两份红绿帖子互换了地方，推给两面，嘴里说道：

“你们都收好。老木，你要点清数目呀。这不是好当玩意儿的，银钱事情……。”

“呃啾”的一声响，爱姑明知道是七大人打喷嚏了，但不由得转过眼去看。只见七大人张着嘴，仍旧在那里皱鼻子，一只手的两个指头却撮着一件东西，就是那“古人

There was not a cheep in the room. Seventh Master moved his lips, but nobody could hear what he was saying. Only his servant heard, and the force of this order entered his very marrows, for twice he twitched as if overcome by awe. And he answered:

"Very good, sir."

Then he backed away several paces, turned and went out.

Aigu knew that something unexpected and completely unforeseen was about to happen — something which she was powerless to prevent. Only now did she realize the full power of Seventh Master. She repented bitterly, and found herself saying:

"I always meant to accept Seventh Master's decision...."

There was not a cheep in the room. Although her words were as soft as strands of silk, they carried like a thunder-clap to Mr. Wei.

"Good!"he exclaimed approvingly, leaping up. "Seventh Master is truly just, and Aigu is reasonable. In that case, Musan, you can't have any objection, since your daughter's consented herself. I'm sure you've brought the wedding certificates as I asked you. So let both sides produce them now."

Aigu saw her father fumble in his girdle for something. The stick-like servant came in again to hand Seventh Master a small, flat, jet-black object shaped like a tortoise. Aigu was afraid something dreadful was going to happen. She darted a look at her father; but he was opening a blue cloth package at the table, and taking out silver dollars.

Seventh Master removed the tortoise's head, poured something from its body into his palm, then returned the flat-looking object to the stick-like servant. He rubbed one finger in his palm, then stuffed it up each nostril, staining his nose and upper lip a bright yellow. Then he wrinkled his nose as if about to sneeze.

Zhuang Musan was counting the silver dollars. Mr. Wei extracted a few from a pile which had not been counted, and handed them to Old Beast. He also changed the position of the red and green certificates, restoring them to their original owners.

"Put them away," he said. "You must see if the amount is correct, Musan. This no joking matter — all this silver...."

"Ah — tchew!"

Though Aigu knew it was only Seventh Master sneezing, she could not help turning to look at him. His mouth was wide open and his nose was twitching. In two fingers he was still clutching the small object "used by the ancients in burials." Indeed, he was

大殓的时候塞在屁股眼里的”，在鼻子旁边摩擦着。

好容易，庄木三点清了洋钱；两方面各将红绿帖子收起，大家的腰骨都似乎直得多，原先收紧着的脸相也宽懈下来，全客厅顿然见得一团和气了。

“好！事情是圆功了。”慰老爷看见他们两面都显出告别的神气，便吐一口气，说。“那么，嗡，再没有什么别的了。恭喜大吉，总算解了一个结。你们要走了么？不要走，在我们家里喝了新年喜酒去：这是难得的。”

“我们不喝了。存着，明年再来喝罢。”爱姑说。

“谢谢慰老爷。我们不喝了。我们还有事情……。”庄木三，“老畜生”和“小畜生”，都说着，恭恭敬敬地退出去。

“唔？怎么？不喝一点去么？”慰老爷还注视着走在最后的爱姑，说。

“是的，不喝了。谢谢慰老爷。”

一九二五年十一月六日。

rubbing the side of his nose with it.

With some difficulty Zhuang Musan finished counting the money, and both sides put away the red and green certificates. Then they all seemed to draw themselves up, and tense expressions relaxed. Complete harmony prevailed.

"Good! This business has been settled satisfactorily," said Mr. Wei. Seeing that they looked on the point of leaving, he breathed a sigh of relief. "Well, there's nothing more to be done now. Congratulations on unravelling this knot! Must you be going? Won't you stay to share our New Year feast? This is a rare occasion."

"We mustn't stay," said Aigu. "We'll come to drink with you next year."

"Thank you, Mr. Wei. We won't drink just now. We have other business...." Zhuang Musan, Old Beast and Young Beast withdrew most respectfully.

"What? Not a drop before you go?" Mr. Wei looked at Aigu who brought up the rear.

"Really we mustn't. Thank you, Mr. Wei."

November 6, 1925

图书在版编目（CIP）数据

彷徨：汉英对照 / 鲁迅著；杨宪益，戴乃迭译
—北京：外文出版社，2010
（经典回声）
ISBN 978-7-119-06679-0
Ⅰ.①彷… Ⅱ.①鲁… ②杨… ③戴…
Ⅲ.①英语—汉语—对照读物②鲁迅小说—选集 Ⅳ.①H319.4：I
中国版本图书馆CIP数据核字(2010)第176838号

策　　划：胡开敏
责任编辑：杨春燕　杨　璐
装帧设计：吾昱设计工作室
印刷监制：冯　浩

经典回声　彷徨

鲁　迅　著
杨宪益　戴乃迭　译
裘　沙　王伟君　插图

出 版 人：呼宝民
总 编 辑：李振国
出版发行：外文出版社
地　　址：中国北京西城区百万庄大街24号
邮政编码：100037
网　　址：http://www.flp.com.cn
电　　话：（010）68320579/68996067（总编室）
（010）68995844/68995852（发行部）
（010）68327750/68996164（版权部）
印　　制：外文印刷厂
经　　销：新华书店 / 外文书店
开　　本：720mm × 1020mm　1/16
印　　张：17
字　　数：130千字
装　　别：平装
版　　次：2010年10月第1版　2010年10月第1版第1次印刷
书　　号：ISBN 978-7-119-06679-0
定　　价：32.00 元　　　　建议上架：双语学习
